ON THE PONY EXPRESS TRAIL

One Man's Bikepacking Journey to Discover
History from a Different Kind of Saddle

SCOTT ALUMBAUGH

TWODOT®

ESSEX, CONNECTICUT
HELENA, MONTANA

For Kazu and Lisa, who wouldn't be caught dead on a trip like this.

A · TWODOT® · BOOK

An imprint of Globe Pequot, the trade division of
The Rowman & Littlefield Publishing Group, Inc.
4501 Forbes Blvd., Ste. 200
Lanham, MD 20706
www.rowman.com

Distributed by NATIONAL BOOK NETWORK

British Library Cataloguing in Publication Information available

Library of Congress Cataloging-in-Publication Data

Names: Alumbaugh, Scott, author.
Title: On the Pony Express Trail : one man's bikepacking journey to
   discover history from a different kind of saddle / Scott Alumbaugh.
Description: Essex, Connecticut : TwoDot, [2023] | "This book is intended
   to provide a humorous and historic overview of the famous (and infamous)
   Pony Express Trail. Maps and route descriptions used in the narrative
   are for general reader orientation purposes and should not be used for
   navigation or as a complete route guide"—T.p. verso. | Includes
   bibliographical references.
Identifiers: LCCN 2022053185 (print) | LCCN 2022053186 (ebook) | ISBN
   9781493068692 (Paperback : acid-free paper) | ISBN 9781493068708 (epub)
Subjects: LCSH: Alumbaugh, Scott—Travel. | Bicycle touring—United
   States—Anecdotes. | Pony Express National Historic Trail—Description
   and travel. | Pony Express National Historic Trail—History.
Classification: LCC GV1044 .A47 2023 (print) | LCC GV1044 (ebook) | DDC
   910.973—dc23/eng/20230109
LC record available at https://lccn.loc.gov/2022053185
LC ebook record available at https://lccn.loc.gov/2022053186

∞™ The paper used in this publication meets the minimum requirements of American National
Standard for Information Sciences—Permanence of Paper for Printed Library Materials, ANSI/
NISO Z39.48-1992.

This book is intended to provide a humorous and historic overview of the famous (and infamous) Pony Express Trail. Maps and route descriptions used in the narrative are for general reader orientation purposes and should not be used for navigation or as a complete route guide. If you want to learn more about the Pony Express Bikepacking Route, the author recommends the *Pony Express Bikepacking Route Guide* published by Bikepacking Roots. You can purchase this guide at https://bikepackingroots.org.

CONTENTS

Part Three: The North Platte—
Julesburg, Colorado, to Casper, Wyoming

Part Four: The Steppes of Central Wyoming—
Casper, Wyoming, to Granger, Wyoming

Part Five: The Wasatch—
Granger, Wyoming, to Salt Lake City, Utah

Preface

ONE EVENING I STUMBLED ACROSS AN ITEM REPORTING THAT A CYCLIST had mapped a bikepacking route along the Pony Express Trail. The route was two thousand miles long, ran across seven states from Missouri to California, and as it followed the trail as closely as possible, was 85 percent off-road. I knew right then I had to ride it. What I didn't know was why.

I used to ride ultradistance cycling events, but that was more than a decade earlier, over paved roads on a lightweight, skinny-tired bike. I had crashed a couple of years earlier and had since only ridden a mountain bike on fun, short, low-speed, off-road trails. Bikepacking was the worst combination of both: long days riding everything from busy highway shoulders to sketchy trails through remote terrain, carrying with me everything I'd need to survive—camping gear, food, clothing, tools, extra water—and doing it all on a slow, heavy bike.

Plus, I had no bikepacking equipment. I owned a full-suspension mountain bike, which could not carry all the equipment and food I'd need. I owned no camping gear, and in fact had not camped in decades—my partner and our teenage son both refuse to camp on principle. Even if I started planning and training and buying equipment like a madman right then, I would still need a year to gather the gear, test it, and train. By then I'd be sixty-two years old, not the ideal age to start a five-week solo ride across some of the most remote areas of the American West.

And yet, there it was: Someone had laid out a Pony Express Bikepacking Route and I knew I had to ride it or regret missing the opportunity the rest of my life. Even if it killed me.

By some turn of fate, not long after I had committed myself to bikepacking the Pony Express Trail, most of us found ourselves locked down under shelter-in-place orders in an attempt to slow the spread of COVID-19. What the stay-at-home order took away from me in terms of training opportunities, though, it gave back in the form of time to research the history of the trail.

As it turns out, there is very little primary documentation about the Pony Express. No one wrote a book-length treatment of the service until fifty years after it ended. By then very few company records still existed, and only a handful of former employees were still alive. As a result of this paucity of documentable proof, at every turn I would read an often-recited "fact" that turned out to be pure fiction. For example, nearly every popular work states that riding for the Pony Express was so dangerous, ads calling for riders specified, "Orphans preferred." No such ad ever ran.

On the other hand, very few Pony Express narratives point out that the owners of the company were slaveholders who supported violent proslavery forces in Bleeding Kansas. This discrepancy is indicative of most Pony Express literature: Chroniclers tend to amplify positive stories about the Pony Express and to downplay, explain away, or most often just ignore the negative aspects. The overall effect of this overwhelmingly positive press is to elevate—almost to canonize—the lone rider and the stouthearted pony as paragons of American fortitude, the Pony Express as the epitome of the determination that won the West.

Once the few supportable facts are exhumed from under the tailings pile of embellishments, however, the Pony Express emerges as one of the least dynamic facets of its era. Reduced to its essence, all the Pony did was substitute riders and horses for electrons, because mostly the Pony just relayed short messages between the easternmost and westernmost telegraph stations. As the reach of the telegraph spread, the route of Pony Express shrunk, until the telegraph wires finally connected from coast to coast and the Pony Express winked out of existence, as if the switch that turned the telegraph on simultaneously turned the Pony Express off.

It came, it ran, it died an ignominious death.

But while the Pony Express may be among the least significant developments of its era, it is the most iconic. As such, it is an ideal perch, a central platform on which to stand and to take in at a glance the panoply of monumental events swirling around it, because one can't really understand the Pony Express—what it stood for, what it accomplished, why it came about at all—without understanding the far more interesting historical milieu out of which it arose: the Mexican-American, Utah, and Paiute Wars; the California and Pike's Peak gold rushes; the overland emigration of hundreds of thousands to Oregon and California; the exodus of tens of thousands of Mormons to Utah. Underlying these monumental events are the equally important political and societal currents of the era: the acquisition of Oregon, California, and New Mexico; the persecution of Mormons across the Midwest; the development of trans-Mississippi freighting and stagecoaching; government and civilian relations with Native Americans; the role of the US Mail in developing the West; the placement and deployment of federal troops and forts along the overland trails; and finally, casting a shadow over every aspect of US history in this period, the increasingly contentious fight over slavery along with the looming threats of state secession and civil war.

At one point in my preparation for the ride, I spoke with a deputy superintendent at the National Park Service about the Pony Express National Historic Trail. She told me that in her view, the trail was like a string of pearls: the underlying string was not so elegant, but it threaded together a collection of pearls, such as the stations and monuments, and the spectacular scenery of the West. As I set out from St. Joseph, Missouri, on the first day of my ride, it struck me that she was half right: sites along the way would probably be highlights in long days of trail riding, but the pearls wouldn't be the stations or landmarks themselves so much as the history of what took place at points along the way.

That is how this book is structured. It follows the course of my ride from east to west and offers pieces of history connected to locations along the Pony Express Trail in geographic rather than chronological order. It is not a book about the Pony Express per se, but rather the history of the American West as viewed along the Pony Express Trail. A view from a different kind of saddle, if you will.

The book starts with a short history of the Pony Express in the context of surrounding historical events. It then follows my ride from St. Joseph, Missouri, to Salt Lake City, Utah, with chapters grouped by sections of the trail. The book finishes with a chapter covering the western third of the Pony Express Trail, from Salt Lake City, Utah, to Sacramento, California. I rode most of that section the summer prior to the ride recounted in this book in a series of day trips to scout portions of the route rather than as a continuous bikepacking adventure.

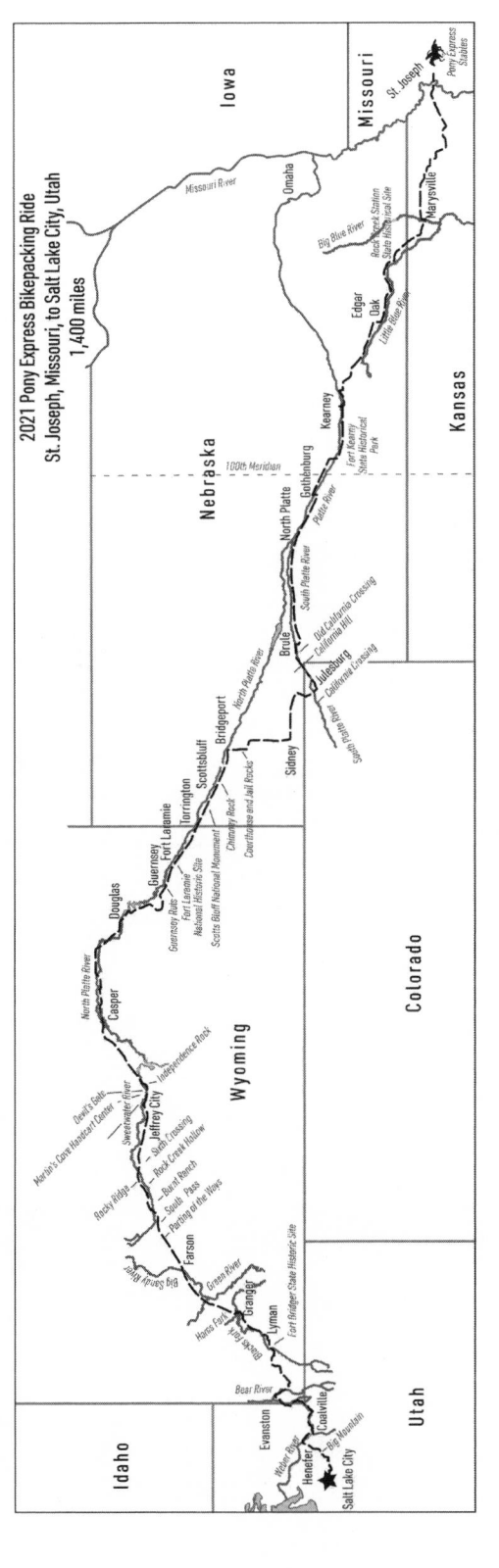

2021 Pony Express Bikepacking Ride
St. Joseph, Missouri, to Salt Lake City, Utah
1,400 miles

INTRODUCTION

FOR ALL THE ACCOLADES, THE DOZENS OF BOOKS, ARTICLES, MOVIES, granite monuments, and bronze medallions, the Pony Express was in reality just a short-lived messenger delivery service: nothing more, nothing less.

Nothing more in the sense that it was not the first nor even the best of its kind: its ponies weren't significantly stronger or faster than other horses; its riders were not braver, tougher, nor more handsome, God-fearing, or proudly American than any other long-distance mail carriers in the West. The owners of the firm behind the Pony Express—Russell, Majors & Waddell—weren't motivated by anything higher than the same object of most commercial enterprises: the desire to stay in business, grow if possible, and continue to make money.

On the other hand, the Pony Express was nothing less than a trans-Mississippi mail service in the mid-1800s. Under the conditions of that time and place, overland delivery service across the American West—at any speed—was literally death-defying. A number of people lost their lives trying to get the mail through; others lost fingers and toes due to frostbite; still others nearly starved. The distance was nearly two thousand miles: The western half, beyond South Pass, Wyoming, was sparsely populated desert and mountains; between Salt Lake City and Carson City, there were no habitations other than the stations set up for the service. Weather was nearly always a problem, from searing heat in the summer, to snowbound passes and subzero temperatures in the winter, thunderstorms, hailstorms, and always, wind. Some rivers were ferried or bridged, but others had to be forded, even when swollen. To set up stations at regular intervals across this expanse, and to keep them staffed, maintained, and safe, was an incredible feat. To ride between them alone on a horse was difficult, dangerous, and maybe a little insane.

Nothing more and nothing less in that there is nothing inherently special about the Pony Express. The idea of a fast horse-relay message line was not unique: Mail contractors had arranged a pony relay to deliver President Buchanan's annual message along roughly the same route just over a year earlier; Herodotus reports that the Persians operated a similar operation in the fifth century BCE. The messages carried by the Pony Express did not directly affect US history in any appreciable way. It accomplished none of the goals normally attributed to it, helped ruin the largest freighting firm of the day, and erased whatever fortunes its owners had or might have amassed.

So the question becomes, why is the Pony Express such an icon of the American West?

I did not start my research with that question in mind. Nevertheless, it is the question that continually arose, and the one I hope to answer throughout the course of this book as I retrace the course of the Pony Express Trail. In order to do so, it's important to know a little about the history of the Pony Express stripped of myths and stories. By way of background then, following is a thumbnail history of the Pony Express in the context of its place and time: the trans-Mississippi West in the mid-1800s.

Ascending Empires: The Mexican-American War and Russell, Majors & Waddell

The Pony Express was a mail service that ran between St. Joseph, Missouri, and Sacramento, California. The service advertised delivery in ten days, as compared to twenty to thirty days or longer for mail delivery by stagecoach or steamship. To achieve this faster pace, riders carried small loads of lightweight mail on horseback and changed horses at intervals around fifteen miles on average. At the end of one rider's route, the mail would be passed on to the next rider to continue it forward. The service operated from April 1860 to October 1861.

The Pony Express was never a company in and of itself, but rather an ancillary operation under the aegis of the Central Overland California and Pike's Peak Express Company (COC&PP). The COC&PP, in turn, was owned and operated by the giant freighting firm of Russell, Majors

& Waddell. Given the inextricable nature of management and finances among the numerous entities with ties to Russell, Majors & Waddell, everyone has always treated all of the related companies as owned and operated by the eponymous firm and its principals: John Russell, Alexander Majors, and William Bradford Waddell. It is the grim faces of this triumvirate that stare reassuringly at the world from countless Pony Express plaques from the Missouri River to the Golden Gate.

The story of the Pony Express, then, starts with the story of Russell, Majors & Waddell, and its story starts with the Mexican-American War.

When James K. Polk became president in March 1845, large chunks of the continental United States as we know it today belonged to two other governments: England, which shared custody of the Pacific Northwest with the United States; and Mexico, which owned everything south of Oregon between the Rockies and the Pacific Ocean, as well as New Mexico. Polk wanted the United States to take sole possession of these lands from both governments.

Americans had been settling in Oregon and California since the late 1830s. By 1845, overland emigrants were organizing themselves into wagon trains each spring and starting west, leaving the Missouri River as soon as there was enough grass along the way to feed their oxen and hoping to cross the Pacific mountain ranges ahead of the winter snows. Most of them wanted their new home to become part of the United States and, like Polk, were willing to go to war with Great Britain and Mexico if necessary.

Happily for Polk and the emigrants, the British had bigger problems at home and gave up Oregon without a fight. Mexico was not so compliant. Polk tried to buy Texas and was turned down. So he went to Plan B: Station troops on disputed land in Texas, provoke a fight, then take all of Mexico's northern lands by force. This land grab became known as the Mexican-American War (1846–1848).

With regard to the Pony Express, the war had two primary results. First, the war gave rise to military contract freighting west of the Missouri River. Second, the United States acquired the present states of Utah and California, along with most of the land that comprises the American West.

The first result, the rise of military freighting, grew directly from the US Army's disastrous efforts to supply its troops. The United States fought the Mexican-American War hundreds of miles from the nearest source of war supplies: Fort Leavenworth, Kansas, on the Missouri River. The only way to keep US Army troops provisioned was to freight materials overland from there. At the start of the war the US Army hired scores of inexperienced teamsters and sent them across the prairie without sufficient training, sometimes without adequate protection, and even without the right destination. The result was a loss of around fifty freighters' lives, untold numbers of animals, and tons of provisions.

The end of the war in February 1848 started the era of permanent military posts west of the Missouri. As with troops during the war, these posts needed to be supplied by wagon train from the depot at Fort Leavenworth. Based on the dismal record of its recent freighting experience, the US War Department decided to get out of the business of freighting and initiate a "contract system." It hired private freighters to haul government supplies at a fixed cost per mile per pound. Over the next half-dozen years, William Russell and William Waddell, as partners, and Alexander Majors, operating on his own, were awarded army freighting contracts under this arrangement.

Starting in 1855, the US War Department simplified the process by contracting with a single firm to service all forts west of the Missouri River. In order to win this lucrative contract, Russell and Waddell joined forces with Majors in December 1854 to create Russell, Majors & Waddell. In 1855, the army awarded the firm a two-year contract, giving it a monopoly on transporting all military supplies west of the Missouri River. Russell, Majors & Waddell borrowed heavily to build facilities in Leavenworth, Kansas (near the army depot at Fort Leavenworth), purchase the needed equipment and animals, and hire crews, but the investment was sound: The firm made solid profits under this first two-year contract. The firm, in the words of historians Raymond Settle and Mary Lund Settle, was an empire on wheels, growing hand in hand with the continental empire of the United States.

The second major outcome of the Mexican-American War concerning the Pony Express was that under the Treaty of Guadalupe Hidalgo, which ended the war, Mexico ceded Utah and California to the United States. To understand the impact of these acquisitions, we have to go back to the 1840s and look at two other Mexican-American War–era events: the Mormon exodus to the Great Salt Lake Valley, and the discovery of gold in California.

COMPETING EMPIRES: THE MORMON EXODUS AND THE UTAH WAR

From the founding of the Church of Jesus Christ of Latter-Day Saints by Joseph Smith, Mormons, as the church's adherents came to be called, were run out of every town in which they'd tried to settle. By 1839 the Mormons had settled in Nauvoo, Illinois. Five years later, in June 1844, Joseph Smith and his brother, Hyrum Smith, were jailed in Carthage, Illinois. On June 27, a mob broke in and murdered them.

After a brief period, Brigham Young assumed control of the church. One of his first orders of business was to relocate the church and its members to a safe, persecution-free home beyond the reach of the United States: he chose the Great Salt Lake Valley, then a remote northern province of Mexico. The first group of Mormon emigrants started west from the Missouri River in April 1847 and arrived in late summer. Unfortunately for them, the United States won the Mexican-American War six months later. The Mormons had started their Salt Lake colony as trespassers on land claimed by Mexico, but then became squatters on the public domain of the United States.

Nevertheless, the Mormons stayed and continued to build a secure domain for themselves. An important part of that security meant being left free to merge, rather than separate, the functions of church and state. But again, the United States got in the way, this time by organizing Utah Territory in September 1850. With that organization, the Mormons lost their right to create a theodemocracy.

To forestall potential Mormon hostility, President Millard Fillmore appointed Brigham Young as governor of Utah Territory. Other appointees, however, were not Mormon, and their attempts to conform Utah Territory to the laws of the United States engendered hostility among the faithful. Mormon antagonism toward non-Mormon officials and

US policies worsened throughout the 1850s. Finally, only three months into office, James Buchanan's administration concluded that Mormon actions in Utah Territory were evidence of "a riotous disposition which could not be tolerated without weakening the fabric of the Union." Buchanan decided to replace Brigham Young with a non-Mormon governor for Utah Territory and to send out a military force to install the new governor in office and protect him against insurrection. This *posse comitatus* became known as the Utah Expedition. Its conflict with the Mormons became known as the Utah War (1857–1858).

Buchanan launched this expedition during summer 1857, which meant the army needed to arrange for wagon trains to haul enough equipment and provisions to support a body of troops through a Rocky Mountain winter. The army turned to its freighting partner, Russell, Majors & Waddell. Most of the firm's freighting equipment, men, and oxen were already spread out across the plains delivering army supplies as previously contracted. Meeting the army's additional request to supply the Utah Expedition would require the firm to purchase hundreds of wagons and thousands of animals, as well as hire anyone they could find to whack oxen across the plains, and to accomplish these tasks on short notice late in the season, which meant greatly inflated prices. William Russell agreed to provide the trains but failed to ask for or receive a written agreement recognizing that the equipment and services he was supplying were over and above the terms of the firm's existing contract with the army. Russell relied instead on the word of the army quartermaster at Fort Leavenworth, who told him that Buchanan's cabinet "assured" the Quartermaster General in Washington that Russell, Majors & Waddell "would not be neglected."

Supplying the Utah Expedition turned out to be financially devastating for Russell, Majors & Waddell. Mormons destroyed wagon trains laden with supplies. The firm's cattle and oxen were either run off or died for lack of forage, exhaustion, and freezing temperatures. When Russell approached the War Department for payment, he was told that the department had already exceeded its yearly appropriation and had no money to pay him. Despite assurances, Buchanan did nothing to compensate the firm for its losses. Although Russell, Majors & Waddell lumbered along for a few more years, the firm was never able to overcome the deficit it incurred in Utah.

STAYING IN TOUCH: GOLD RUSHES, STAGECOACHING, AND OVERLAND MAIL

The second Mexican-American War–era event that impacted the Pony Express was the discovery of gold in California. James Marshall discovered gold on January 24, 1848, less than two weeks before the United States and Mexico signed the Treaty of Guadalupe Hidalgo. The ensuing rush of Forty-Niners created a critical mass of Americans in California, all of whom, it seems, wanted mail. The United States began providing mail service to the Pacific Coast in 1849 by steamship via Cape Horn and across the Isthmus of Panama. Mail was so popular that when the monthly steamer arrived a canon was fired on San Francisco's Telegraph Hill, "followed by bedlam throughout the city." Men waited in line for days or paid others to stand in line for them.

Californians soon demanded faster service. In 1856, one year before the Mormons started girding themselves for a US invasion, Senator Weller from California presented a petition from his constituents to his colleagues calling for better roads and overland mail service. It was the largest collection of signatures submitted to Congress at the time.

In response, Congress approved an overland mail route to California. In 1857, Postmaster General Aaron Brown awarded this route to Butterfield and Company.

For a number of reasons—primarily the difficulty of traveling over the Rockies during the winter, and the fact that the United States was technically at war with the Mormon church—Postmaster Brown specified that the line run along what came to be known as the Southern Route. The Southern Route started from two cities (St. Louis, Missouri, and Memphis, Tennessee), and converged at Little Rock, Arkansas; from there it ran just north of the border with Mexico to Los Angeles, California, before going north to Sacramento. This service, operating as Butterfield Overland Mail, received a six-year, $600,000 per year subsidy, which was by far the largest overland mail subsidy at that time. The contract gave Butterfield and Company one year, until September 1858, to set up stations and get the line ready to run.

The Butterfield Overland Mail route was instantly derided as the "ox-bow" route due to its roundabout course. The route was 2,800 miles long, nearly a third longer than the South Pass route travelers had been taking to California for twenty years. The route over South Pass—that is, the Oregon, California, and Mormon Pioneer Trails (collectively the "Emigrant Trail" or "Emigrant Trails")—became known as the Central Route. Newspapers in California led the call for a second, presumably faster mail line over the shorter Central Route. The argument over the competing routes, Central and Southern, became a proxy argument over the issue of slavery. The mail route was largely thought to be the precursor to a transcontinental railroad route; Postmaster Brown, so the reasoning went, was a Southerner, and as such, was hoping to lay the groundwork to help ensure the railroad connected the American South to the West.

At this point, history seems to repeat itself. Just as James Marshall discovered gold in California at the close of the Mexican-American War in 1848, Green Russell discovered gold near the future site of Denver, Colorado, at the close of the Utah War in 1858. And just as the California Gold Rush led to a massive surge in overland emigration to California that shifted the country's focus to the West Coast, the Pike's Peak Gold Rush led to an even larger flood of emigration that refocused the country's attention to the front range of the Rocky Mountains.

Military freighting had whetted William Russell's appetite for government contracts. Butterfield Overland Mail's $600,000 per year contract had drawn Russell's attention to potentially lucrative US Mail subsidies. The Pike's Peak Gold Rush was to give him the means to have both.

Throughout fall 1858, news of the gold strike at Pike's Peak raised a flurry of excitement, but the season was too late to start serious prospecting. Like other Missouri River entrepreneurs, Russell wanted to cash in on the gold rush that would erupt the next spring.

Despite Russell, Majors & Waddell's dire financial situation, William Russell proposed that the firm start a stagecoach line to the settlements growing up around Pike's Peak. Russell's partners, Majors and Waddell, demurred. So Russell turned instead to a former freighting associate, John S. Jones. In February 1859, Russell and Jones started their stagecoach line, the Leavenworth and Pike's Peak Express Company. They borrowed heavily, and in a rush of activity, scouted a new route, purchased equipment, posted temporary stations, and stocked the line before launching the service about ten weeks later, in April 1859.

Within weeks after it started operations, Russell and Jones went even further into debt to purchase a rival stagecoach line owned by John Hockaday. Hockaday's line, which ran between St. Joseph, Missouri, and Salt Lake City, Utah, came with a US Mail contract and subsidy. The contract specified that the line run along the Central Route, so Russell and Jones abandoned the route they had just scouted and supplied and set about relocating their stations and equipment to comply, which necessitated more borrowing. Even with the mail subsidy, the passenger traffic was not enough to meet operating costs (which is one reason Hockaday had sold out). Within six months, the Leavenworth and Pike's Peak Express was hopelessly insolvent. In October 1859, Russell, Majors & Waddell purchased the Leavenworth and Pike's Peak Express from Russell and Jones in order to protect itself from Russell's creditors.

Which brings us at last to the Central Overland California and Pike's Peak Express Company, the business that ran the Pony Express.

THE SHORT HAPPY LIFE OF THE PONY EXPRESS

In November 1859, one month after Russell, Majors & Waddell took control of the bankrupt Leavenworth and Pike's Peak Express, Russell started the COC&PP to assume control of the defunct stagecoach company's operations. At some point over the following winter, Russell hit upon the catastrophically bad idea of supplementing the COC&PP's stagecoach and mail service by starting the Pony Express along the same line. There are multiple versions of who first came up with the idea, why Russell pursued it, and why his reluctant partners eventually agreed to support it. Whatever its origins, Russell intended to use the Pony Express to position the COC&PP to replace the Butterfield Overland Mail as the provider of overland stagecoach and US Mail service to California; moreover, Russell was certain he could do even better and win a million-dollar contract to operate over the Central Route.

Russell rushed the Pony Express into service much the same as he had the Leavenworth and Pike's Peak Express just a year earlier. At first, the rush seemed justified. The COC&PP launched its Pony Express on April 3, 1860, to great acclaim. By mid-May it had a stagecoach, mail line, and Pony Express running two thousand miles between St. Joseph, Missouri, and Sacramento, California. These were halcyon days for Russell, Majors & Waddell. Newspapers, particularly in California and along the Missouri River, lauded the Pony Express and its owners in profusions of purple prose.

These happy days, however, were short-lived.

Just one month after the Pony Express started running, the Paiute War broke out in western Nevada. In late May 1860, bands of local Native Americans attacked hastily built stations along the Pony Express line and killed several station keepers. On May 31, the Pony Express temporarily suspended operations through Nevada. Even after it started up again, Pony Express runs were disrupted throughout June 1860, and bands of Native Americans continued to harass stations from central Nevada to Utah through the following October. In addition to the death of its employees and the loss of livestock, Russell, Majors & Waddell had to rebuild and reinforce a number of stations throughout the Great Basin, incurring even more unforeseen expenses.

Meanwhile, Russell, Majors & Waddell was sinking deeper into debt faster than prairie schooner wheels into East Kansas mud. The US Mail subsidy was insufficient to support the stagecoach line; the company lost even more money every time a Pony Express rider jumped on his mount, waved his hat, and hollered, "Giddyap!" Russell borrowed whatever he could under increasingly unfavorable terms. After he'd exhausted all other sources, he became involved in the embezzlement of government bonds, which he used as security for loans. In December 1860, the government official who loaned Russell the bonds had a crisis of conscience and confessed. On Christmas Eve, Russell was carted off to jail. And though the case against him was dismissed due to a technicality in February 1861, Russell, his partners, and their firm were thoroughly disgraced.

Throughout this period, the country had been slouching toward civil war. In December 1860, while Russell was being ratted out in Washington, DC, South Carolina seceded from the Union. Texas followed in February 1861. Soon after, the Butterfield Overland Mail line through the south was "cut up by the roots."

In light of the increasing likelihood of war between the North and South, the allegiance of California and its immense wealth became a critical issue. Under its constitution, California was a non-slave state, but there was a substantial proslavery faction, as well as a rival movement for independence. In order to keep California and its gold in the Union, the Lincoln administration thought it essential to keep California connected to the North, primarily through its stagecoach travel and mail communication. The question was how.

The government's options were few. The Butterfield Overland Mail line through rebel territory had been broken. The COC&PP and its Pony Express still operated along the Central Route, but given the company's poor financial status and Russell's involvement in the recent bond embezzlement scandal, the government couldn't reward the firm with a huge subsidy.

In the end, Congress passed a bill directing Butterfield and Company to relocate its Butterfield Overland Mail operation to the Central Route. To expedite the move, Butterfield and Company subcontracted with the COC&PP to operate the eastern half of the route, between St. Joseph, Missouri, and Salt Lake City, Utah. The bill compensated Butterfield and Company for damages to its line, reimbursed it for having to relocate to the Central Route, and somewhat ironically, increased the overland mail subsidy to $1 million. Russell's dream of a million-dollar overland mail contract had come true at last, but for someone else.

This same bill specified that the Pony Express continue operating, but that the service was to expire as soon as the transcontinental telegraph was completed. With the joining of the wires on October 26, 1861, the Pony Express became obsolete; by the end of November, it was gone. Even with the increased subsidy under its subcontract with Butterfield and Company, Russell, Majors & Waddell wasn't able to earn enough money to pay off its debts. Less than six months later, the assets of Russell, Majors & Waddell were sold at auction and the partnership dissolved.

PART ONE

THE PRAIRIE—
ST. JOSEPH, MISSOURI, TO
KEARNEY, NEBRASKA

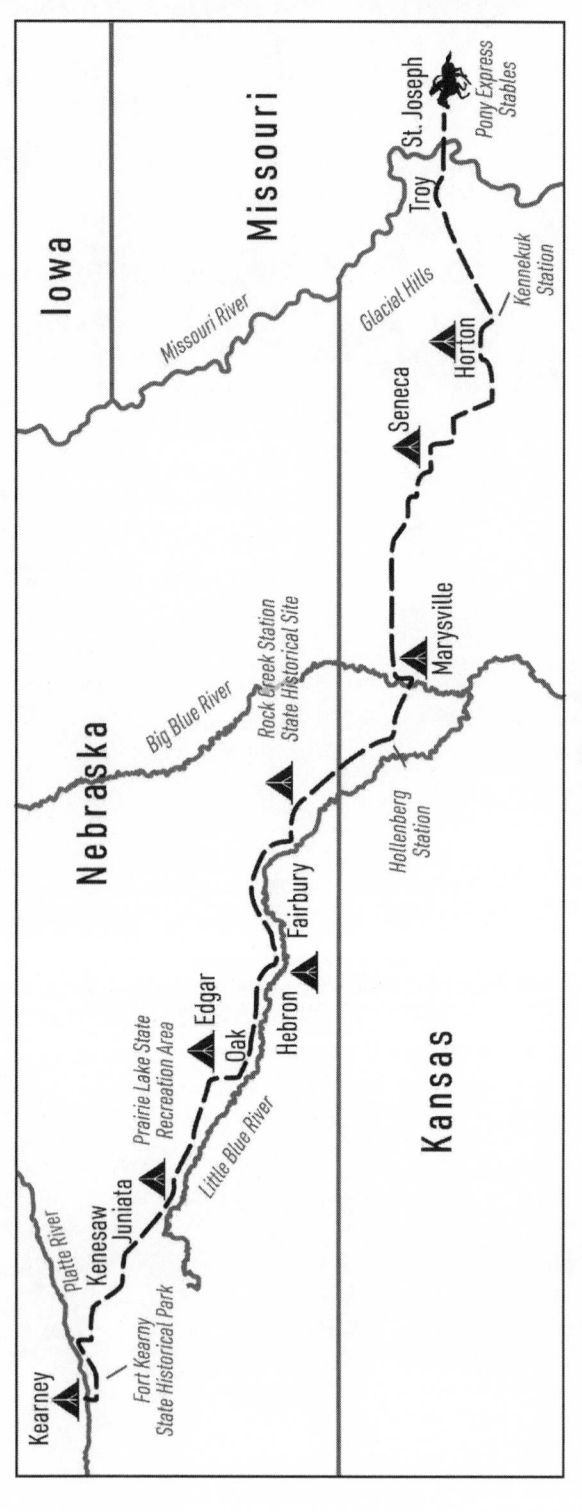

The Prairie

St. Joseph, Missouri, to Kearney, Nebraska

362 miles

CHAPTER ONE

What I Learned about East Kansas

HERE'S WHAT I LEARNED MY FIRST DAY BIKEPACKING THE PONY EXPRESS Route. Despite what you may think, northeastern Kansas is not flat: it is as hilly as San Francisco in places. And despite what anyone may tell you, northeastern Kansas doesn't have mud: it has glue-impregnated clay.

The ride started out fine. Actually, it didn't. As I was ready to roll out from St. Joseph, Missouri, I found I had a flat front tire. It was a new tire and had been holding air, so after a few minutes of panicking, I decided to pump it up and just see what happened. I'd know within five or ten miles whether I needed to turn around.

Running Tubeless

As with most mountain bikes, I run tubeless. The advantage of tubeless tires is they virtually eliminate puncture flats, the bane of off-road travel. The disadvantage is they require an absolutely airtight seal. My best guess was that the seal had most likely been broken through the rim tape (which keeps air from escaping through the spoke holes), which meant that the leak would be slow. The prudent move would have been to stay put another day and fix the leak, as there weren't any bike shops on the route for 350 miles. But I was impatient to get started.

On my way out of St. Joseph, Missouri, I swung by the Patee House, headquarters of the Pony Express ("Where the Pony Express started and Jesse James stopped!"), and the Pony Express Stables (Mile Zero of the Pony Express Bikepacking Route) before crossing the Missouri River on the Pony Express Bridge into Kansas. The ride went fine, at least as far as Wathena, Kansas, about ten miles west of the Missouri River. I didn't know it then, but that was the longest stretch of flat I'd ride until I reached the Platte River, three hundred miles away. Riding the Pony Express Route west across northeast Kansas, from the Missouri River to the Little Blue River, takes you across an endless succession of creeks and streams, all running north and south. The route constantly drops down to a creek bottom, then climbs back up the other side.

I should have been better prepared. The elevation profile told me I'd climb two thousand feet that day, but I'd ignored it: It's Kansas, how bad could it be? Had I reviewed my research, I might have been reminded how bad. Back in the 1940s, Irene Paden wrote a book titled *The Wake of the Prairie Schooner* based on summer trips she and her husband had spent crisscrossing the West in a station wagon, dragging their growing son along, while they retraced the old emigrant routes to Oregon and California. After climbing up and down the steep hills in East Kansas, she wrote, "Driving an ox team over these endless, rolling hillocks was a task from which the very imagination recoiled." Yeah, well, so is riding a bike hauling forty pounds of trailer and gear.

The gravel roads were damp, but solid. Cars and trucks had left packed tracks to follow after the rain the day before. But dirt is different from gravel, and when I turned from the latter onto the former, I bogged down immediately. Twice.

The first time, I recalled the advice I'd received from Emma and Derek, cyclists I'd met in St. Joseph. "It's okay to ride dirt roads after it rains, so long as they still have puddles," Emma told me. What if they're wet but the puddles are gone? "No puddles means the mud has absorbed the water," Derek said, "which makes it very dense, like peanut butter. It'll rip your derailleur off."

Bearing that in mind, I stayed on the Pony Express Route when it called for a turn onto a puddled, muddy road, but slowed considerably, and advanced cautiously. Every inch I moved the wheels sank deeper, so I stopped the bike before the mud stopped me. I extracted myself from that morass and found an alternative route on gravel and pavement. Francis Parkman, who traveled through Northeast Kansas in 1846, was not so lucky on his first encounter with Kansas mud. Not long after starting out from Westport, he encountered a "deep muddy gully, a species that afterward became but too familiar to us; and here, for the space of an hour or more, the cart stuck fast."

I rode the detour to my first waypoint, Troy, Kansas, site of the first Pony Express station west of the Missouri River. There were two types of stations on the Pony Express: swing (or "relay") stations and home stations. Swing stations, like Troy, were brief stops along the way where Pony Express riders changed horses; home stations marked the beginning and end of a section, the places where one rider would hand the mail off to the next, then lay over for a day or more before making the mail run back.

My first impression of Troy was that it was red. The streets and most of the buildings were made of brick. The red was broken here and there by white limestone walls and foundations, concrete curbs, and painted crosswalks; all of it was set in the ridiculously verdant midwestern green of lush grass and leafy trees. Even so, Troy struck me as predominantly, overwhelmingly red. I'd never seen anything like it. As corny as it sounds, my thought on entering downtown was, "Toto, I've a feeling we're not in California anymore." I parked the bike and had a snack, then took a couple of pictures of the Pony Express marker on the northwest corner of the Doniphan County Courthouse grounds before moving on.

A couple of hours later, I had just topped a hill and started down when I saw, and ignored, a sign that said, "Gravel ends." I didn't see any puddles, which meant the road was probably peanut butter, but it looked solid enough and I was picking up speed on the downslope and didn't want to stop. By the time these thoughts zinged through my brain I was furrowing deeper and deeper into the muck until the bike just stopped dead, nearly throwing me over the handlebars. The wheels were locked, packed so full of mud they wouldn't budge. It took me three trips to carry everything (bike, trailer, gear bag) back up the hill to the gravel section. It felt like walking on flypaper, mud adhering to the mud already adhered to my shoes. Every fifteen feet I had to stop and scrape my soles in the weeds along the side of the road.

While I was schlepping all this gear, a pickup stopped. The driver, Carla, lived in the house just before the end of the gravel. She asked if I'd like to use their hose to wash the mud off my bike. I thanked her and told her I'd be okay. By the time I had carried the last load back to the gravel, she was crouched next to the bike, scraping mud from the back tire with a butter knife she'd retrieved from the house. I joined in, digging mud out from the frame using a twig I'd found. Once the bike and trailer could roll, I got them to the hose and spent twenty minutes trying to wash enough mud off to make everything operable. Carla offered me water, lunch, a snack, like a worried mother. She asked where I was headed, and wrote down phone numbers of people to call—including her mom—in case I needed help. Carla was a godsend, uncommonly sweet and generous, and meeting someone like her so randomly almost—*almost*—made me feel less embarrassed about getting stuck in the mud like an idiot when I should have known better.

I later learned Doniphan County, which I'd been riding through all morning, is part of a unique section of Kansas called the Glacial Hills, notable for both its hills and mud.

"When the glaciers receded north, they left behind a unique, scenic landscape of rolling, wooded hills and valleys with clear, running streams." Rolling hills? The elevation profile for the route I'd mapped was jagged as a saw blade. They might seem rolly in Irene Paden's station wagon, or maybe on a lighter bike. But all morning I'd been down in first gear, crawling up hills at around four miles per hour.

The peanut butter mud is attributable to loess (pronounced "luss"), the special soil of the Glacial Hills. Loess is outwash deposited by meltwater from glaciers during the Ice Age and is composed of fine particles of silt and clay that tend to interlock.

"Silt and clay" with "exceptionally fine particles" that "tend to interlock." Right. Just add water.

From Carla's house, I avoided further encounters with Kansas glue-mud by detouring onto the paved highway, rolling easily south and west, passing the tiny hamlet of Bendena, skirting by Denton, and stopping in Everest, Kansas, where I took a snack break in the local park. None of these towns has any real significance to the Pony Express, or for that matter, to anything related to the westward emigration of the mid-1800s. None of them were here.

Past the town of Everest sat a collection of monuments for Kennekuk Station, the first Pony Express home station west of the Missouri River. When I was planning my ride, I had considered riding from home station to home station, each day's ride re-creating the ride of every Pony Express rider. But I soon found that identifying home stations was not as straightforward as it might seem. The statement above, "the first home station west of the Missouri River," carries far more ambiguity than its declarative form suggests.

Home stations were on average between seventy-five to one hundred miles apart. Kennekuk is within that mileage range from St. Joseph, but so are the next two Kansas stations, Seneca and Marysville, both of which also claim to have been home stations. According to the Kennekuk Station monument, it was only a home station for the first two months of the Pony Express, from April through May 1860. The monument in Seneca states that it became a home station in July 1860 (leading one to wonder where the home station was during June). On the other hand, a plaque on a stone barn in Marysville claims *it* was the "Original Pony Express Home Station No. 1," which directly contradicts both the Kennekuk and Seneca monuments.

In fact, there is no definitive list of Pony Express stations. There is an "official" post office list, which identifies 138 stations. But trying to identify, locate, and name a complete list of Pony Express stations is like trying to change a tire on a moving car. Throughout the Pony's eighteen-month existence, stations were constantly added, removed, abandoned, and relocated. According to the National Park Service, which administers the Pony Express National Historic Trail, there were eighty-six stations when it began, and 147 by mid-1861. Trail historian William Hill states that "By the end of the express, the number [of stations] could have grown to between 190 and 200, but some may not have been used." Could have? May not have been? How useless is that?

You can take your pick of station lists; no choice is wrong because none is unquestionably right. Even the "official" government post office list is just a snapshot of a moment in time.

And these lists are less illuminating than they seem. Many stations were known by different names by different groups at different times. Between Troy and Kennekuk, for instance, stood a relay station known variably as Lewis (also spelled "Louis"), Cold Spring, Chain Pump, Valley Home, and Valley House Station. Experts even differ on the actual location of many stations. Historians place Kennekuk Station, for example, in two different places, five miles apart.

So when I was standing in front of the bronze Pony Express medallion mounted on a concrete post in the corner of someone's front yard at a gravelly intersection, I may or may not have been on or near the site of Kennekuk Station, which was a home station for two months, though possibly three, before being replaced by a station either in Seneca or Marysville, Kansas.

The long and short of it is that I decided not to base my ride days on home stations.

From Kennekuk, I detoured north off the Pony Express Route to Horton, Kansas, a quiet little town of shady, tree-lined streets. My destination was Mission Lake, just north of town, where I'd planned to camp. A week or so earlier, I had gotten in touch with Mike, the caretaker of the lake, to see what's what: Did I need reservations? Where should I find him to pay? Did they offer tent sites? We had a pleasant if disjointed conversation. In the end he assured me I'd have a spot with access to water, toilets, and a shower. Mike asked my name and I told him. He hesitated. I spelled my last name for him. After another moment's silence, he said, "I'll just mark you down as 'Scott on the bike.'"

Two days before in St. Joseph I'd decided to put off starting my ride for a day due to rain. When I called Mike to change my reservation, he said, "Sure. Scott on the bike. From California. No problem." In fact, he told me, some people had been tent camping there and had left that afternoon ahead of the rain. "They loved the spot," he said. "I guess they like primitive camping."

Primitive camping?

I asked him how he thought the area would be just one day after the rain.

"Oh, it'll be nice," he said. "Maybe a little muddy, but we'll deal with it. It'll be okay."

When I arrived, I found Mike and his family in a large trailer next to the camp's maintenance building. I introduced myself. He studied my rig for a moment. "When you said 'bike,' I assumed you meant motorcycle." Once we'd cleared that up, I asked him about the tent camping area. It turned out to be three-quarters of a mile away, and in addition to being "not too muddy," had no electricity, no running water, and only pit toilets. I could do without electricity (I carried a solar charger) and didn't mind the toilets. But I'd had enough mud for one day, and did not want to walk a mile and a half for a shower. I haggled with him for a while and he finally agreed to let me take one of the many unused RV spots close by even though they were reserved for people staying a week or longer.

The campsite was nothing special: a patch of gravel to park an RV next to patchy grass on which to pitch a tent. But it sat on the very edge of Mission Lake. The breeze had calmed and puffy white clouds seemed to float in the perfect blue mirror of the small reservoir. It was a peaceful place to rest after a tumultuous first day.

CHAPTER TWO

Hippogriff in Flight

THE NEXT MORNING DIDN'T START WELL. AS IT WAS MY FIRST NIGHT camping, I didn't sleep comfortably, slept in later than I had wanted, and then took all kinds of time to pack up to go. My front tire was completely flat. It had lasted through yesterday's ride, so I felt comfortable continuing, but my daily routine would have to include pumping it up every morning. I just hoped the leak wouldn't get worse.

Someone from a radio station in nearby Hiawatha, Kansas, had heard about my ride and wanted to do a phone interview at 9:30 a.m. I had planned to eat breakfast in Horton, do the interview, and still be on the road by 10:00 a.m. I wasn't even packed until 9:30. I saw Mike, the caretaker, on my way out. "Look me up if you come by here again," he said. "I may not be here, but look me up anyway."

I was worried about the weather because the morning was absolutely clear and it was already approaching eighty degrees. In Davis, California, where I live, summer mornings like this are the kiss of death, because you know it'll be one hundred degrees by 4:00 p.m. Nevertheless, I had to eat, so I stopped in at Grandma's Depot.

It was a nice little restaurant on Highway 20, which runs along the north edge of Horton. The server was very pleasant, but also very slow. She'd bring one thing to my table at a time (fork, knife, coffee, creamer). It was a small place, and there was only one other customer, but she was in no hurry. Neither was the cook. On one of her trips to my table, the server told me I had beautiful eyes, so I was inclined not to get upset at the delay. But God help them if they ever have a rush.

Speaking of God, someone had wandered in announcing he'd felt the call to preach the Book of Revelation at Grandma and whoever else happened to be sitting with her (maybe the cook?). The itinerant was older, gray, and gaunt; he reminded me of Royal Dano, the minister from *The Right Stuff* who showed up whenever a test pilot crashed. His style was Socratic, posing questions designed to solicit "I don't knows" so he could provide answers. I didn't follow much of what he said—he equated aliens with the devil and talked about specific numbers of people who'd be taken in the first rapture, who'd be left, and how God would choose—but the cadence of his voice, his old-school proselytizing, seemed oddly appropriate to that time and place.

When breakfast finally arrived (talk about the Second Coming) I hurried through my meal, a plate-sized pancake and two eggs. The food had a certain taste. I couldn't place the flavor, but I'm sure it came from something long-since banned in California. The entire meal came to less than $5. Even leaving a 40 percent tip (see the comment above about eyes), I got out of there for about the price of a double espresso in Davis.

I came out of the restaurant to a welcome surprise: Puffballs of fair-weather cumulus had sprouted like mushrooms across the field of the sky. Most of the morning I had wonderfully cool temps. Even when the cloud cover thinned in the afternoon it never got much above eighty degrees. Warm, but not as hot as I had feared.

Back on the road the hill country continued, but I was smarter about the mud. The gravel road I was on transitioned to dirt on the far side of an intersection. The surface was wet, but the road looked solid. Even so, I turned right, opting to stay on gravel, and headed north toward the highway. Just east of the intersection, someone had installed a large metal Pony Express sculpture. It was the iconic image—rider leaning forward in the saddle, spurring his pony on, mane flying, tail pointed straight back like a starched flag—that captures perfectly the hallmarks of the Pony Express: Speed, endurance, and commitment. The image is powerful, but misleading.

Pony Express riders did not gallop between stations. During the day they rode at about the same pace I kept on my bike—which I can tell you after riding 1,400 miles of the Pony Express Route is not very fast.

According to Pony Express historian Joe Nardone, "This idea of a gallop. No they didn't do that. . . . At nighttime they were probably doing three to five miles an hour and in the daytime ten to twelve miles at a trot or a lope, not a gallop."

There were rare occasions when riders were expected to gallop: when being chased, for instance, by some pesky Shoshone horsemen. Rather than fight, Pony Express riders were supposed to run, relying on their horses being able to outpace any pursuers. Actual attacks, by Native Americans or otherwise, seem to have been few and resulted in only one death: Bart Riles (or Riley), reportedly killed by Shoshones near Smith Creek Station in Nevada. In fact, more riders died in accidents, such as being thrown from their horses. Nevertheless, being chased by Native Americans was a regular feature of Pony Express riders' stories, likely because in recounting their time with the Pony Express, the former riders found racing for their lives a far more compelling tale than, say, tripping over an ox.

The other reason to ride a horse at a gallop was the rare occasion when the Pony Express pulled out all the stops to race a particularly important message across the continent. Such events required special preparations and were planned well in advance. The record-breaking run was the delivery of President Lincoln's inaugural address to California. Lincoln's address was telegraphed ahead to Fort Kearny, then carried by Pony Express from there to the next telegraph point: Fort Churchill, Nevada; Placerville, California; or Folsom, California, depending on which account you read. To help ensure the fastest time between the east and west telegraph terminals, each horse only traveled about ten miles, rather than the twelve to twenty miles of a normal run. Even so, a number of horses were ridden to their death. As profligate as the Pony Express was in practice—it is estimated to have lost between \$100,00 and \$500,000—the company wouldn't have sacrificed horses intentionally on every scheduled run.

Not that the truth ever got in the way of a vivid depiction. From the first, the Pony Express has inspired writers and artists to idolize this simple mail service, idealize it, elevate it to the level of myth. The mount wasn't merely a horse, but "the veritable Hippogriff who shoved a continent behind his hooves so easily." Riders had to be "young, skinny, wiry fellows," and, due to the danger of the work, the archetypical Pony Express want ad allegedly specified, "Orphans preferred." No such advertisement for riders ever existed. I have read through all of the lists of Pony Express riders I could find, and have not found one rider identified as an orphan.

Yet "orphans preferred" is probably the most quoted phrase of Pony Express "fakelore," to use Joe Nardone's term, blithely repeated in virtually every account of the Pony Express. The only known ad for riders asked simply for "men, familiar with the management of horses." But that wouldn't suffice because like their supernatural horses, Pony Express riders had to be quintessential horsemen, the epitome of American bravery and élan. They are idealized throughout the literature as "clean, God-fearing, worthy of trust, and modest in the extreme." A typical description describes them as "picturesque and romantic in their buckskin jackets, their spurred boots, their pistols thrust through a gaudy sash!"

A bit much? Sure, but let's face it. Who would be inspired by a sculpture of a slouching cowboy delivering a few pieces of mail on a trotting horse? And I have to admit, as I looked up at that sculpture while climbing up to the highway from a creek bottom, the jet-black silhouette of the hippogriff in flight against the cerulean sky did cut a striking image.

I worked back to the gravel roads of the Pony Express Route and made it to my stopping point, Seneca, Kansas, midafternoon. Coming into town on Seneca's red-bricked Main Street, I heard music: "Venus" (by Shocking Blue, not Bananarama), and "Fame" by David Bowie. I wondered for whose benefit the music played. Downtown was quiet. There was little traffic, and fewer pedestrians. It seemed so anachronistic to hear these tunes piped into speakers all along a quiet, brick-laid street bordered by buildings more than a hundred years old.

Seneca has a couple of Pony Express monuments, as well as a Pony Express museum. I took pictures of the monuments, noted the museum's limited hours (because I wanted to stop in the next morning), and kept on to my spot for the night, Bailey's RV Park, on the outskirts of town. A billboard at the entrance said to get a campsite at Bailey's, you call. So I called. Thirty seconds later, a golf cart sped up, and the camp host led me over to the tent-camping area—a grassy patch all of a hundred feet from the entrance where RVers took their dogs to poop—then walked me over to the showers and restrooms, told me what it cost, and where to drop the check (I swear campgrounds will be the last businesses in America to accept checks). Fifteen seconds later, he was back home, because the hosts' trailer was only another hundred feet from the tent area.

I wrote out a check and walked it over. Then I had the rest of the afternoon to set up camp, take a shower, recharge all my devices, wash a load of muddy clothes, and try to get a better night's sleep for the next day's ride.

CHAPTER THREE

The Butt Goes First

NEXT MORNING I BACKTRACKED A MILE TO SENECA, KANSAS, TO DROP a postcard, grab breakfast, and see the Pony Express Museum, which was supposed to open at 9:00 a.m. I stopped in at Sweet Pea Bakery, which I thought offered breakfast, only to find it didn't. No matter. I ordered an Americano and ate the sweetest cinnamon roll I hope I ever come across as long as I live.

While I was eating, a woman came up and apologized for interrupting me. She introduced herself as Dana, then told me she was Carla's cousin (remember Carla with the butter knife?). Carla had asked her to look out for me in case I needed any help in Seneca. I was touched. How very sweet of both women. Dana took a selfie with me to send to Carla, then went back to a table and rejoined her friends.

I sat in front of the Pony Express Museum listening to the Main Street jukebox ("Happy Together," by the Turtles, among other golden oldies) until about 9:10 when I finally read the fine print on the door, which stated, "By Appointment Only." I thought about calling the number, but didn't know how long it would take for someone to get there, and as it was warm already, didn't want to sit around much longer.

I rode north out of town to the gravel roads of the Pony Express Route. All went fine for a mile or so, until I turned west and ran smack into a headwind. The wind wasn't always on my nose. It played with me all day long, sometimes in front, sometimes on the side, sometimes disappearing altogether; never, however, from behind where it would do some good. Between the wind and an increasing soreness in my backside, I had a less-than-stellar day on the bike.

Two months before I left home to start this trip, I broke my collarbone in a low-speed crash on my Schwinn cruiser (falling onto grass in a green belt, of all places). Eight weeks was enough time to heal before my Pony Express ride, but my injury kept me off the bike when I should have been training. That worried my partner, Lisa, or at least concerned her. She asked whether I would be in good enough condition to ride. I assured her I had trained plenty up to that point, and while the first week or so might be rough, I'd be up to the challenge.

All, that is, except for my butt, because when you stop riding a bike, the butt goes first. Legs, arms, neck, wrists, cardio—that conditioning lasts longer and comes back quickly. But sitting for seven or so hours on a bike saddle takes some getting used to, and you have to get reacquainted, as it were, every time you're off the bike. If you think about it, sitting in or on anything for that long is not really comfortable. That being said, saddle discomfort is a particular bummer because if you can't sit, you really can't ride for very long.

Saddle or Seat?

There is some controversy among cyclists over which term is correct, saddle or seat. From the earliest days, when inventors were trying to solve the challenge of creating a "mechanical horse," saddle was the proper term. In the late 1800s, when the safety bicycle was invented (two-wheeled, chain-driven bikes like we have today), the term "seat" came to be used. Today, most people use the terms interchangeably.

Sheldon Brown, a well-respected expert on bicycles, maintained that "saddle" was still the proper term: "A seat is something you sit on, and is designed to bear essentially your entire weight. . . . A saddle is intended to carry some, but not all of your weight. The rest of your weight is mainly carried by your legs, and some by your hands and arms."

Bicycle historian David Herlihy attributes the usage of the respective terms to different types of cyclists: "[T]he vernacular might speak of bicycle seats. . . . But for those thoroughbreds more attuned to the bicycle's equestrian roots, 'saddle' was—and remains—the preferred term."

Though I do not consider myself a traditionalist, saddle seems the more appropriate term. I ride a Brooks saddle, which is a relatively heavy saddle made of leather stretched over a metal frame with no padding other than the give of the leather. Perhaps counterintuitively, I (and many other ultradistance cyclists) find it the most comfortable saddle on long rides—that is, once you're rehabituated.

Thirty minutes out of Seneca, I started to pay the price of not training in the saddle. It made the day extra-long, not just because the pain interrupted my bike-daydreaming by focusing my attention in the moment, but also because I used every downhill to stand and get some relief, which slowed me some. The good news about saddle discomfort is that it's not a linear progression of pain. Soreness one day does not necessarily mean more the next. Of course, it also doesn't necessarily mean less. You just have to grind it out until the discomfort ceases to be an issue.

I rolled into Marysville, Kansas, around 3:30 p.m., dropping south into town on a shaded multiuse trail along the Big Blue River. Marysville is notable in that it seems to be noted by everyone who passed through here during the mid-1800s and bothered to write (which does not include Pony Express riders, because on the whole, they weren't the scrivening sort). Though Kansas Territory stretched to the summit of the Rocky Mountains, the Big Blue was the boundary of the true frontier until the late 1850s.

It was originally known as Palmetto; a man named Frank Marshall set up a ferry here in the early 1850s, and a town (named after his wife) grew up around it. For emigrants, Marysville was a place to repair and reorganize gear. At the same time, it was hazardous. Cholera rampaged through camps along this part of the trail in the late 1840s and early 1850s. After disease, death by drowning at this river crossing and others along the way was one of the largest killers of emigrants.

The wide streets in the center of town, as with Seneca and Troy, were paved with brick and bordered by brick buildings. I rode around an enormous Pony Express sculpture (the same postage-stamp image of a racing horse and rider as the sculpture near Horton) and straight into Marysville City Park, which has sites for RV and tent camping.

This feature of the Midwest—camping in the city park—was completely new to me. I've never lived in a town that allowed, let alone encouraged, transients to stay overnight. Civic campgrounds seem to be a feature all across the Midwest. Some of the towns charge a nominal fee. (Marysville was free, though the town did accept donations.) Apparently, there are public corrals across the Midwest as well, holdovers from overland emigrant days when they served as overnight camping spots for wagon trains.

The park was part of a wonderful complex of greenbelt, campsites, and a water park where 1980s hits blasted out over the screams of swimmers all through the hot afternoon. All in all, a pleasant place to spend an early-June day. I found a shady site under some beautiful old lindens and started to set up camp. Off the bike, I felt mentally slow: thoughts seemed to take too long to register; my movements felt clumsy, awkward. I realized, in a cloudy sort of way, that I might be dehydrated and underfed. I found a bench nearby to rest and ate and drank there until I felt I could think reasonably clearly again.

While I was stabilizing my system, a woman approached and apologized for bugging me. She then introduced herself as Betty, Carla's mom. It seems Betty was in Marysville getting her hair done, and Carla had asked her to look out for me, so before Betty returned to Seneca, where she lives, she took a turn through Marysville City Park on the off chance I might be there. She saw my orange bike and stopped to say hi and ask if I needed anything.

Like cousin Dana in Seneca, Betty took a selfie with me to send to Carla. Before she left, she told me that the Pony Express Museum people in Seneca (whom I didn't call to come open up) were the folks Carla had told me to look up if I needed anything there. I should have called the number on the museum door after all. I felt bad about missing that opportunity.

I hoped to make up for it by visiting Marysville's Pony Express Museum. By the time I arrived, however, it had just closed. One of the volunteers, Chuck, was still standing outside. He told me he lived on a farm just outside town and had chores to attend to, but said he'd rather talk than work. He walked me over to the original stables (where the "Original Pony Express Home Station No. 1" plaque was mounted), then we sat down on a bench where Chuck held forth for the better part of an hour. He was proud of the museum and the town, was knowledgeable, certainly, and a good storyteller; but more than that, it seemed Chuck *really* did not want to go back to the farm and his chores, preferring instead to tell me all he could about the history of Marysville and the Pony Express Museum founding and improvements. He walked me over to the post office to show me an oil painting of the Pony Express stables hanging in the lobby. And despite the museum being closed, he unlocked it and ushered me inside and pointed out different exhibits he recommended I see when the museum reopened the next day.

On toward evening, too late to attend to his chores, Chuck decided to leave me with some closing thoughts.

"You know what created the Pony Express?" he asked.

I shook my head.

"Hollywood."

"I thought it was Buffalo Bill's Wild West Show."

He shrugged. "Like I said, Hollywood."

Chuck then confided that he could not figure out why anyone would be stupid enough to ride their bike the length of the Pony Express Trail. I told him he was in good company, as my partner, Lisa (who'd started identifying herself as "married to the nut"), felt exactly the same. Chuck got a good laugh out of that.

CHAPTER FOUR

Dark Night of the Soul

THE NEXT DAY STARTED THE NIGHT BEFORE, WHICH IS TO SAY I DID NOT sleep well in Marysville's Central Park. Bright lights lit the area all night. I'd set up camp directly under one and had to lay a shirt over my eyes to simulate nighttime. Also, it was loud. Very loud. The park sat next to the train yard, and freight trains came and went all night long.

Nevertheless, I got off to a decent start, until a mile or so later when halfway across the Big Blue River I realized I had left my water bottle at the campground. No sweat, it was still there when I went back. But that was a dumb mistake and an unnecessary delay.

Emigrant guidebooks from the mid-1800s advised that if they hadn't been setting a night guard, once overlanders crossed the Big Blue they should start or risk losing their livestock. For the most part, overlanders left their animals outside the ring of wagons to graze at night. There was always a danger of losing livestock to a stampede, or to wolves driving the animals off, at any point in the overland journey. But the area between the Big Blue River and the Platte River was considered Pawnee country, and the Pawnees had a reputation as master horse thieves.

Travelogues and trail guidebooks of the era singled out Pawnees as "treacherous and predatory people," predisposing overlanders to view them as such. The stereotypes were compounded by emigrants' fear of all Native Americans, along with their ignorance of Plains Indian customs. The situation worsened when emigrants failed to follow common sense. Especially vulnerable were men who rode off individually or in a small group to hunt game in country where experienced men knew better than to take such a risk. Sometimes they were killed. More often they would escape an encounter with just the loss of their horses or their clothes.

In any event, overlanders were now setting night guards, the most detested duty for teamsters and emigrants alike. In addition to being uncomfortable, night duty could also be dangerous, though more often than not, the nervous guard was the cause of danger. Overlanders shot at one another, as well as oxen, mules, horses, sheep, and even saddles and blankets, mistaking them for marauding Indians.

Telling Time on the Prairie

On the long nights of guard duty, overlanders relied on the stars to tell them when their shift was over. They would tell time by noting the relationship of the "dipper" end of Ursa Major as it rotated around Polaris. It takes a little computation, but is not overly complicated. I thought I might try this method, but was generally asleep well before I could make use of it. Besides, I was traveling with two mobile phones, a tablet, and a satellite tracker. More often than not I couldn't avoid seeing what time it was.

The next Pony Express station west from Marysville was Hollenberg Station, which sits across a divide between the Big Blue and the Little Blue Rivers. It was the last Pony Express station in Kansas, and worth seeing because the building is one of the very few unaltered Pony Express stations still on its original site. When I arrived, however, there was a handwritten note on the Visitors' Center door: "Sorry but the center is closed today." The author included a smiley face, I guess to make disappointed visitors like me feel better about being turned away.

From Hollenberg Station, the Pony Express Route turned northwest to follow the Little Blue River nearly as far as the Platte River. The original Pony Express Trail (as well as the Oregon and California Trails) trended northwest for 120 miles along the banks of the Little Blue to Thirty-Two Mile Creek (near Ayr, Nebraska). Since that time, the land has been surveyed, settled, and farmed, making it impossible to follow the original trail in most places along the Little Blue. Instead, the Pony Express Route I was riding, like the National Park Service's Auto Tour Routes, made northwest indirectly by stair-stepping north and west on roads laid out along the survey lines.

Like Hollenberg Station, I had been looking forward to this part of the route along the Little Blue River. Emigrants needed three things every day on the trail: a campsite, water, and forage for the animals. The Little Blue River had all of these in abundance, and as a consequence, it was fondly remembered in the overlanders' diaries.

The change in direction seemed to augur a change in my mood, because soon after leaving Hollenberg, my energy level steadily dropped. The breeze was about fifteen knots out of the south, which meant I had a tailwind or crosswind all day. Not the worst direction, but it was a desiccating, enervating wind that sucked the hydration out of me on the cross and didn't cool me at all when blowing from behind. The forecast high was ninety degrees, and it felt at least that hot. Not a cloud in the sky until a few cumulus clouds formed in the late afternoon.

I am usually fine riding in hot conditions. But (like the saddle thing) my body needs to acclimate, and I had not had that opportunity. I was sucking down water and electrolytes but still suffering—and now worrying about having enough water to last the day.

Just shy of the Nebraska state line I saw a tractor pull in next to a farmhouse and start to refuel. I stopped to ask for water. The driver told me it wasn't his house, just where they kept the fuel he needed, but that his cousin, Eunice, who did own the house probably wouldn't mind. Eunice's tidy house sat at an angle to the road, surrounded by a prim patch of lawn. You'd almost expect to see an apple pie cooling on the windowsill.

As I refilled my water bottles, I mentioned to Eunice's cousin how I was looking forward to riding along the Little Blue after reading so many nice things about it, thinking he might appreciate an outsider appreciating the area in which he lived. He didn't respond in words. Instead, he gave a wry smile and surveyed the dusty gravel fueling area and the dry fields across the road before looking at me again, the expression on his face all but saying, "I don't know as I'd describe it as that exactly." I thanked him again and got underway.

I crossed into Nebraska, passed an unmarked Pony Express station site, then came across a huge, triangular Oregon Trail memorial, the engraved words eroded to illegibility on the weather side. A nearby sign indicated the path of emigrant-era wagon ruts. The roads ran north and west; the wagon ruts cut diagonally northwest across an intersection, parallel to the Little Blue (which was out of view). The direction was right, but the tracks looked no different from tire ruts, and while I had no reason to doubt the veracity of the claim, it was hard to be impressed. Or maybe it was just my downward-spiraling mood.

Because not long after, I started to despair. Suddenly, it hit me that I was going to be out on roads like this for a very long time, looking for station markers that might not exist, fighting the wind and the heat, not sure where I'd sleep every night, or whether I'd even be able to find a place. It struck me in a way it never had before that not only might I not complete the trip, I might not even *want* to complete the trip. I had always been unsure I could do the whole thing. In fact, the morning I left St. Joseph I actually stayed in bed as late as I could because I knew once I got up, the trip started and this was it. But that was a different, more intellectual fear than the physical realization, this feeling in my gut, that I just might not be up to the journey I had set for myself.

Further along I stopped under a rare patch of shade cast by a tree barely hanging out over the road across from a dusty farmhouse. The right edge of the roadbed sloped down to a creek. I got off the bike to take a break and set the trailer kickstand. The rig listed a little to starboard, toward the slope, but seemed stable enough; that is, until it capsized and sent everything cascading down the slope. I ignored the mess until I was able to gather up the energy to gather up my gear, then slowly, methodically stepped down through the grass, unhooked the trailer, and one by one, hauled every item back up.

This was only Day Four. How would I ever make it five or six weeks?

I limped along the remainder of the way to Rock Creek Station State Recreation Area, the campground where I had planned to stay. I could no longer push the pedals. I had to choose the gear that would allow the pedals to turn with the least effort. I stood whenever I could and coasted.

It felt like it took forever. Then, as I approached the campground, two things happened that perked me up.

First, a cloud passed overhead, covering me in a shadow and cooling the air. I couldn't believe how grateful I was. Seconds later I was coasting downhill and a deer bounded across the road. I took that as a good sign. Belatedly, my exhausted, slow-working mind realized that a few seconds sooner and that deer would have wiped me out. But now I had dumb luck to add to my two other signs of good fortune.

I should have stopped by the Rock Creek Pony Express monument, where a young Wild Bill Hickok shot the owners of the site, but I was too tired. Not even the grisly lure of murder and mayhem by a genuine Western icon were enough to distract me from making it to camp.

Once there, I opted to pay $25 for an RV spot with electricity rather than $15 for a "remote" campsite without, mostly because the RV spots were closer to the showers. After I dropped my envelope into the irretrievable payment receptacle, I went back to the site I'd chosen and found the 110-volt outlet didn't work. Part of me wanted to laugh and just think it figured. But part of me was utterly despondent because I had *devices* that needed *charging*, and even though my backup batteries would do the trick, I couldn't help feeling that it was hopeless. Give it up. You're hosed.

Bonking will do that to you.

"Bonking" is the cyclist term for Hitting the Wall, Nothing Left in the Tank, etc. It is a feeling of absolute depletion, zero energy, helplessness, and hopelessness. The kind of feeling that first makes you feel like you're going to die, then degenerates to where you fear you won't. My despondency over the broken electrical outlet at my campsite was just the latest manifestation of my failure to replenish the calories and nutrients I'd been furiously burning since leaving St. Joseph. There had been signs throughout the day—forgetting my water bottle in Marysville that morning; parking my bike too close to the edge of the road that afternoon—and had I been paying better attention I might have taken longer beaks, eaten and drunk more. I might have been able to keep myself from sinking this low.

Just then the camp hosts, Dale and Marilyn, pulled up in a golf cart. I told Dale about the broken electrical outlet and he said he'd bring a voltmeter over and check the socket. He did, and sure enough it was dead. He said he had a 30-to-20-amp converter but returned a short time later saying he couldn't find it. Then he noticed my bike, and as he was a cyclist, we got to talking. Two years earlier Dale had been in a bike wreck and had shattered his femur and hip socket. He was seventy-nine years old then, and his doctor told him he'd be in really bad shape if he fell again. Rather than give up cycling, Dale bought a recumbent tricycle—a serious, carbon fiber rocket ship of a trike—and once he healed went back to riding. "I'm not sure how I healed so well," he told me, "except maybe it's because I ride in a mission-supporting fundraiser every year. I think the Lord just wanted me to raise more money for the church."

I wandered off to take a shower. As I was returning to my site, I was thinking about how I really needed to eat to get my levels back up, but was also depressed by the unappetizing prospect of dehydrated meals and energy bars. When I passed by the camp hosts' RV, Marilyn stepped out and asked if I'd like to join them for dinner. I saw Dale cooking chicken over the grill. I thanked Marilyn and told her I didn't want to appear rude, but that I was vegetarian. She said, "Well, do you like potatoes and onions and carrots and coleslaw? And would you maybe like some fruit?" I said I would be back shortly.

I hung some clothes to dry and went back to Marilyn and Dale's. Their friends Denny and Connie were also over for dinner. We talked until the chicken was ready, then moved to the picnic table and said grace and got to it. I was voracious. I felt like the planet-sucking doomsday machine from *Star Trek*, sucking down anything that crossed my path. Marilyn kept offering me more food, until I finally said, "I will eat everything you put in front of me, so don't offer unless you're sure you can do without." She kept passing me something to eat whenever my plate started to show some white. At some point Connie went to their RV and brought back desert: cantaloupe and rhubarb cobbler, complete with Miracle Whip. After dinner we went back to the comfy chairs and talked some more and by and by it got to be evening. Before I left, Marilyn said she'd send Dale over with a cup of coffee for me in the morning.

To run into people this generous, who seemed to sense what I needed even if I didn't, especially after the afternoon I'd put myself through, was too much. My eyes teared up with gratitude on the way back to my camp.

CHAPTER FIVE

Cholera and COVID in the Great American Desert

As promised, Marilyn sent Dale over with a cup of coffee first thing. Then she called across the camp to ask if I wanted orange juice, and I said no thank you, but she came over and stuffed a bottle in my hand anyway. When it was time to go, we joined in a little huddle and they prayed for my safety on the road. It was a great send-off.

I rode into the town of Fairbury, Nebraska, for a second coffee and a fritter from a grocery store bakery. Outside the store I talked to a man who'd stopped to ask where I was headed and he left me saying, "God bless you and have a safe trip." I am not in the habit of praying, or being around those who do, at least publicly. There was something comforting about having so many blessings come my way that morning.

North of Fairbury, I found the monument for Virginia Station. The station was also known as Whiskey Run because whiskey was dumped into the nearby creek (or "run") to keep some people from getting their hands on it. A plaque at the site states that "Indians traded for whiskey at the station and harassed the emigrant trains. The whiskey was dumped in a nearby creek." An earlier historical account reports that US soldiers seized several barrels of whiskey from a freighting outfit who were selling it to whites and Indians along the trail and poured the contraband whiskey into the stream.

Along the Pony Express Trail I'd often come across a monument that presented a biased version of a historical event only to learn after researching about another version that painted a broader picture. It is one thing to say "Indians traded for whiskey . . . and harassed the emigrant trains"; it is quite another to write that US soldiers confiscated and dumped contraband whiskey from a (white-owned) freighting outfit illegally selling it to American Indians. I wondered where the balance lay between leaving a historical monument in place in respect of its age—the monument itself being a historical artifact—versus allowing it to stand and miseducate anyone who accepted its statements at face value.

From the Virginia Station site, I took a detour off the Pony Express Route to look for an important landmark on the Oregon Trail: George Winslow's grave. My map showed the gravesite next to a gravel road. The site is marked by a granite obelisk, erected in 1912, so it should have been easy to spot. I rode back and forth searching for it, but no luck. The only marker I came across was a small wooden sign with sun-faded paint that read "Oregon Trail," and below it, the dates "1830" and "1871." George Winslow died while emigrating along the Oregon Trail, so I knew I was on the right track. But the dates made no sense.

There are many dates to choose from as the start of the Oregon Trail. The 1830 date the sign makers selected probably referred to the Smith-Jackson-Sublette caravan of 1830, the first wagon train to take the Platte River route west. The travelers weren't emigrants; they were engaged in the fur trade and were freighting goods to the summer rendezvous in the Rockies. The first overland emigrants on this route were the missionary Jason Lee and his party, who crossed the continent with Nathaniel Wyeth in 1834. The first overland emigrant wagon train on this route, the Bidwell-Bartleson Company, came through here on their way to California in 1841. The onset of the emigration era is sometimes tabulated from 1843, the year of the so-called Great Migration, which included the Cow Column, named for the slower-moving emigrants herding draft animals to help colonize Oregon. Any of those years might have been appropriate.

On the other hand, the end date on the sign, 1871, seemed completely arbitrary. Jess Unruh's opus on the overland emigration, *The Plains Across*, stops at 1860. The emigration continued past that date, but largely tapered off by the time the transcontinental railroad was completed in 1869. Wagon trains took the trail through the 1880s, and as late as 1912.

I had no idea how these sign makers arrived at their Oregon Trail dates and it bothered me. A minor discrepancy. Petty. But I was irritated I hadn't mapped the location of the gravesite more accurately and was venting my frustration on the makers of the old Oregon Trail sign.

Nebraska has a lot of roadside landmarks marking and memorializing the Oregon Trail. The road is marked by granite trail markers set in place around 1912. The funny thing, though, is none of the people who used the Emigrant Trail through Nebraska wanted to stay here. The early emigrants crossed two thousand miles to get to the wet, wooded Willamette Valley in Oregon, which was a lot like the farmland they had left. No one knew what to do with Nebraska: the empty space, the apparent lack of water, the incessant wind.

This vast, treeless expanse formed part of the Great American Desert, which had been considered unsettleable, uncultivable, since Major Steven Long's Expedition in 1820. Everyone passed through Nebraska on their way to someplace better: Oregon farms, California gold, Mormon Zion. Everyone passed through as quickly as they could. I found it ironic that Nebraska took so much trouble to honor people who would have preferred it wasn't in their way, and thought about that every time I passed a landmark to the hundreds of thousands of emigrants who were just passing through. It also made me better appreciate the Nebraska Tourism Committee's slogan that year: "Visit Nebraska. Honestly, it's not for everyone."

George Winslow was one of them. He died of cholera on June 8, 1849. He was twenty-five years old, and like so many that emigration season, was headed for the California goldfields. His death was by no means extraordinary. Disease caused nearly nine of every ten deaths for overland emigrants, with cholera being the number one killer. Cholera was rampant along the Missouri River and followed the emigrants up the trail as far as Fort Laramie, Wyoming. One emigrant wrote that "The road from Independence to Fort Laramie is a graveyard," and estimated the number of burials from 1,500 to 2,000.

But while George Winslow's death is not extraordinary, the fact that his grave was marked by a tombstone still identifiable in the early 1890s, more than forty years after his death, is exceptional. It has been estimated that there is an average of one grave for every eighty yards of the trail. But of the tens of thousands who died from cholera and dysentery, drowning, accidental gunshot wound, being run over by a wagon or by oxen, snakebite, and fights with indigenous Americans, few gravesites are known today. Cholera victims in particular were treated worse the further along the trail they contracted the disease. A "spirit of gloom" coupled with a sense of panic that they might not cross the final mountain ranges before the first snows led emigrants to tend less to the dead and dying further along the trail. Burials were "performed perfunctorily, sometimes with indecent haste"; sometimes a wagon train would leave watchers to bury the victim once they passed; other times, the dying were simply abandoned. Diarists wrote of watchers digging the grave within the dying companion's sight, and even burying people before they were dead.

There are stories of numerous victims buried near a campsite, sometimes in a mass grave. Caskets were sometimes improvised from discarded wagon parts; other times, victims were buried in nothing but a blanket. A wagon party might stop the night only to find that wolves had dug up recently interred remains, scattering their burial clothing, exposing their partially eaten bodies. Emigrants started honoring their dead by erasing the burial sites rather than marking them, burying bodies in the middle of the trail so oxen hooves and wagon wheels would eradicate any trace to protect them against human and animal predators. Irene Paden gives a particularly poignant description of such a scene:

> Picture a trail-side camp in the early morning. In the trail itself a grave has been dug during the night. Wrapped only with blankets and soft buffalo robes the precious contents are gently lowered into it. If the neighborly occupants of near-by wagons have been able to find cactus, a layer of its protecting spiny joints is carefully tamped in next to the beloved dead and a shuddering prayer breathed that it may be enough. Next, the earth is packed above it firm and smooth. The bereaved family must go on. There is no help for it. The wagons are loaded and ready, and wait for the word which must be given. It is given. The slow-moving oxen move forward and onward. The

creaking, rambling wagons lurch and roll. The whole inexorable march, from this moment on, flows westward over all that was mortal of their loved one—forever obliterating the last resting place and effacing it from the memory of man.

George Winslow had the good fortune to die early in the trip, surrounded by friends. They hadn't reached the point, as many did months later, when the numbers of deaths along the way, coupled with exhaustion, had desensitized them, made them callous, interested only in moving on as quickly as possible to get over the mountains ahead of winter snows.

When I tried to find George Winslow's grave in early June 2021, COVID-19 had been raging for over a year. Vaccines had been available for months, but millions across the country didn't take the pandemic seriously at all. When I started on my trip, infection rates were dropping. By the time I finished, the Delta Variant was driving those rates up, largely due to people who refused freely available vaccines.

One of the ironies of studying history is to think we are better off than our forebears in part because we are more knowledgeable. George Winslow and his friends had no idea what caused cholera or how to prevent it. And the disease was frightening. General knowledge of germs was still in the future, making the disease "more mysterious and dreaded by the utter ignorance of the emigrants as to what caused it." In extreme cases a traveler might get up as usual in the morning and be buried at the noon stop.

Today, we know precisely what causes cholera and what conditions encourage its spread. We can look back on George Winslow and his friends and the unsanitary conditions in which they traveled in 1849 and say no wonder so many died and if they only knew. But here we were in the midst of the COVID pandemic, knowing the answers, having vaccines and the knowledge how not to spread it, and yet were unable to stem the spread of the devastating disease due to some twisted logic of individual freedom. We had the benefit of science, the experience of past epidemics. We knew better. And yet, here we were.

Eventually, I discovered where George Winslow's gravesite lay. Though my map showed the site off a dead-end road, it was actually on a knoll about a quarter mile down an overgrown trail behind a locked gate off a dead-end road. I only saw it from over my shoulder, as it were, on my way back to rejoin the Pony Express Route.

Riding away from George Winslow's grave, I wondered whether I was complicit. What is more iconically American than the Pony Express, the trail I was following? What screams Individual Freedom more loudly than the image of a lone rider racing across the landscape, braving the dangers of the trail? I didn't see myself that way—I wasn't riding the route to test myself, but because it had caught my imagination; I wasn't riding alone to prove anything, but because I couldn't talk anyone into riding with me. Nevertheless, just by exposing myself to people along the way, I was risking contracting the disease, and worse, bringing it back home. To that extent, I had to consider that maybe my behavior was not so different from the anti-maskers and anti-vaxxers whose intransigence I condemned.

On the fourth day of my ride, I had questioned whether I could finish it. On the morning of the fifth, I questioned whether I should have started the ride at all.

CHAPTER SIX

A Bone in Her Teeth

AFTER MY UNSUCCESSFUL DETOUR TO VISIT GEORGE WINSLOW'S GRAVE, my fifth day of riding became a lot like the fourth, except in one key regard: I did not despair. My energy quickly and steadily drained through the day. By the time I rolled into Hebron, "Nebraska's Porch Swing Capital" and my stopping place for the night, I felt like I was knocking and pinging like a car running on fumes.

Along the way I had passed a granite monument for the Little Sandy Station (a stagecoach station with no connection with the Pony Express); the town of Powell, Nebraska, which so far as I could tell consisted of a dilapidated wooden building listing hard to port with a peeling "Town of Powell" sign hanging from the lintel; and just west of there a stainless-steel post, barely taller than the cheat grass brake in which it stood, marking Big Sandy Pony Express Station.

I wished I'd had more energy to enjoy these sites and the scenery along the way. On the other hand, I had every reason to be tired. The weather was hot (ninety degrees) and windy (fifteen–twenty knots), and there was a fair amount of climbing some more stupidly steep hills. The difference was now I knew I could finish the trip. The unridden miles ahead didn't overwhelm me. I just had to take each day as it came, and all I had to do that day was make it to Hebron. Which I did.

I woke the next morning to a wind that blew twenty knots and better all day long. A sailing buddy of mine had a saying whenever the breeze stiffened: "The wind's got a bone in her teeth." That phrase pretty well described my ride all day.

Before heading out, I took a turn through Hebron to see the world's largest porch swing and drop another postcard home. I felt like the anti-Pony Express: instead of delivering mail across the country, I was posting it from little towns along the way.

I had gone off course from the Pony Express Route to stay in Hebron the night before. I could have backtracked a couple of miles east to rejoin the route from where I left it. But there were no Pony Express stations to see, and the wind was straight out of the south. I decided instead to take Highway 81 north out of town for the first three or four miles and let the breeze push me along for a change.

The highway was two lanes in each direction, with a broad median, six-foot-wide shoulder, and a rumble strip. Nearly every car and truck that passed me, even the semis, moved over to the center lane to leave a lane between me and them. Similarly, Kansas and Nebraska drivers almost always moved over and slowed, rather than pass me, on any two-lane road when we neared the top of a hill with limited visibility. They had been, in a word, cautious and courteous.

But as polite as Nebraska drivers were, they seemed to have no concept of the amount of dust their vehicles kicked up. Riding gravel and dirt roads, I found myself smothered in clouds of dust every time someone passed me from in front or behind. The friendly Nebraska drivers moved all the way over and smiled and waved (the Nebraska wave: lifting one finger off the wheel), but they didn't slow down at all. As a result, I got thoroughly dusted—eyes, mouth, a new layer glued to my skin by sunblock—every time. It's possible that rural Nebraskans live in so much dust they didn't even notice. Still, I hoped at least some of them looked in their rear-view mirror, wondered where I disappeared to, and put two and two together before they met another rider.

Midwest Gravel Roads

Cyclists spend a lot of riding time staring down at the road. Ask any rider you know and they will be able to tell you the condition of any local road, where the pavement is rough, where it's broken or littered with glass and debris. Studying the road ahead is essential to keeping the rubber side down (i.e., avoid crashing).

In Kansas, I passed over sections of gravel road that had recently been repaired. The repairs were easy to spot because they were made not with fine gravel but with ¾-inch rock poured across the roadbed. I had originally thought I might use lighter-weight tires on this part of the trip to make better time. After coming across these patches, I was glad I had stuck with my oversized knobbies with their reinforced sidewalls. The sharp rock in these sections could easily have sliced a lighter tire.

Nebraska's gravel roads, as a rule, were softer. But that presented a different problem. They were rideable when the surface was compressed, but tricky to navigate in long sections where the top layer was loose. It often felt like trying to ride through a riverbed, with the river still in it. Loose gravel roads are notorious for turning a front tire and causing a spill. I was constantly shifting across the entire road searching out the smoothest, hardest spots to roll through. Happily, traffic was so light I could swerve across the roadbed at will.

At the end of this brief northerly leg, I stopped at a pull-out to see a memorial for the Oregon Trail and the 1960 Pony Express Centennial Re-Run. There had been a couple of previous re-rides in 1923 and 1935, as well as a 1954 reenactment that rode between Ogden, Utah, and Colorado Springs, Colorado, nowhere near the original route. The 1960 Centennial Re-Run, memorialized just north of Hebron, Nebraska, does not seem to have been one of the better-coordinated events. San Francisco and Sacramento got into a scrape over which should be declared the western terminus of the Pony Express. One of the re-riders staging the cross-country mail run accidentally shot another. The re-riders were unable to bring the mail overland on time and their tired horses had to be put on a truck. When they arrived in Sacramento, they found they'd left the mail pouch somewhere behind.

From here I turned west, and Nebraska finally started acting like the Midwest state it's supposed to be: miles of crops in every direction, wide-open views under a cornflower sky, the land stretching out into broader vistas the way we who do not live there imagine it would. Only less flat than I had imagined. I still found myself climbing grades and was repeatedly surprised (and annoyed) that they seemed so much steeper than they appeared to be. Without realizing it, I had fallen victim to an illusion of the prairie. The spaces are so large it appears flat, whereas it isn't flat at all. You may not notice it in a car, but on a bike, especially a bike laden with camping gear, you notice every incline.

Descriptions from emigrant days all liken this part of the country to the ocean. The image dates as far back as Coronado's expedition in 1540 to find Quivira, the Seven Cities of Gold (which, improbable as it may seem, turned out not to be in central Kansas): "I travelled five more days as the guides wished to lead me, until I reached some plains, with no more landmarks than as if we had been swallowed up in the sea. Santa Fe trader Josiah Gregg wrote that "not a single landmark is to be seen for more than forty miles." He referred to Independence, Missouri, as the port of embarkation for the "prairie ocean," proposed that maritime law be adapted for use in freight caravans, and is credited with coining the term "prairie schooner." Comparisons of the prairie to the sea in terms of its expanse, its monotony, and its romance recur throughout overlanders' accounts from the mid-1800s.

So far it had been hard for me to picture landscapes described by emigrants from the mid-1800s, and even by Irene Paden in the 1930s. West of Hebron I got my first sense of the rolling landscape resembling ocean swells. This was easy land to disappear in before it was carved into rectilinear parcels. Coronado's men had to make landmarks out of buffalo dung to find their way back to camp. I never had to worry about losing my way because there were landmarks everywhere—farmhouses, radio towers, water towers, street signs. Still, at the top of a rise, where I could survey the distances, I could at least get a sense of the immensity earlier travelers must have felt.

Twice along this empty stretch farmers stopped on the road to talk to me. Just rolled up to me and stopped their huge pickups in the middle of the road to ask where I was headed and what I was doing and to tell me what I might want to look for in the next town as if we were acquaintances passing each other on a sidewalk. At least they didn't dust me.

The only town I passed through all day was Oak, Nebraska ("Hub of the Oregon Trail"). Oak was very small and seemed to have no functioning

businesses along its short main street. Then again, it was Sunday, so it's
more likely everything was closed. It did have Oregon Trail Park, though,
with shade and water and a Little Blue Station marker and a couple of
doorless (though odorless) concrete pit toilets that seemed as if they had
not been used, well, since Oregon Trail days.

Most of the historical markers in and around Oak commemorate
the ordeal of local settlers who were victims of coordinated raids during
August 8–10, 1864. The attacks, by Cheyenne, Arapaho, Southern Brulé,
and Southern Oglala warriors, targeted settlements and travelers across
four hundred miles of the Emigrant Trail, from Julesburg, Colorado (on
the South Platte River), to this section of the Little Blue.

Historian Merrill Mattes found the Native Americans' "mood of vengeance" understandable in light of massacres of Lakota at Ash Hollow in
1854 and of the Cheyenne and Arapahoe at Sand Creek, Colorado, ten
years later. George Stewart agrees, noting that after Harney's massacre at
Ash Hollow there was peace, "but the Sioux remained grumpy and things
were never quite the same."

The Lakota who lived along the Emigrant Trail were no doubt grumpy:
they had a number of legitimate complaints. But as George Hyde points
out, the August 1864 attacks were primarily led by Cheyenne and Arapahoe warriors, not Lakota. Hyde also cites more immediate provocations.
In April 1864, Cheyennes were blamed for running off herds of cattle east
of Denver. The Cheyennes denied responsibility, saying the animals had
stampeded and the careless herders reported being raided to avoid blame,
a practice Kit Carson later testified was common. Nevertheless, the Colorado cavalry, staffed by volunteer troops who felt "Indians were twopence
the dozen and that shooting them was a public service," marched through
Cheyenne country attacking all Indians met. By midsummer the Cheyennes and Arapahoes were "goaded into madness by the wanton attacks
of the cavalry on their people."

Estimates of Euro-American deaths in the raids range between
fifty and one hundred. I haven't come across any estimates of Cheyenne,
Arapahoe, or Lakota deaths. Late that same fall, in November 1864,
Colonel John Chivington led a retaliatory raid on a peaceful encampment under Black Kettle at Sand Creek, Colorado, and killed around 230

Cheyenne and Arapahoe people, "composed mostly of women, children, and the elderly." Unlike other engagements known alternately as either a "massacre" or a "battle," depending on one's perspective, Chivington's slaughter is unequivocally known as the Sand Creek Massacre. Mattes qualified his empathy with the Native American "mood of vengeance" of the summer of 1864 by disparaging their methods as "barbaric." As the Sand Creek Massacre demonstrated, there was no shortage of barbarism among war parties on either side.

Not far past Oak is a section of trail known as the Narrows, a bottleneck where the trail was squeezed between the Little Blue and nearby bluffs. At one point, the bluffs extend westward like an arrow pointing nearly into the Little Blue. I'd hoped to see this spot to try to understand why the emigrants felt forced to take this hazardous passage. Unfortunately, the Narrows were on private property. In any case, changes in the course of the river and erosion along the bank have obliterated the Oregon Trail along this stretch, so there was no longer anything to see.

This seventy-mile section of the Pony Express Route, from Hebron to Ayr, Nebraska, did not have any campgrounds or motels. I didn't see that as a problem when I was planning the trip. My attitude then was if I could average fifty miles a day, I could do seventy in a pinch. Given the fact that under actual conditions I was wiped out after forty- and fifty-mile rides, I needed to find someplace closer to stay. In Hebron, the night before, I'd found a website for the town of Edgar, Nebraska, about five miles off the Pony Express Route. The town offered camping in its South Park. So just past the Narrows, I left the Pony Express Route and detoured to Edgar for the night.

I turned my back to the wind, which still had a bone in her teeth, and had an easy downwind run to Edgar on a nicely paved road. Once in Edgar, I asked at the local market (the only place open on a Sunday afternoon) about camping in South Park, got directions, and made my way there. The grounds were covered in a nice layer of grass, shaded by lindens, with a few lichen-covered picnic tables. The small park also featured 1937 river-rock monuments built by the Works Progress Administration, as well as a river-rock WPA picnic shelter in the center, which looked as disused as the pit toilets back in Oak.

It seemed like a nice place to play frisbee, or maybe run a dog, but it was a complete disappointment as a campground. There were four spaces for RVs at the south edge of the park, but the electrical outlets were all locked, as were the water hydrants. Clearly, Edgar's camping season hadn't opened yet. Then it struck me that it probably hadn't been open for two years due to COVID, which also explained why the WPA shelter looked so disheveled. Understandable. But then I realized there were no restrooms in the park and was seized by a minor panic. I spent thirty minutes on Google Maps frantically trying to find a nearby town with accommodations but came up with no good options. So it was time for a little pep talk.

You're a bikepacker, I said to myself, *you have everything you need to be comfortable here for the night*. No water? There's enough left over from the day for everything you need. No electricity? You have a solar-charged battery. No bathroom? There are some convenient bushes across the street next to the RV pump-out station. I started to relax and to accept that this park would be fine for the night. There was nothing to prevent my sleeping here, just small inconveniences. If I wanted convenience, I should have planned a completely different trip.

Given the locked outlets and water hydrants, I wasn't certain the city was welcoming overnight campers. So, I rolled my bike next to a bench in the middle of the park and set up my tent, making it as obvious as possible to anyone passing by that I was camping in the park even though there were no restrooms, water, or electricity. I figured if the cops didn't roust me by sundown, I'd move everything into the tent and take my chances.

No one came around. After the sun set, the breeze finally laid down and the town became blissfully quiet. Except for the trains. Freight trains and their whistles woke me up all night long. I had no idea how anyone in town could sleep through them. At one point, I heard two, at different pitches, alternating back and forth. I braced for a big crash. It didn't happen, of course. But then I kept myself up for a while wondering if different trains had differently pitched whistles, and whether people could identify different trains from their sound. Random thoughts like these kept me occupied all through that night of intermittent sleep.

CHAPTER SEVEN

The Little Blue

Morning in Edgar, Nebraska, was as quiet as the night, if you take the trains into account. I was in that park from 3:30 p.m. or so until 8:30 the next morning and no one used it in that time, not even to let their dog do its business on the grass. I went by the market in town and bought some bottled water to refill my supply. The market didn't have a bakery section. After waffling for a nanosecond, I bought a six-pack of pecan rolls for the road and wolfed two down as soon as I got outside.

As I was getting ready to leave, a guy in a pickup (there are a lot of guys who drive pickup trucks in the Midwest) stopped to talk about my trip for a moment. He seemed to search for a memory, then told me Edgar was a railroad town, one of an alphabetical string of towns all named by a now-defunct railroad whose name he couldn't recall. He smiled in a self-congratulatory way and said, "There's a little local history for you anyway."

I later retraced the towns. From east to west they start at Alexandria and run through Bruning, Carlton, Davenport, Edgar, Fairfield, Glenvil, Hastings, Ingleside, Juniata, and Kenesaw. The line eventually extended to Grand Island, Nebraska, but I couldn't trace it any further than Kenesaw. The railroad was the St. Joseph and Grand Island Railway, the third successor to the original line, the Palmetto and Roseport Railroad. The railroad was intended to continue the Hannibal & St. Joseph Railroad (which delivered mail from the East to the Pony Express) as far as Marysville (Palmetto), and eventually, the West Coast. The railroad's ambitious goal was one reason the Pony Express started in St. Joseph, Missouri.

In early 1860, when Russell, Majors & Waddell was setting up the Pony Express, two towns competed to be the eastern terminus: Leavenworth, Kansas, and St. Joseph, Missouri. The firm's freighting operation had been based in Leavenworth since 1855, so that town seemed like the logical choice. St. Joseph, however, had a couple of advantages: the only telegraph terminal and train depot that reached as far west as the Missouri River were located there. To tip the scales, St. Joseph offered a few incentives. Among other provisions, St. Joseph gave the firm, "exclusive privilege of carrying express matter" over the nascent Palmetto & Roseport Railroad for twenty years. Pony Express historians Raymond Settle and Mary Lund Settle cite this concession as proof of Russell's foresight.

Unfortunately, within two years Russell's questionable business acumen destroyed the transportation colossus that was Russell, Majors & Waddell. The firm collapsed before the partners could take advantage of this exclusive railroad privilege.

Rather than ride south from Edgar to regain the Pony Express Route, I rode due west, powering through a six-mile crosswind run. That meant skipping a few miles of the trail, but nothing of enough historical interest to justify a difficult upwind ride.

Back on the route, I zigzagged north and west, following the northwest course of the Little Blue while adhering to the grid-like property lines. I'd been having issues with the app I used to navigate. It had been glitchy, crashing on me, failing to track, and was slow to acquire a GPS signal. As a result, I took a couple of wrong turns, lost some time, and gained some unnecessary miles. In reality, I didn't need the app through this stretch. The Pony Express Route followed the National Park Service's Local Tour Route for the Oregon, California, and Pony Express National Historic Trails through this section. I could have just followed the Park Service's signs.

It was hot and windy (again) and I was slugging down more water than I had planned (again) and started worrying (again) I'd run out. I carried two large bottles strapped to my forks specifically to carry extra water. I had been leaving them dry, thinking I'd rather drink less and not have to carry the extra weight, which was stupid. You'd think I would have learned to carry more water after I'd had to stop and refill at Eunice's place in Kansas.

The truth is, I'd expected to find more farmhouses along the way. During the western emigration, it was said there would be lines of wagons miles long through this section of the Emigrant Trail. In 1849, wagon trains extending five or six miles and taking more than two hours to pass were a common sight. It appears that once the wagon migration dropped off, life along the Little Blue fell back to its pre-emigration quietude. Between that and the large tracts of farmland, houses (along with my chances to refill water), were scarce.

At one point I saw a woman giving three kids a joy ride on a golf cart near a farm and asked permission to top off my water. I was fortunate to find people like her along the way who allowed me to refill on these long summer days. Otherwise I would have been in bad shape.

I could have been in worse shape. As taxing as it was riding in heat and wind, riding in rain would have been worse. While rain had delayed my start by a day, I didn't see any more until weeks later, in Casper, Wyoming. The 1844 emigrants were inundated with rain for the first month of their overland trek. One diarist wrote that in the first two months of travel, there were only eight days without rain. It took one party nearly a month to travel less than a hundred miles from the Missouri River. When they came to the Black Vermillion River, it was too swollen to cross safely. "This little stream that at low water could be stepped over detained us seventeen days in one camp."

Soon after I refilled, I came to a place where I had to cross a railroad track to get to my next turn, just on the other side. A freight train was stopped there, blocking the intersection. I knew I was starting to bonk again because the longer the train didn't move the more imperative it became that I figure out how to get around it and keep to the Pony Express Route rather than simply backtrack a few miles and go around. For a brief moment I even weighed the chances of passing between the cars. Common sense prevailed. Instead of risking my life to save a couple of miles, I dropped my bike and trailer into a ditch that ran along the track, dragging and bouncing them over the damp, uneven ground for about a hundred yards to get to my next turn.

A little further, I came to the next turn on the Pony Express Route, which dropped down to Thirty-Two Mile Creek, only to see a "Bridge Out" sign. I kept on to the next intersection, a mile further, and hoped the bridge on that street was still standing. Happily, it was. I looked for the Thirty-Two Mile Pony Express Station, which was supposed to be nearby. I even parked the bike and walked up and down the street thinking I might have ridden past, but no luck. By then the day started to feel like it was slipping away, so I focused on getting to Prairie Lake Recreation Area, Nebraska, my stopping place for the night.

When I made it to the campground, a couple of cars were parked near the entrance, but there was no ranger station, nor any obvious place to camp. I called the district that runs the area for advice. The park ranger I spoke with said, more or less, "Anywhere you want," then tried to direct me to the "rustic" camping next to the lake with an older pit toilet, no electricity, and presumably, a lot of dirt. He added that there were some nice old shade trees down there.

At the time I was standing in a brand-new "covered area," an open structure with a roof overhead. It had a level concrete pad with four picnic tables, running water, electricity, and a new pit toilet building close by. The covered area sat on a rise overlooking the lake and was surrounded by a level grass field. The area was being developed for RV camping and, like all such areas in every campground I stayed in, was better groomed and had more conveniences than the primitive section the ranger was pushing. I told him I'd prefer to stay where I was. He said it would be fine to camp anywhere other than under the covered area, to which I agreed; he failed, however, to say anything about commandeering the covered area, which I did as soon as I was off the phone.

I washed some laundry with the hydrant water and strung a line to dry in the wind, started plugging in everything I could on one table, and took over another table to air out my gear. There were no showers. Neither were there any people. I stripped down to my boxers and gave myself an open-air sponge bath of sorts using the cold hydrant water. The air temperature was still in the upper eighties, the wind still well into the teens, so I was dry in minutes. I spent the rest of the afternoon sitting at a shaded, level picnic bench, wearing only a T-shirt and boxers, and worked on my journal until it was time to make dinner and set up the tent and go to bed. It was a long, lovely, peaceful afternoon.

This would be my last night on the Little Blue. The campground sat near where the Emigrant Trail came to its first dry crossing: a twenty-mile drive over the sandy, windy divide between the Little Blue River and the Platte River, a difficult pull in emigrant days. With this crossing, the Emigrant Trail entered the transition zone between the prairie and the plains.

Riding the Little Blue Valley the previous few days had not been as inspiring as I'd hoped, hidden as it was by farms, the river itself rarely accessible. Nevertheless, before leaving the Little Blue, it was nice to reflect on its legacy as part of the emigrant experience crossing the prairie.

CHAPTER EIGHT

The Coast of Nebraska

I woke at my Prairie Lake campsite to the sound of birds. Screechy, early rising harpies is how they struck me at the time. The forecast was the same as nearly every day so far—hot and windy—so my goal was to get underway by 8:00 a.m. I made it out of the campground by 8:30 a.m. Close enough.

The town of Juniata, Nebraska, was less than ten miles away, so I detoured off the Pony Express Route to stop in at Karen's Scrumptious Bakery. One cinnamon roll (not nearly as sweet as Sweet Pea Bakery in Seneca) and a cup of pod-brewed Starbucks later I was off to rejoin the route.

The wind was mostly behind me, and but for the loose top layer of the Adams County roads, I made it along pretty well. I stopped in Kenesaw, Nebraska, for a cold bottle of electrolytes and grabbed an apple for later. Two towns in one morning! I hadn't seen that much civilization in one day's ride since St. Joseph, three hundred miles back.

Outside Kenesaw, near the summit of the divide between the Little Blue and Platte Rivers, I stopped by Susan Haile's grave. It was known in years past as the "Lone Grave." The site was fenced off; inside was a monument placed in 1960 over the spot where the original marker had lain. The monument indicated the year of Susan Haile's death (1852) and the cause (drinking from a well "poisoned by Indians"). A signpost nearby told the story of how her grief-stricken husband returned to Missouri to purchase a gravestone, then carried it back. Most of those heartbreaking statements are also most certainly false.

Contrary to the memorial, cholera, not a poisoned well, caused Susan Haile's death. For one thing, her husband's later recollections recorded that she died of cholera. For another, it is unlikely the well was poisoned. The Pawnees who traveled in the area were not warlike or hostile, did not have a poison that would be effective in a well, and in any case, would have drunk the same water themselves.

Nor was Susan Haile's lone grave. The cholera epidemic swelled in cycles on the Emigrant Trail, and 1852 was a particularly bad year. Her grave lay in the midst of the "cholera corridor," the trail between the Missouri River and central Nebraska. Probably a hundred or so other emigrant graves lie near Susan Haile's, but hers is the only one that has been located.

As for Susan Haile's tombstone, there are multiple iterations of the emigration-era story of husbands carting gravestones across the prairie in wheelbarrows for their deceased wives' graves. Retracing the Oregon Trail in 2011 on a mule-pulled wagon, Rinker Buck noted, "Over the summer I would encounter four more versions of the wheelbarrow story at trail graves farther west, and there are any number of stories like it on other overland trails." The wheelbarrow stories are considered apocryphal, fables of undying love. And possibly indicitive of husbands' regrets for forcing their wives to make this fatal journey. Historian John Faragher wrote that the decision to emigrate as a family was always made by the husband, never the wife. Historian Lillian Schlissel notes that some women's diaries contain "detailed tabulations" with "a bookkeeper's care for detail" of the number of graves passed, and finds in these women's meticulous notes that "resentment against the decision to go West seems to surge up and fill the pages."

The Sand Hill Pony Express Station monument (also known as Summit Station) lay near the site of Susan Haile's grave. Emigrants had their first view of the Platte River from here. I wasn't able to see the river even though it was just ten miles away. In fact, I didn't get my first view of the Platte until the road I had taken from the Sand Hill Station dead-ended into the riverbank.

That road ended up being a tedious slog. As if on cue, once I passed west of the Sand Hill Station marker I ran into the deepest, loosest, sandiest road yet. At times I was in first gear, even on downhill grades, fighting my way through sand drifts, struggling to keep from getting bogged down to a stop. This was not a happy stretch of road.

One thing riding the Pony Express Route has taught me is an appreciation of the functional nomenclature. A name like "Sand Hill Station" doesn't mean nearly as much when you read it in a book as it does when you read it in situ, as it were, sweating and cursing while wrestling a bike over a sand hill.

Another thing riding the Pony Express Route has taught me is empathy for how difficult it must have been to get a wagon overland in the mid-1800s. Not that my travails in any way compare, but I got more of a taste for traveling in emigrant times than I had imagined I would—much more, certainly, than had I driven the route. I'd read accounts of emigrants having to double-team wagons—adding six or eight more oxen to the six or eight already pulling—with all hands pushing on the spokes of all four wheels to extract their wagons when mired in mud or sand. Sitting in my house, complacently planning my route while sipping coffee and listening to classical music, I might have given a passing thought to how strenuous and tedious these exertions would have been for the emigrants. It never occurred to me that 160 years later I'd encounter the same lousy roads. And yet here I was, day after day, getting stuck in glue-impregnated mud, frantically and futilely spinning through intractable sand. The modern roads over the Emigrant Trail were improved from emigrant times, of course. Through Kansas and Nebraska, at least, they were graded and plainly marked on maps as public roads. In a car they probably would have been interesting, quaint. On a bike, they were often a pain.

At last I reached "The Coast of Nebraska," the apotheosis of the ocean-like prairie. The phrase refers to the resemblance of the banks of the wide, flat Platte River to the seashore of the Atlantic Ocean. During the spring flood, the sand hills along the Platte River Valley led emigrants to describe their wagons as ships moving through the sea of waving grass.

The Platte River was originally referred to both as "Nebraska" and "Platte." Sources agree that "Nebraska" derives from a Native American word. What is less certain is from which language, and what the word means. Mattes holds that Nebraska "is the approximate Omaha Indian equivalent for 'flat water,' and the French word 'Platte' is synonymous." Another source states unequivocally that it is an Otoe word meaning "weeping water."

The Pony Express Route turned west to follow the Platte. A few miles along I stopped at a sandhill crane viewing platform to take a break. The platform, just a few feet above the level of the river, gave a clear view in both directions. In emigrant days the river was reported to be as wide as three miles. Then, as now, it separated into as many as ten channels as it threaded its way through countless midstream islands.

Despite its imposing breadth, the Platte was shallow. Even before the river was dammed and its water siphoned off for other uses, the water was four feet deep or less. One traveler looking at the river thought it could float a war ship, and was surprised to see a man jump in and wade a considerable distance without wetting his breeches. This shallowness made it fordable—which was fortunate because it could not be ferried—but also made it largely unnavigable along its length (though that didn't stop people from trying).

The overlanders could forgive the river for being ridiculously wide and misleadingly shallow. What irked them was the poor quality of the water. The river water carried so much sand it had to be treated to be palatable. One method was to dig a hole two to four feet deep in sandy soil near the river level to let groundwater seep into it. Another method was to let the mud settle out in a pail, maybe speeding the process by adding a little alum. Some advocated boiling, "not to kill bacteria, which they had never heard of, but to immobilize the 'wiggle-tails.'"

These salient features of the Platte make it the most maligned river in the world. The Platte carried so much sand that emigrants accused it of flowing bottom-side up. Historian Bernard De Voto described it as "one of the most preposterous [rivers] in the world, a bottomland through which a mile-wide trickle of water you had to chew made its way along cottonwoods and quicksands."

Another surprising feature of the river was that its banks were bare of trees. For campfires, overlanders instead used buffalo dung, or more politely, buffalo chips. For two hundred or so miles along the Platte, emigrants carried bags during the day's walk to collect this fuel for their campfires.

Yet for all its absurdity as a river, Platte River Valley provided the trunk line of westward travel. The Oregon, California, Mormon Pioneer, and Pony Express Trails all ran along its banks. Unfortunately, all of this traffic also led to the Platte River Valley being one of the worst areas for the spread of cholera.

An hour or so past the sandhill crane platform I took another break at Fort Kearny State Historical Park. From its founding at this location in 1849, Fort Kearny was the first real settlement since Marysville, Kansas. It marked the halfway point from the Missouri River to Fort Laramie, Wyoming, over three hundred miles further west. For emigrants, it was the end of the shakedown portion of the journey across the prairie and the beginning of the more challenging voyage across the Great Plains. It wasn't a fortification—no battle of size was fought within a radius of one hundred miles—but rather it was an oasis of civilization, a place for emigrants to recuperate and reorganize. Just as importantly, it was a place to get repairs made and purchase supplies. Emigrants who traveled north of the Platte River sometimes even crossed the river here to purchase supplies and drop off or retrieve mail.

I walked the Fort Kearny grounds, nearly deserted on that early June day. I was glad I stopped. There were some nicely preserved buildings, stone monuments, a comfortable guest center. It was hard for me to capture the significance of the fort as a haven, a settlement that would be so welcome to emigrants and freighters after days and weeks of empty prairie. A highway runs by the front door; traffic races by on an interstate not far behind. Even though the fort is not close to a town, it's not so far removed as some of the historic sites further west, as I would later discover. Still, I enjoyed a pleasant walk, if not a particularly enlightening one.

Fort Kearny sat on a reservation ten miles square. Just before the eastern border (near the sandhill crane viewing platform) was Dogtown (known more respectfully as Valley City), and just west of the western border sat Dobeytown (*dobe* meaning *adobe*). Both operated as Pony Express stations. Dobeytown (later dubbed Kearney City) in particular had a reputation as being a wicked town, the "the worst place on the entire overland route." It was "a squalid settlement of 'dobe huts whose very mention was next door to an indelicacy," the "ordinary type of hell-hole that clung to the fringes of any military reservation." The bars there sold a whiskey dubbed "pop skull" and "tanglefoot," so damaging that wagonmasters sometimes avoided camping nearby for fear of losing some of their bullwhackers. One writer noted that the cemetery was larger than the town.

Time has erased both settlements. Near the former site of Dogtown I saw a place renting yurts for $125/night to watch sandhill cranes. The site of Dobeytown has a Nebraska State Historical Marker; across the highway is a modern residence, complete with a manicured lawn.

My stop for the night was the town of Kearney (the "Heart of Nebraska"). Kearney (a misspelling of "Kearny," pronounced "Carny") was about seven miles west of the old fort. I took a break at a rest stop before crossing the Platte River and heading into town. The wind was so strong it blew my helmet across the table. Not a gust of wind, but the steady baseline breeze, which I'd estimate at least eighteen knots. I'd ridden in wind this strong nearly every day of my ride, the only variable being the direction from which it blew. Fortunately, it was behind me as I rode the main drag into town from the south.

My plan was to spend two nights here, following the practice of some overlanders to rest one day every seven. When leading freight caravans across the prairie, Alexander Majors rested his crews on Sundays to observe the Sabbath and recruit the oxen. He carried this practice into Russell, Majors & Waddell. The firm printed a handbook for its wagonmasters, which stated in part: "We expect our trains to observe the Sabbath, and whenever an opportunity occurs to hear preaching, embrace it." In order to take a day off, it was necessary to camp near good grass and water. Wagon-masters often avoided having to give their bullwhackers a rest day by making sure not to camp near such a spot on Saturday night.

Emigrants who rested regularly made better time on the road. Many emigrant trains adopted constitutions before setting off to govern the train on their journeys, and some of these constitutions included a provision requiring the train to observe the Sabbath by taking a day of rest. But like Alexander Majors's wagon trains, the regulation was one of the most violated.

As Fort Kearny was a way station for emigrants, Kearney, Nebraska, felt like a way station for me. It wasn't Sunday, but like the more practical emigrants, I thought it wise to rest "according to the dictates of geography rather than the Old Testament." The shakedown part of the ride was over. It wouldn't hurt me to take a day here to wash, reprovision, rest, and recruit before getting back on the road.

Recruiting the Oxen

The word "recruit" appears in commentary in and about this period to mean resting draft animals (e.g., "recruiting the oxen"). The word originally comes from Latin for "grow again." It is usually not applied to humans, but to the extent my legs were doing most of the work to propel my rig, the termed seemed apt.

PART TWO

THE GREAT PLATTE RIVER ROAD— KEARNEY, NEBRASKA, TO JULESBURG, COLORADO

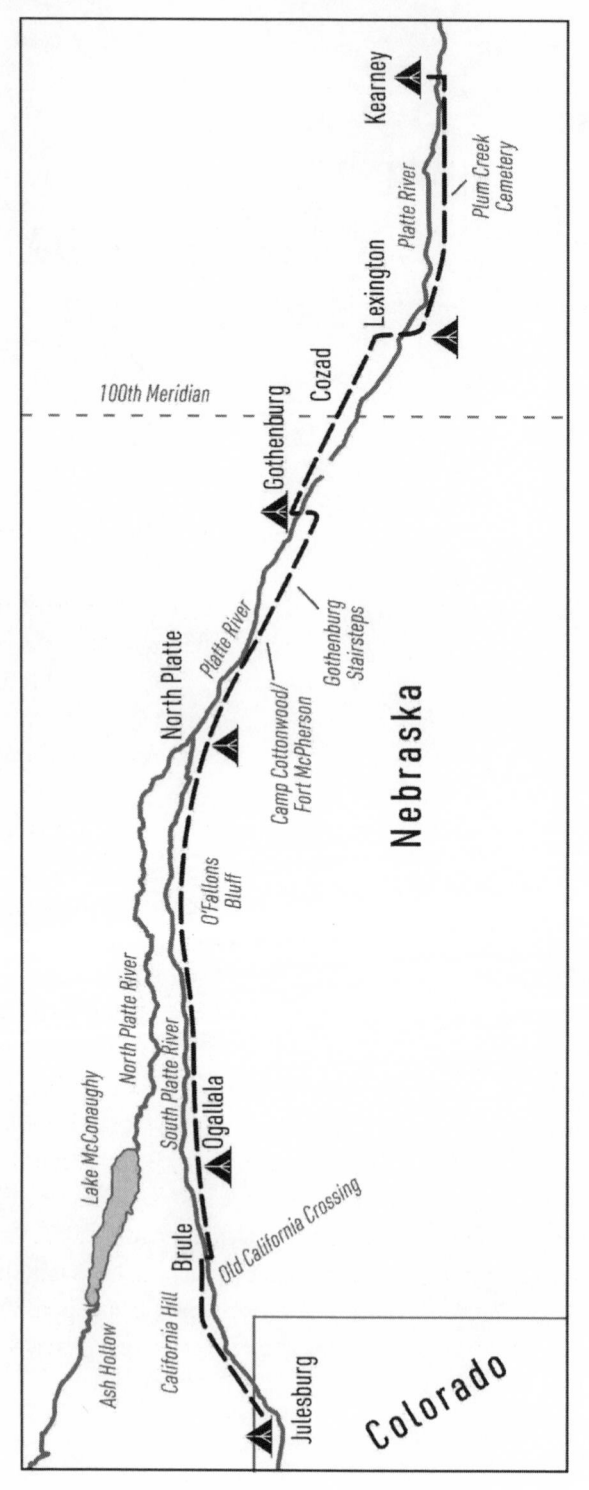

The Platte River Road
Kearney, Nebraska, to Julesburg, Colorado
255 miles

CHAPTER NINE

The Great Platte River Road

My first day riding the Great Platte River Road felt like cheating. I had booked a hotel room in Lexington, Nebraska, my next stop west, because the forecast called for thundershowers, and I did not feel like waking up in a rainy campground. The hotel check-in time was 2:00 p.m.; I arrived at 1:56. I had no idea I'd get there so early.

I had spent the day before washing and tuning up the bike and trailer, trying (unsuccessfully) to repair my tire's slow leak, reprovisioning, doing laundry, replenishing electrolytes, and preloading carbs. All in all, though, my busy day off felt strangely refreshing.

During the emigration, women would spend layover days in a similar way: washing clothes, cleaning, and cooking. Enjoying the relative leisure of doing chores while staying put instead of while on the move. The key word being "relative." Women's lot on the trail can only be defined as incessant, taxing work.

Laundry duties fell exclusively to women. That is, when there were any in the company. During the California Gold Rush emigration of 1849, roughly sixty thousand men emigrated west, but only about six hundred women. Outside the influence of women, men traveling west rarely washed their bodies; some bragged that they never once took their clothes off during the months-long trip, not even their boots. Clothes would be soiled with "layers of sweat, grease tar, salt, dirk, alkali, lice, and effluvia from too-delicate-to-mention sources," yet men were reluctant to wash their clothes. One affliction that might drive men to wash was lice. Apparently, stagecoach drivers and station stock tenders were sometimes covered with them. Even then, in lieu of washing, they would delouse their clothing and blankets by leaving them out on an anthill for a few hours, a trick the emigrants picked up.

In addition to clothes washing, women always did the cooking. They also helped pitch the tents, unloaded and reloaded the wagons at river crossings, yoked and sometimes drove the oxen. In many ways, the overland journey reduced women to tasks only fit for hired hands.

Conversely, men would often use off days to play, usually by hunting buffalo. Given the slightest sign of a distant buffalo herd, even men who otherwise stressed the importance of keeping on the move would stop, saddle anything that could run, and head off to hunt. They justified it by claiming to be hunting for food. But that was disingenuous. The amount of usable food they brought back was dismally low.

Heading out from Kearney, Nebraska, the temperature was warm (upper seventies and rising), the humidity high (eighties). I started perspiring as soon as I mounted the bike. There was a strong crosswind, but under the conditions, it was welcome; I might otherwise have drowned in sweat.

My first thirty miles were on virtually flat, lightly traveled pavement. For the first time since Wathena, Kansas, no hills! I was zipping along the Great Platte River Road, the "superhighway of westward expansion." Writers from the period, and writers writing about the period, drape garlands of superlatives about the superiority of the road along this stretch. The road was described as "a broad, smooth, beaten track, fully three hundred feet wide, swept clean by the wind." Mattes claims that "From Fort Kearny to the lower ford of South Fork . . . a distance of 120 miles, the Great Platte River Road was one of the finest natural roads in the world." Such praise comes up again and again.

Unfortunately, conditions weren't always ideal. During the rainy season mud along the road could mire wagons axle deep. Wet conditions also brought out mosquitoes and buffalo gnats. At the other extreme, dry spells brought excessive dust and blasts of sand.

I don't know to what extent development and agriculture have lessened the blowing dust, sand, and alkali in the area. I can report that it has done nothing to abate the wind. As for irritation, I didn't wear goggles, but I did have a very good, protective pair of sunglasses and plenty of eyedrops, both indispensable throughout the trip.

Some Plains tribes referred to the Platte River Road as the Great Medicine Road because of its ability to produce endless waves of emigrants. One irony of the Platte River Road is that while the four major overland trails (Oregon, California, Mormon Pioneer, and Pony Express) converged and ran together along the river, there was no single road, per se. Unlike other areas of the Emigrant Trail, there are no wagon ruts to view because wagons, horses, emigrants, and herds all spread out across the valley on both sides on the river. The "trail" along the Platte was often five miles wide, or as much as twelve miles total, including both banks.

I passed easily along this stretch, breezing along with relative ease thanks to the smooth pavement, the quartering wind, and the gentle, imperceptible, upward slope that runs a thousand miles or so from the Missouri River to South Pass in Wyoming. Occasionally the road turned to gravel and the going was slower. But at every point I was already so far along on the day's ride it didn't matter. About the only event of note was getting a quick tasty lunch at Taste of India, an Indian restaurant tucked into a truck stop near Overton, Nebraska. I had to fight the wind for two miles to get back to the Pony Express Route, but that hardly seemed worth complaining about.

Riding fifty miles along the Platte River Road felt nothing like fifty miles had the week before, though I would attribute that more to the road than to my acclimating to the ride. Maybe the writers who praised this stretch were on to something.

Somewhere during the day, I passed the spot where, in 1858, the captain of a wagon caravan hauling freight to Salt Lake City engaged a Native American hunting party in a standoff. The captain was Jack Slade, who later worked as division superintendent for the Central Overland California and Pike's Peak Express (parent company of the Pony Express). Soon after the freighters left Fort Kearny, lines appeared on both sides of the road. The lines turned out to be hundreds of Native Americans who wanted compensation for crossing their land. Slade held his gun on the leader until all of the wagons were safely past.

55

This type of exchange—a request for tribute—was one of the most common, or at least one of the most commented on, interactions between Native Americans and overlanders traveling through their lands.

In the early period of the overland emigration, the land west of the Missouri River was home to several nations of American Indians who lived there, including those tribes forced to relocate from the East. Federal laws, designed to protect the tribes from emigrants and settlers, defined the area west of the Missouri as "Indian Country." Emigrants and freighters crossed this territory not by right, but under sufferance. Among other provisions, these laws prohibited settlement or habitation of the land, required travelers to carry passports establishing the length of their stay, and allowed passage through Indian Country only on well-defined roads.

By the mid-1840s, Native Americans were complaining to Indian Agents that overlanders were killing and scaring away buffalo and other wild game, overgrazing prairie grasses, exhausting the timber and water resources. They felt overlanders had no right to be in their country without their consent.

In the absence of government action, Native Americans along the Emigrant Trail sometimes sought tribute payments from overlanders, usually in the form of provisions, as recompense for losses to their sustenance. Sometimes the person requesting tribute would present a paper, called a "recommends." These started as letters from sympathetic Indian Agents who explained the nature of the payment as compensation for the tribe's losses. On occasion, the recommends had a positive effect, reassuring emigrants of the bearer's good character. Other times, emigrants wrote their own recommends, some of which derided the bearer, who couldn't read English. Irene Paden wrote that, "As often as not the treasured note read in effect: 'Look out for him. He is a thief and a liar.'"

Some emigrants thought the tribute reasonable and paid accordingly. Others submitted out of fear. Still others reacted more like Captain Slade in the vignette above, by threatening violence at gunpoint, preferring to fight rather than acquiesce to what they considered blackmail. What the overlanders didn't realize, or perhaps didn't care about, was that their threats and actual use of force led to reprisals: sometimes in nighttime theft of cattle, other times in retribution taken against the next group of travelers. What they also didn't realize was that reciprocal gift giving was a strong tradition among Native Americans. The people who lived along the trail felt they were giving the overlanders the gift of allowing them to cross through their lands and use their resources. By Native American tradition, it was the overlanders' turn to reciprocate. Overland emigrants, who thought they had an absolute right to the trail and its resources, did not feel the same way.

Hugo Koch told the story of Jack Slade facing down a hunting party single-handed as a way of demonstrating Slade's courage. But the confrontation didn't end when Slade's freight train and the hunting party went their separate ways. What we don't learn from Koch is whether any of the freight train's animals were taken that night; whether the hunting party raided a subsequent train; to what extent Slade's defiant refusal further escalated bad feelings between Native Americans and overlanders along the Emigrant Trail.

Further along I stopped by a memorial at the site of the 1864 Plum Creek Massacre. This attack, carried out by Cheyenne warriors against a freight caravan, was the first action in the August 1864 raids along the Emigrant Trail from Julesburg, Colorado, to Big Sandy Station on the Little Blue River. A mile or two west of the site is the Plum Creek Cemetery where the bodies of eleven men killed in the raid lie in a mass grave. Also in the cemetery is a headstone for Sarepta Gore Fly, who died of unknown causes while returning to Missouri from Colorado in 1865. Her headstone was discovered in a nearby field, but the exact site of her grave is unknown. Like Susan Haile, whose gravesite is back near Kenesaw, Nebraska, Sarepta's husband is said to have carted her headstone across the plains in a wheelbarrow to this site. The interpretive sign at the site states, "like other similar wheelbarrow stories, this one is probably pure myth."

A series of occurrences took place at an emigrant campground in this same area eight years earlier, on June 14, 1846, which constitutes a microcosm of the emigrant experience on the Emigrant Trail. Three companies of overland emigrants all encamped within a two-mile radius.

Over the course of one day and night, a child was born, a young couple was married, and a small boy was buried.

The birth, marriage, and burial were recorded by Edwin Bryant, who was traveling to California. Bryant had some training as a physician. He wasn't fully qualified, but given the lack of medical resources on the trail, he acquired a reputation as a doctor, and that reputation spread among the emigrants who sometimes desperately sought his help. On this Sunday in mid-June, a group of men rode twenty-five or thirty miles back along the trail to ask Bryant's help with a boy whose leg had been crushed after being run over by a wagon. They also wanted him to look at a number of others in the train who were ill. Bryant felt they would not take no for an answer. He agreed to ride forward with them and try to help.

It was late afternoon when they reached the wagon train, which was in camp. Bryant went straight to the boy, whom he had assumed had suffered the injury the day before. The boy was laid out on a bench made of planks; Bryant realized he was expected to operate. It turned out that leg had been crushed nine days earlier and that nothing had been done to treat the wound. Gangrene had set in and the area was infested with maggots. Bryant had enough medical experience to know the boy would soon die. He refused the boy's mother's pleas to operate, explaining that amputating his leg would only increase his suffering and hasten his death. The mother insisted someone try to save her son's life. Another member of the emigrant train agreed to operate. The details Bryant relates about the amateur amputation are horrific; he seems genuinely relieved when he writes, "A few drops of blood only oozed from the stump; the child was dead—his miseries were over!"

Bryant then went to see the boy's father, who had been unable to walk or even sit upright for four weeks due to an inflammatory rheumatism from wading through streams and being exposed to rain. He could do nothing for the boy's father or for the other adults he visited, except to recommend that they not take too much medicine. What they needed most was rest, but the wagon train would not lay over for fear of becoming snowbound in the mountains.

Bryant was then summoned by a friend in a different wagon train camped about three-quarters of a mile away. While there, he joined in a wedding celebration. As he left the newlyweds, Bryant could see the light of torches and lanterns for the funeral of the boy he was too late to save. While he watched the funeral procession, a man arrived from a third encampment nearby and told him that the wife of one of the emigrants in their train had just given birth to a son.

All along the trail emigrants left their names wherever they could: carved with a knife, written in lead pencil, or scrawled in gunpowder, tar, or buffalo or axle grease onto land formations, loose rocks, trees, and even animal and human skulls. Experiences like these—where so much life, including death, took place at such an unmemorable place as an overnight campsite—must have made the emigrants realize how ephemeral their lives were. The Emigrant Trail was like a palimpsest, each campsite erasing the signs of the previous night's campers. No wonder emigrants left their names wherever they could. It was an attempt to leave some record of their passing against the day when they would be gone.

CHAPTER TEN

The Hundredth Meridian

SPEAKING OF EPHEMERA, REMEMBER YESTERDAY, WHEN LIFE WAS SWEET, fifty-mile rides were easy, the wind a friendly nudge from abaft the beam? Forget all that. I woke at six the next morning to howling wind. The weather forecasts had been wrong about the rain: the thunderstorm that was supposed to pass through the night had detoured north. What the forecasts got right, however, was their high-wind prediction. If anything, they underestimated it.

I considered staying at the motel another day. The clerk who'd checked me in the day before had warned me about the weather. He'd pulled out his smart phone and while checking a weather app mumbled about seventy-knot winds and hailstones and weather watch until 11:00 a.m. In any case, I woke to clear skies and dry roads, but there was still this matter of the wind. It had clocked from southeast to due north, following the low-pressure system as it tracked east. My course for the day, for the next two days in fact, was west-northwest, which meant the wind would be quartering on my starboard bow rather than my larboard aft as it had the day before.

Translation: Headwinds. The prediction was for twenty-five knots, so more accurately, *wicked* headwinds.

I decided to set a low goal for the day: I'd only ride thirty miles, to Gothenburg, Nebraska, with a bail-out option at seventeen miles in the town of Cozad if weather conditions deteriorated. And rather than ride south to regain the Pony Express Route (which would mean riding wind-blown gravel roads on zigzag segments with due-north legs directly into the wind), I would power north into downtown Lexington, then take Highway 30, which runs on the oblique, north of west. The first leg would be tough, but that would be my only directly upwind stretch. What's more, from Lexington the highway ran more or less dead-straight through Cozad to Gothenburg: both towns had Pony Express station buildings I wanted to see—buildings I would miss if I stuck to the Pony Express Route.

As expected, the first leg from the motel up to Lexington, Nebraska, and Highway 30 was tough. It felt like a hill climb: low gear all the way, downshifting into gusts to keep from being slowed so much I couldn't turn the pedals. After I made downtown Lexington, I stopped in the lee of a two-story building to catch my breath and let my heart rate subside. Just for giggles, I checked the wind speed: twenty-five knots, gusting to thirty-four knots.

I set out on Highway 30 and did what you do when you ride into a strong wind: Stop worrying about it, put your head down, and ride. There's just no other way. Plus, this was an interesting wind. Even though it was blowing hard, it wasn't angry. The Santa Anas in Southern California, where I grew up, are angry. So are the winds in and around in the Sacramento Valley, where I live now. They have an edge, a vengeful harshness. This wind was different. It was bossy—it pushed me all over the six-foot shoulder on the highway—but it wasn't angry, and somehow that made it less annoying than it otherwise might have been.

I made Cozad, Nebraska, in two hours, which meant a pace of just under eight miles per hour. Much better than I had anticipated. Willow Island Pony Express Station stands in Cozad Central Park. More importantly, though, Cozad has the 100th Meridian Museum. That was what I really wanted to see, because the hundredth meridian is the beginning of the American West. And what traveler can resist geographic lines, demarcations between here and there?

The transition from the wet, fertile prairie to the drier, harsher Great Plains starts further back at the ninety-eighth meridian, which crosses the Pony Express Trail near the point it hits the Platte River. Wallace Stegner called it "that all-but-mystical line at which begins another climate, another flora and fauna, another ecology, another light, another palette, another air, another order of being." The Great Plains environment was so different from what settlers had experienced east of the Missouri River they didn't attempt to settle the plains until the 1860s. In part, this was because they had no tools effective in the Plains environment. According to Walter Prescott Webb, settlement only became possible courtesy of two inventions—the Colt revolver and barbed wire—and two innovations: plains-adapted plows and windmills.

For 250 years, the Plains Indians kept out Spanish, English, French, Mexican, Texan, and American invaders and withstood missionaries, whiskey, disease, gunpowder. One reason they were so successful at defending their domain was that Plains warriors carried carried from twenty to thirty arrows and could shoot them so rapidly from a running horse they could keep one in the air all the time. The revolver was the first weapon that could compete with the Plains Indians' skill on a horse with a bow and arrow.

The Homestead Act of 1862 granted adult heads of families 160 acres of surveyed public land for a minimal filing fee and five years of continuous residence. But in a country without rocks or trees, it wasn't until barbed wire was first sold in 1874 that homesteaders had an effective, affordable means to build a fence to keep cattle out of crops. The flat plow of the east was useless against the matted grasses of the plains; farmers modified the plow to give it a point, and later created the disc plow. The wind-driven windmill, which also came into large-scale production in the 1870s, made homesteading the dry plains possible by using wind to bring water to the surface from depths of 50 to 250 feet.

Webb characterizes the West as "lawless," in the sense that laws enacted east of the Missouri River didn't make sense in the West. Land allotments under the Homestead Act were too small to be viable. The water laws developed in the wet regions of England and the eastern United States did not work because unlike those well-watered environments, there wasn't enough water to go around.

Clearly, there was a lot more going on in the Great Plains than I had realized, which made me look forward even more to a museum dedicated to the hundredth meridian, this climatological border where the ways of lives and living shifted from East to West.

When I arrived, the 100th Meridian Museum was closed. Remembering my error in failing to disturb the museum keeper back in Seneca, Kansas, I called Judy, the board member listed as a contact. She said she'd come right down. And she did. She opened the museum and it turned out not to have anything whatsoever to do with the Great Plains, the hundredth meridian, Walter Prescott Webb, or the Great American Desert. It was a museum dedicated to—Cozad, Nebraska. The museum acquired its propitious name because the town's founder, John Cozad, picked this area to settle when he saw, while riding on a train in the 1870s, a "100th Meridian" sign placed by the railroad at this spot.

Judy gave me a lovely tour. She was in the process of moving herself and her husband into town from the farm where they'd lived for forty-something years, but unlike Chuck back in Marysville, she wasn't dodging work; you could tell she loved her town and was pleased to show someone around the museum who would bother her to open it up. The museum was nice, had well-designed exhibits, and the tour was interesting, fun. Not what I expected, but very pleasant. I thanked her and left a donation.

Cozad, Nebraska, wasn't on the Pony Express Trail. The closest Pony Express station, Willow Island, sat about six miles southeast of town, across the Platte River. In 1936, the Dawson County American Legion Post No. 77 purchased the Willow Bend station building and relocated it to Veteran's Memorial Park. Seeing as the good people of Cozad had taken the time to preserve it, I decided to swing by to pay my civic respects.

Like most things that have achieved mythic status, the station building was unprepossessing in real life. It was small, squat, built of hand-hewn logs, and looking at it, all I could think was, *Man, what a lousy place to live.* The sole purpose of swing stations like this was to have a pony saddled and ready so the Pony Express rider could exchange a tired horse for a fresh one as quickly as possible. Seeing this station building—a one-room hovel with (originally) a sod roof, a dirt floor, and cloth for windows—showed more than any words ever could that swing stations were all about the horses. And this was one of the nicer ones. Other stations were constructed of adobe bricks, still others of loose stones, and some were mere holes dug in a hillside. Most had dirt floors, beds were pole bunks built against the walls, and the furniture consisted of boxes, benches, or whatever was at hand. And as bad as Nebraska might be in winter, other stations were in even harsher, more barren locations.

Having seen the Cozad sights, it was time to brave the wind again. On my way through town, I passed a white board in the window of the Green Apple Café that said, "Skinny people are easier to kidnap. Stay safe and eat lots of pie." So I stepped in for coffee and a slice of blueberry pie while I wrote a postcard home to send from the Cozad post office (because how many people have a postmark from Cozad, Nebraska?). As I was leaving the café, my museum tour guide and her husband were coming in. She said he'd gotten new shocks for his truck; somehow, that meant he had to take her to lunch.

Another ninety minutes in the wind and I was in Gothenburg, Nebraska. In 1992, the state legislature designated Gothenburg as the "Pony Express Capital of Nebraska." There's even a "Pony Express Capital of Nebraska" memorial brick in front of the Gothenburg Post Office. All this recognition even though the Pony Express Trail never ran on this (north) side of the Platte.

The town itself was a little bigger than Cozad, and despite being west of the hundredth meridian, its lawns were lush and its trees as leafy as any town I'd passed through so far. In 1931 the people of Gothenburg moved a small building known as Machette Station a few miles north from its original location to where it now sat, in Ehmen Park, and turned it into a Pony Express museum. The station building, however, has a murkier provenance than the Willow Island Station in Cozad. Some historians doubt the Machete site was part of the Pony Express route. It is also possible that "Machette" was a corruption of the name "McDonald," which was an alternate name for Cottonwood Springs Station some miles further west.

In any case, the log structure was built in the 1850s, and the town has made it into a cozy little one-room Pony Express museum with free admission. So, I stopped in. If possible, seeing the inside of the swing station in Gothenburg was even more depressing than imagining it from the outside in Cozad. The Gothenburg Pony Express Museum was very

nice—it had a small library, some artifacts, and was very neat and clean—
but living there? Through a Nebraska winter?

I chatted with the volunteer about the station and its history, then got
to the real issues: Where was the best camping nearby? The best lunch?
Breakfast? I didn't get any good restaurant info. I did learn, however, that
the campground where I'd planned to stay south of town was closed, but
that Lafayette Park, on the northern edge of town, offered nice campsites.

Before heading out to the campground, I stopped in at the local grocery store to stock up on liquids and snacks. As I was leaving, an old guy
with a cane, wearing a VFW hat, shuffled up the sidewalk. He stopped and
looked my bike and trailer up and down and said, "Got an air conditioner
on that thing?" We talked a few minutes, and as he walked into the store,
he said rather wistfully, "Wish I had an air conditioner to loan you."

The campground at Lafayette Park was the nicest I'd stayed in
yet. While the RV and tent sites were separated, the tent sites weren't
"remote" or "primitive." They had electricity, a fire grill, a picnic table on a
level concrete pad, and were close to the restrooms and showers. Instead
of train whistles, I heard neighing horses and twittering birds. All for ten
bucks a night.

My first day in the American West ended peacefully. The blustery
morning gradually mellowed into a golden summer afternoon: The wind
slowly subsided, the leaves on the cottonwood trees quietly fluttered, the
grass glowed yellow-green in the slanting afternoon sun. Sure, insects
kept biting my legs, but not everything can be perfect.

CHAPTER ELEVEN
Stair-Stepping through History

I HAD A HARD TIME GETTING OUT OF GOTHENBURG THE NEXT MORNING. Maybe it was the light, or maybe my lighter mood, but everything I saw seemed photo worthy. I wanted to stop everywhere, take a picture of everything. In fact, a photographer could easily spend a day in every town I passed through taking pictures because there was so much to see: historic buildings, brick streets, the rivers, the fields, the hills, the midwestern sky.

Not to mention lawn art. One thing I'd noticed along the way was that the houses on the country roads in Nebraska shared two characteristics. For one, virtually all had the family name engraved, emblazoned, or at least painted on some slab of stone, or burl, or thick piece of wood prominently displayed in their front yard. Some were quite ornate, decorated with a little tableau like a farm scene or a forest animal diorama. If I'd stopped for every piece of lawn art, I'd still be out there. The other thing is every ranch house had a front lawn, and every lawn looked like new-housing-development sod, freshly laid just last week. Maybe the grass was still coming in for the season, but it always had that tenuous, light-green hue, like if you stepped on the grass you would crush it and sink into the mud below.

South of Gothenburg, I crossed back over the Platte River and turned west. The wind had backed 120 degrees or so overnight and was now blowing out of the southwest. It was still fighting me, but thankfully, not as forcefully as the day before. It was forecast to build to the high teens by the afternoon, just strong enough and contrary enough to be obnoxious.

Backing and Veering

When a wind "veers" or "clocks," it changes direction in a clockwise direction, say from 0 degrees (north) to 90 degrees (east). A "backing" wind is the opposite, a counterclockwise shift: in this case, for instance, from 0 degrees to 240 degrees (southwest).

The Pony Express Route through this area followed the original 1913 route of the Lincoln Highway, the "Main Street across America." It was one of the original coast-to-coast highways. Unlike modern interstates, where armies of engineers and road builders survey a route and plow under and pave over everything in the way in the name of interstate transportation and Dwight D. Eisenhower, Lincoln Highway existed mostly on paper as a set of directions to help a driver navigate town to town to get from New York to San Francisco. When it "opened," less than half the highway was improved. Early Lincoln Highway motorist guides described the transcontinental trip as "something of a sporting proposition" taking twenty to thirty days. Motorists were advised to pause their journey if it rained and to give the roads a day or two afterward to dry out. This guide was still good advice in 1919. The US Army sent its first transcontinental motor convoy across the country on Lincoln Highway that year. At times, it had to send out scouts to find the road, and like the overland emigrants seventy years earlier (and me one hundred years later), had to deal with muddy roads and getting stuck in deep sand.

This stretch of Lincoln Highway is a tourist attraction known as the "Gothenburg Stairsteps." The original 1913 route stair-stepped north and west through this area, following the surveyed land tracts. I would say it seems incongruous for anyone to want to drive the older, slower, more tortured original route of the highway, but seeing as I had been stair-stepping for four hundred miles or so trying to follow an even older route, I could understand the novelty.

Despite it being remembered as an automobile highway across the United States, the League of American Wheelman, a cyclist advocacy group, were among the most active groups pushing for improved roads. The

67

Lincoln Highway and other early interstate "trails" grew out of the Good Roads movement of the 1890s, an effort to persuade government officials to improve rural roads so bicyclists could ride without injuring themselves or scaring the horses.

It is difficult at this remove to remember a time when the automobile was not the primary mode of transportation for most Americans. According to bicycle historian David Herlihy, by the 1890s, the height of the Good Roads movement, the bicycle had become the "people's nag," the "long-coveted mechanical horse that provided, above all, practical transportation." One benefit of this evolution in transportation was the push for the better roads we take for granted today.

I enjoyed riding this little piece of highway history. The roadbed was well paved, smooth, and lightly traveled. The Platte River Valley had narrowed. Unlike the flat roads I'd ridden the last few days, at times I rode up small rises over the skirts of the low hills that form the valley's southern border. These were described as "sandhills" in the mid-1800s. To the emigrants, they were a novelty, yet another feature they hadn't seen east of the Missouri River. When I rode through the sandhills along this stretch, they didn't look sandy at all, but were green, enviously green to this child from California where the hills are deep-baked golden brown by that time of year.

I passed by a marker for Gilman's Pony Express Station, all but hidden behind overgrown roadside grass. I also passed a few local monuments along the way. One marked the location of McDonald Ranch (the mangled version of which became known as "Machette's," the original location of the station/museum I visited in Gothenburg). The inscription on the stone monolith read:

OVERLAND RANCH OF CHAS. MCDONALD
EST. AT COTTONWOOD SPRINGS ON OREGON TRAIL
JAN. 1860 / HIS SON W. H. WAS
BORN HERE JUNE 14 1861
BEING THE FIRST WHITE CHILD
BORN IN THIS COUNTY.

McDonald's ranch was one of many "ranches" that sprung up along the Emigrant Trail, habitations that served as temporary havens for overland emigrants. In fact, by 1860 and the era of the Pony Express, the overland journey resembled the overland treks of the early 1840s in name only because hundreds of supportive facilities had been established along the route.

Presumably, in recognizing the birth of W. H. McDonald, the benefactors of the McDonald's Overland Ranch monument were celebrating the first non-Native child born in the county. Still, I wondered whether anyone noted the first African American baby born in these parts. Somewhere between 7,500 and 15,000 African Americans, both enslaved and free, passed through here during the overland emigration. Unlike white settlers, however, there are few contemporary accounts. For the most part African Americans' passage went undocumented. Many traveled as enslaved servants, and slave codes in the South made it illegal to teach enslaved people to read or write. Some whites were so concerned that African Americans might "learn that a man's rights do not depend on his color," Congress declared in 1802 that "no other than a free white person shall be employed in carrying the mail of the United States." The prohibition stood until 1865.

Overland emigration was tough for anyone. Imagine how much more danger, hardship, loneliness, privation, and fear African Americans had to endure. Most of the jumping-off towns for overland emigration were in Missouri where the law *presumed* all African Americans were enslaved unless they could prove otherwise; free African Americans had to carry papers or risk being jailed as runaways. African Americans, free and slave, had to guard against being kidnapped and sold, either into slavery or to a new enslaver, because slave hunters kidnapped free people and even stole slaves to collect a bounty.

On the trail, enslaved people had to carry extra burdens, work extra duties. Some slaves were promised release from slavery once on the West Coast; nevertheless, enslavers sometimes went back on their word. Free Blacks struggled to find a wagon train that would accept them. The constitution of the Great Migration to Oregon in 1843, for example, stated, "No Black or Mulatto person shall, in any case or any circumstance whatever, be admitted into this Society [wagon train], or be permitted to emigrate with it."

And once African Americans reached Utah or the West Coast, they were often no more welcome than they had been east of the Missouri River. Horace Greeley, credited with coining the Manifest Destiny tagline, "Go west, young man," also wrote, "all the unoccupied territory of the United States, and such as they may hereafter acquire, shall be reserved for the benefit and occupation of the white Caucasian race." Sanctioned discrimination, in the form of Black Laws, followed African Americans across the plains. African Americans faced state and territorial laws restricting their freedom, their rights, even their ability to settle in the state. Utah, for instance, legally recognized slavery in 1852 even though Joseph Smith, the founder of the Latter-Day Saints, called for the elimination of slavery in his 1844 presidential platform. Similarly, even though California barred slavery in its state constitution, according to historian J.M. Guinn it had the most odious laws in the nation against African Americans. At least one slaveholder emigrated to Wyoming in light of the Emancipation Proclamation because "out West a man could still be free to own another man without government interference."

It took a lot for anyone to emigrate on the Emigrant Trail. It took even more for African Americans, especially in the years before the Emancipation Proclamation. The McDonald Ranch monument memorializing the birth of the first white child seemed to perpetuate the emigrant-era tendency to render African American emigrants and settlers invisible. In light of the racism and hostility that hounded African Americans all the way to the Pacific Coast, it seemed an insult, unnecessarily preclusive.

Less than half a mile further I came to a monument for Fort McPherson, which read on one side, "This Fort Made Possible the First White Settlement in Lincoln County Located Here and Known as Cottonwood Springs."

Like the "first white child" monument for McDonald's Ranch, I presumed the folks who erected this monument meant Cottonwood Springs was the first non-Native settlement. If so, the inscription might as easily have declared that the fort made possible the first "permanent" settlement in the county. It would have been historically accurate, and possibly less offensive—except maybe to the Lakota who used this area extensively prior to the coming of the settlers.

The crossing of the Platte at Cottonwood Creek was the best available in the area. There was good forage for the Lakota animals in summer and winter. Cottonwood Canyon was wooded, furnishing fuel and protection, and afforded an easy passage to the hunting areas to the south. The military established Fort McPherson at the mouth of the canyon in 1863 to control Lakota movements north and south across the Platte River. Six months later, in April 1864, Brigadier General Robert B. Mitchell traveled to Fort McPherson (popularly called Fort Cottonwood) to meet with "Shan-tag-a-lisk" (Sinte Gleska, or Spotted Tail, of the Brulé), "O-way-see'-cha" (Bad Wound of the Oglala), and other Lakota leaders.

As it turned out, the Lakota had long wanted a council with the US Army at Camp Cottonwood but had avoided the camp because the troops stationed there used any Native Americans they spotted for artillery target practice. Once gathered, General Mitchell's message to the Lakota was simple: "[T]he white man wanted peace, *and wanted the Sioux to keep out of the Platte Valley*." He explained that Lakota would still be allowed to cross the Platte River, but only under escort. The Lakota leaders protested and the council broke up without resolution, all parties agreeing to meet again. The parties met twice more but resolved nothing. General Mitchell ultimately issued a warning: the Lakota had taken the land from other nations that had occupied it before their arrival; accordingly, "rights to land, if accumulated by conquest by the Indians, could be accumulated by the whites."

A few months later, in August 1864, Cheyenne, Arapahoe, and Lakota staged the coordinated raids discussed earlier at Plum Creek and in Oak, Nebraska, along the Little Blue River. The August 1864 raids were not the Lakota's reaction to the establishment of Fort McPherson— the raids were led primarily by Cheyenne and Arapahoe warriors—but

Lakota braves participated. The question of access to the Platte River Valley would be decided by war.

Plopping a fort down at the best crossing of the Platte seems akin to poking the Lakota in the eye and daring them to do something about it. In the following months and years, Native Americans, settlers, emigrants, freighters, soldiers, and mail carriers all paid a terrible price in human suffering.

I understood the locals' desire to erect this monument commemorating their history by celebrating the beginning of settlement in this area. But following so close after the McDonald monument, the Fort McPherson monument struck me as almost jingoist. It seemed that in fairness there might also be some recognition of the manner in which the fort came to be—that in settling the American West it wasn't only "whites" who strove and accomplished, suffered and lost, were given birth and died.

CHAPTER TWELVE

C-Store Caravanserai

MY STOP FOR THE DAY, A CAMPGROUND NEAR THE TOWN OF NORTH Platte, Nebraska, felt like the antithesis of the previous night's camp in Gothenburg. Instead of lush grass, the ground cover was spotty; rather than listening to horses and birds, I had the constant roar of interstate traffic on US 80, about 250 yards away. I was back to the "primitive" section of the campground, which meant no water at my site, and the restrooms and showers were on the other side of the phalanx of RVs parked between me and the one building with washroom facilities. I did snag the only spot with 110-volt electricity nearby, so there was that.

And, oh yeah, "primitive" camping cost twice as much here as in Gothenburg.

The guy who ran the campground was nice ("How are we doing today?" he said to everyone.) And I did have a choice: there was a higher-rent campsite just down the road. I cannot say how much nicer it might have been, but it cost ten dollars more, and by the time I found this campground, I was ready to stop. Had I known how wind-blown and exposed and loud and lacking in amenities this place was, I might have chosen differently. Though I will admit I appreciated how fast my laundry dried in the full sun and whipping wind.

It was also possible that tent sites in the other campground were all taken. Every campground I stayed in was full every night, overflowing with vehicular "campers." After fifteen months of COVID, RVing America was on the road again, with a vengeance. "Camping" (as opposed to, say, bikepacking) is very eye-opening in a way. Cohabitating among

73

these gargantuan RVs, the trailers and the mammoth pickups pulling them, the patio gear, town cars, motorcycles, boats, etc., I was astounded at the hundreds of thousands of dollars invested in each family's rig. Not that I would have turned down an invitation to sit in any one of these air-conditioned monstrosities of an evening, sip mai tais, and yell out questions to Alex's replacement host on *Jeopardy.*

I rose at six the next morning, prompted by chirping birds and the fact that I had oriented my tent to face the rising sun. I needed to make Ogallala, Nebraska, sixty-five miles west. The forecast was low nineties, and even though the wind was holding its daily routine of building to the upper teens from the south, my pattern was not.

The Platte River Valley doesn't run straight, but in sort of a sinusoidal wave. The first peak of the wave was where I hit the Platte River, near Grand Island, Nebraska; the first trough was at the city of Kearney, Nebraska. Since that point, I'd been riding north and west (stair-stepping, as it were) to the next peak, here at the town of North Platte. Continuing west, the valley dips down again toward Julesburg, Colorado. As a result, I would be riding south and west the next two days, which meant headwinds on the southerly legs. Kind of a bummer, but there wasn't much to do about it, except what I was doing: getting an early start.

It was going to be a long, hot, windy ride on a route that didn't pass through any towns, so I filled the spare water bottles I carry on my forks for the first time. I skipped cooking breakfast, thinking I would stop in at the local Denny's on I-80 and grab a quick Grand Slam breakfast. It still took me over an hour to get rolling. Normally, though, it took closer to two. Packing was never a quick process for me.

Denny's turned out to be Flying J Truck Stop–adjacent, built into the gas station convenience store (like Taste of India back in Overton), only Denny's hadn't opened yet and didn't look as if it would anytime soon. I rummaged around Flying J for something to eat without sausage, bacon, or any other type of breakfast meat (because I'm vegetarian), and finally came up with a sort of Egg McMuffin on French toast. I went outside and started breakfast, only to find that I had not read the sandwich label closely enough. I opened it up, discarded the bacon, and (because I am not so adamantly vegetarian I refuse to eat food that has touched meat) wolfed down the rest.

74

Had I a mind to tarry, I might have ridden into town and toured Scout's Rest, Buffalo Bill's ranch. As the true father of the Pony Express—not the real-life 1860 Pony Express, but the storybook version we're all taught to believe—I might have paid my respects. Were it not for Buffalo Bill Cody, I would not have attempted this ride, because without Buffalo Bill, the Pony Express would have been no more than a footnote in the history of the development of the West.

How then did the Pony Express become such a revered institution? The primary reason is that Buffalo Bill's Wild West Show, the most popular traveling show of the era, thrilled audiences throughout America and Europe for more than thirty years with its exhilarating Pony Express segment. A horseman would gallop down the bandstand, check his pony within one length, and just as quickly the mail bag would be on another pony galloping off at full speed. It was a showstopper. Buffalo Bill's Wild West show became the self-designated keeper of the Pony Express legend.

Around this same time the Pony Express started appearing in print as well. In *Roughing It*, Mark Twain included a couple of pages of exuberant prose, widely reprinted ever since, describing the excitement of seeing a passing Pony Express rider. Twain published this book in 1872, nearly a dozen years after the demise of the Pony Express. Buffalo Bill published his autobiography just a few years later, in 1879. In that book he padded his résumé by falsely claiming to have been a Pony Express rider, one of the most often-repeated untruths about the Pony Express. Buffalo Bill never rode for the Pony Express: the closest he came was to ride within a three-mile radius of Leavenworth, Kansas, as a messenger for Russell, Majors & Waddell. He held that job for two months in 1857, when he was eleven or twelve years old.

Never one to let truth stand in the way of a good story, Buffalo Bill's autobiography is replete with harrowing scenes of outriding Indian attacks, facing down a gang of desperadoes, and braving a near-record 322-mile ride. He claimed to have been hired by Jack Slade, the most notorious figure of the Pony Express, and to have joined a group of riders who set out to chastise a local tribe who had stolen Pony Express horses, the posse led by none other than Wild Bill Hickok (even though at the time Hickok was busy killing the McCanles clan a couple hundred miles away at Rock Creek Station in Nebraska).

With these two works, Mark Twain and Buffalo Bill Cody set the mold for nearly all of the Pony Express literature that followed. Most of the subsequent writings on the Pony Express are not factual, but rather, "undocumented historical material"; that is, "the story of the Pony Express without reference to sources by acceptable historical professional standards." In addition, most of these publications often incorporate these undocumented "facts" from earlier works.

Which would be fine, except that with the accretion of years these undocumentable stories have evolved into a doxological canon, with writer after writer heaping unqualified praise on this interstitial, short-lived failure that for a period of eighteen months bridged the gap between the three-week stagecoach mail service and the lightning-quick telegraph. Even the works of Raymond Settle and Mary Lund Settle, authors of the authoritative works on the Pony Express, are at times uncritically romantic.

I blame Buffalo Bill. Still, I had to tip my helmet to the old scout, because even if I didn't know it when I decided I'd attempt this ride, his dreamy-eyed version of the Pony Express had set me on the path. Nevertheless, I passed on the chance to stop by Scout's Rest due to freshening wind, rapidly climbing temps, and the long ride ahead. But the truth is, I likely would have passed even if the weather were more favorable. There was nothing for me to learn there.

North Platte, I thought as I turned my back to it, *you might be a lovely city, but I did not give you a chance. Your interstate convenience stores and gas stations are as unpleasant as any. But it's not your fault.*

My first five or so miles were on pavement. I stopped at a drinking fountain/pedestrian rest area dedicated to the memory of a cyclist, Patty Evans, silently praying it wasn't installed, like a ghost bike, because she had been killed by a car on that street. I later found she hadn't, but rather was an avid cycling advocate, mostly for women. She was my age when she died, sixty-two, which gave pause for thought.

I passed a memorial for the Cold Springs Pony Express Station buried in overgrown weeds off a busy road with no turnout, making it impossible for anyone driving to stop and pay heed. It seemed like a waste of the cost and effort of marking the spot, but that's up to North Platte, I guess.

Checking In

At the Cold Springs site, I realized I had forgotten to send my morn-ing GPS message and to turn on my tracker. I carried a satellite tracker in case I needed emergency help once I reached remote country. Happily, I did not. But in the meantime, family and friends had expressed an interest in following my progress, which the tracker updated every hour. I sent out messages every morning when I started and every afternoon when I stopped to let folks know I was okay. Some mornings, like this one, I was a little scattered and forgot to send the messages before getting underway, so I found a pullout and took a moment. Communication duties attended to, I moved on.

Once I settled into the ride, it went reasonably well. Some of the low roads were sandy, but not horribly so. As advertised, the wind was due south: nasty headwinds on the too many southerly legs, tailwinds on the precious few northerly legs, annoying crosswinds the rest of the time, which was most of the route.

Midmorning I arrived at the next landmark of the mid-1800s emi-gration, O'Fallon's Bluff. The sandhills of the Platte River Valley, which had up to this point politely kept their distance, now crowded the Platte River, leaving no way for emigrants, freighters, or me to get to the Pacific Coast except by going over them. One freighter wrote that the sand was so deep in places, heavily laden freight wagons "would often sink to the hubs" and that it took "an entire day to again reach river trail, which was hard and smooth."

Just as O'Fallon's Bluff signaled the end of the easy-going Platte River Valley for emigrants, so it did for me. Miles and miles of climb, descend, repeat, over and over. Now that I was deep in them, I found the sandhills of the valley were in fact sandy. There was no shade anywhere. Occasionally trucks sped past at speed, each spreading a new layer of dust to refresh what-ever dust my sweat had washed away. The tops of the hills were windy, the bottoms stiflingly hot for the absence of wind, the scenery bland and sere. When I rode south, into the teeth of the wind, my pace slowed to a crawl.

This was not a great time. And that was before the bugs.

At one point I topped a hill, tongue probably hanging out from thirst even though I was constantly drinking, and saw a golf course, the last thing I would have imagined coming across after all the sand and sage I'd ridden through. There were two couples at a hole nearby, sitting in separate golf carts: white, middle-aged, sporting polo shirts, khaki shorts, and golf visors, laughing heartily about something. Probably the sweaty guy on the bike with his tongue hanging out. Golfing there must be a hoot. Signs scattered about specified that all alcohol drunk while golfing must be purchased at the golf course store. Maybe that explained the couples' mirth.

On the far side of the golf course, I started picking up insects that hitched a ride then bit me by way of saying thanks. While I struggled up sandy hills. In the heat and wind. Things went on like this for a while, improving a little with the miles as the bug population decreased and the hills flattened some. By then, however, I was in bad shape—feeling very tired with twenty-five or so miles of a sixty-five-mile day still to go.

Then, like a beacon of salvation, I saw a gas station sign. All day long the route had been playing tag with I-80, touching it then running away south only to meet it again further west. This station sat at an offramp for the town of Paxton, Nebraska. I carried with me everything I needed— water and electrolyte mix, energy bars, gels, and caffeinated goo—but something different, anything ice cold, and preferably enjoyed in a pneumonia-conducive atmosphere, sounded so good.

And it was. I pulled in, spent way too much money on drinks and snacks, and got permission from the owner to sit in the empty lobby of the adjoining Days Inn to enjoy it all in air-conditioned comfort. Until then I had seen c-stores as eyesores, blemishes, places of last resort. Not anymore. This little store was an oasis of respite. A temporary sanctuary. C-store caravanserai.

Back out into the heat and wind a half-hour later, I passed the Paxton Cemetery, where the halyards on a series of two dozen or so flagless flagpoles clanged against the metal like halyards on masts in a harbor. Each pole rang out in a different tone, and together they made a beautiful music.

Just past the cemetery I detoured off the Pony Express Route to go by another station site. The first mile or so reeked as if I were riding downwind from a feed lot, which I'm sure I was. When I came to the turnoff for the Pony Express station, I weighed whether it was worth the effort. The site was two miles downwind, which meant two tough miles back upwind, and I didn't know whether there was even a marker to see; under the conditions, I didn't care enough to find out. From there, I had one more upwind mile, then unbroken crosswind over an unbroken line of hills for twelve torturous miles to get to Ogallala, Nebraska. Those miles dragged on and on. Talk about tedious.

I had rented a motel room the night before while sitting in that scruffy little campground in North Platte, knowing it was going to be a long, hot day and knowing as well that at the end of that day a primitive or rustic or grassy or undeveloped or remote campsite just wasn't going to cut it. Somewhere along the way I had passed out of Central and into Mountain Daylight Time, so I was too early to check in. I found a place nearby to get a salad and a shake while I waited because here I was at yet another I-80 interstate off-ramp, all four corners of both sides of the free-way crammed full of places to eat, shop, fill up—whatever. Three c-store interchanges in one ride. It was a record.

When it was finally time to check in, I made my way back to the motel. The clerk asked about my bike and my ride. She told me that in prison she'd read Cheryl Strayed's book *Wild* about hiking the Pacific Crest Trail. "I've always wanted to try something like that," she said. "Maybe after my next divorce."

CHAPTER THIRTEEN

Crossing to California

I ROSE EARLY THE NEXT DAY, THANKS IN LARGE PART TO THE GUY WHO ran his diesel truck in front of my room for half an hour starting at 4:30 a.m. I stopped by McDonald's for breakfast, but even as voracious as I was, still found the hash browns inedible. Salted cardboard was how they struck me at the time. Popped across the street to Casey's (c-store) to get some electrolyte drink for down the road (another hot one), and, while I was there, a couple of donuts, because—donuts!

Ogallala, Nebraska, has a Pony Express monument for Sand Hill Station. True to the station name, unpaved roads through the area were hilly, sandy, and slow, though not as bad as back at O'Fallon's Bluff. The wind had veered a few degrees and was now west-southwest: In other words, more directly against me. The good news is while the contrary direction of the wind slowed my pace and made me work harder, it cooled me enough to keep me from the full force of the heat. I'll take that trade-off on a ninety-five-degree day.

The Pony Express Bikepacking Route stayed south of the South Platte River between Ogallala, Nebraska, and Julesburg, Colorado, to take advantage of the lightly traveled unpaved roads. Pony Express station monuments, however, were located along Highway 30, which runs parallel to the route but a couple of miles north, across the South Platte River. I wanted to swing by those station sites, as well as California Hill, an important landmark on the Oregon Trail. So about twelve miles into the ride, I left the route to detour north and catch Highway 30 where it passes through Brule, Nebraska.

Downtown Brule was small and very quiet, the only activity being a few people going in and out of the postage-stamp-sized post office. I turned west there onto Highway 30, passed the Diamond Springs Station monument a mile or so past town, then came to a historical marker for California Hill.

A little geography:

The main Emigrant Trail ran along the south bank of the Platte River. Heading west toward California, the Platte River splits into north and south forks just east of North Platte, Nebraska (near the site of Buffalo Bill's ranch). The South Platte River makes a wide southwest arc from the forks at North Platte to Denver, Colorado; the North Platte River angles northwest toward Casper, Wyoming. South Pass, the only wagon pass through the Rockies along this route, lay west of Casper. Consequently, anyone following the Emigrant Trail to a destination on the other side of the Rockies had to cross the South Platte River to follow the North Platte River toward Casper. Prior to 1859, the most popular crossing, known as the California Crossing, was just west of Brule.

For the emigrants, crossing any river was a difficult, dangerous task. Drownings were the most common fatal accidents on the trail. The South Platte was not the most treacherous crossing, but it was still arduous. Though on average the river was relatively shallow, it was deepest after the spring flood, when most emigrants traveled. It was also wide, anywhere from a third of a mile to over a mile, according to diarists. The bottom was uneven, with deep holes and steep sandbars, neither of which were constant, but instead were constantly shifting in the current. The bed of the river was often described as quicksand. As long as the animals kept moving, they were fine; if they stopped, sand would instantly gather around their legs and start to bury the wagon wheels, miring everything in place and soon drowning the animals. Emigrants would try to protect their belongings by caulking the wagon beds and raising them on blocks, but sometimes that wasn't enough to keep rushing water from flooding the beds. It's no surprise that after crossing, some "took a turn at the jug for Spiritual consolation."

After fording the South Platte, travelers had to cross the divide between the forks to reach the North Platte River. The steep climb up to the divide was known as California Hill, one of the steepest grades on the trail. The area is marked by a Nebraska Historical Marker near the base of California Hill (which notes that the owner of the property donated the land in memory of trail historian Irene Paden). You can drive to the top to view wagon ruts. The Oregon-California Trails Association has erected a fence with a narrow gate allowing access to tourists on foot but preventing damage to the historic swales by vehicles (and presumably, mountain bikes).

Up to this point in the trip, the only trail ruts I'd seen were way back on my first day in Nebraska. I had planned to climb California Hill and view the ruts there, but once again, the elements convinced me otherwise. The climb looked steep, the day was already hot, the wind steadily building, and I still had an upwind run into Julesburg, Colorado, ahead of me. It struck me that being just a couple of miles off the highway, I could drive there another time and walk the ruts at my leisure. I opted to roll on. While I rode though, I kept glancing downhill to the Platte on my left and uphill to the right, imagining a line of white-topped prairie schooners climbing up from the river and disappearing over the back of California Hill. It must have been something to see.

California Hill led to Ash Hollow via Windlass Hill, two other areas mentioned often in emigrant diaries and trail histories. But the Pony Express did not go that way, so neither did I.

Some miles further along, I dropped down from the bluffs and rode southwest through Big Springs, Nebraska, crossed into the northeast corner of Colorado past the South Platte Pony Express Station monument (where a donkey across the road yelled at me the entire fifteen minutes I spent resting and refueling there), and eventually made it to Julesburg, the "Gateway to Colorado."

The Emigrant Trail did not come this far along the South Platte River until just prior to the time of the Pony Express. No one continued west past the California Crossing near Brule, Nebraska, because there was nowhere further along the South Platte to go. Until 1859, that is, when the Pike's Peak Gold Rush got into full swing.

The previous summer, gold had been discovered at Cherry Creek (where Denver, Colorado, sits today). As mentioned above, the South Platte River makes a wide southwest arc to Denver. It was easy enough for anyone wanting to get to the gold diggings to follow the Emigrant Trail, and rather than cross the South Platte at the California Crossing, continue following the river southwest. Consequently, starting from spring 1859, travelers on the Emigrant Trail had two primary destinations: overlanders headed to Utah or the Pacific Coast crossed the river to head northwest to South Pass; argonauts and others headed for Denver City continued along the south bank. Julesburg, Colorado—about twenty miles west of the California Crossing at Brule, Nebraska—became the point where these two paths diverged.

In a similar way, Julesburg also signifies the point at which the firm of Russell, Majors & Waddell diverged. Up until 1859, it was a freighting firm: A mammoth, hugely successful firm, but nearly the only thing it did was haul freight, mostly to US Army posts west of the Missouri River. Rushing headlong in order to take advantage of the Pike's Peak Gold Rush, William Russell ignored Majors's and Waddell's advice and diversified the firm over their objections by launching Russell, Majors & Waddell into stagecoaching, mail delivery, and ultimately, the Pony Express.

No one knew how large the Pike's Peak strike might turn out to be, but there were plenty of people in addition to Russell who wanted to profit from the rush of gold seekers. One of these was William Larimer, an experienced town promoter. In late summer 1858, Larimer headed out to the Pike's Peak gold diggings to make money by setting up a town and selling lots. On his way he stopped in Leavenworth, Kansas, and met with Russell. Larimer secured Russell's agreement that if Russell, Majors & Waddell established stagecoach service to the Pike's Peak Gold Rush area, Larimer's town (wherever that ended up being established) would be the terminus. In exchange, Larimer promised Russell a share in the town he was going to create, which effectively gave Russell about thirty acres in the heart of what was later known as Denver, Colorado.

Russell presented this opportunity to his partners, who flatly refused. Majors and Waddell found the prospect unacceptably risky: it was too early to tell whether the Pike's Peak Gold Strike would be substantial or turn out to be a flash in the pan. So during winter 1858–1859, William Russell came together with one of his former partners, John S. Jones, and created the Leavenworth and Pike's Peak Express Company to carry freight, passengers, and express matter between Leavenworth, Kansas, and Denver City (in what was still Kansas Territory).

Russell and Jones borrowed heavily with an eye to having the stagecoach line ready in just a few months so they could be in a position to handle traffic in time for the spring rush to the mines. They purchased the finest stagecoaches made—Abbot-Downing Concord coaches—along with hundreds of mules to pull them. They also sent out a surveying party to map out a more direct route across Kansas to Denver City, rather than having their stagecoaches run on the more roundabout Emigrant Trail, so they could advertise their line as the quickest conveyance to the gold fields. By the time the Leavenworth and Pike's Peak Express Company was up and running in April 1859, Russell and Jones had spent "something near a quarter of a million dollars in their preliminaries, equipment, and in completing arrangements before turning a wheel."

There was nothing legal to prevent Russell from creating such a company, but it was only his position as a principal of Russell, Majors & Waddell that enabled him to borrow the money to finance this new venture. Waddell understood that, and in a series of letters, excoriated Russell for tying Russell, Majors & Waddell's reputation to such a speculative undertaking.

What Waddell didn't understand at the time was that Russell would never let fear of taking risks prevent him from plunging ahead, especially if he ran those risks with other people's money. That is not meant as a compliment. Russell acquired a reputation as a "plunger," that is, "a risk taker, a gambler, a speculator." By one estimate, Russell and Jones's stagecoach venture cost $1,000 a day to operate. They ran the Leavenworth & Pike's Peak Express Company for about six months, until October 1859. By then, the company owed creditors over a half-million dollars. Russell, Majors & Waddell took over the company and assumed its debts to protect its investment and credit. So it happened that even though Majors and Waddell initially had no interest in Russell's boondoggle, he'd backed them into stagecoaching and carrying US Mail.

Despite monumental failures like the Leavenworth & Pike's Peak Express Company, William Russell is often described as bold, visionary, as in this strident defense: "Lesser men of his day and since, either through ignorance or misunderstanding, have flippantly labeled him an impractical visionary or reckless gambler. The fact is, he was neither. . . . The very worst that can be said of him is that he was an irrepressible speculator."

Maybe. I think Russell's actions in regard to the Leavenworth & Pike's Peak Express Company support a different conclusion. In their effort to mythologize the Pony Express, most writers characterize Russell's actions in the best possible light. To do so, stories about the Pony Express avoid or neglect an aspect of Russell's character: namely, as one writer bluntly states, "Russell was dishonest."

And, I would add, not particularly astute. Just weeks after spending a quarter of a million in setting up their stagecoach service, Russell and Jones spent another $144,000 purchasing a rival stagecoach line, an ill-advised purchase, which in addition to being expensive, fundamentally altered the Leavenworth and Pike's Peak Express Company's operations.

During this time, John M. Hockaday ran a stagecoach and mail line between St. Joseph, Missouri, and Salt Lake City, Utah. Hockaday's route followed the Emigrant Trail: In fact, his US Mail contract required he use that route. He relied, as all stagecoach lines did, on his mail contract to supplement income from passengers, which alone wasn't enough to cover the cost of operating his line. Hockaday had operated his stagecoach line for nearly a year when two unexpected events occurred in March 1859.

The first was Congress's failure to pass its annual postal appropriations bill. Instead of being paid, the best the postal department could do was to give Hockaday certificates of indebtedness. Hockaday could in turn sell these certificates, but only at a severe discount.

The second event was the untimely death of Postmaster General Aaron V. Brown. There were two opposing schools of thought regarding US Mail contracts in the West. One was that mail contracts should "subsidize public transportation to the West in order to speed its development and strengthen its ties with the East." The other was that "every mail route must pay for itself out of the revenues it earned." Postmaster General Brown, who'd awarded Hockaday's contract, was of the former, subsidizing school. Unfortunately, he died suddenly in the spring of 1859. The new postmaster general, Joseph Holt, was firmly of the latter school. One of his first actions in taking the office was to review all trans-Mississippi mail contracts with "a jaundiced eye." As a result, Hockaday's subsidy was reduced by one-third, and Hockaday was ordered to reduce the frequency of his mail service even though, as Hockaday explained in his appeal, such a decrease in service would actually increase his costs.

Between the postal department not paying Hockaday the money it owed him and Postmaster General Holt reducing his subsidy going forward, Hockaday's prospects were bleak. Luckily, Hockaday's "splurging new competitor," Russell and Jones's Leavenworth and Pike's Peak Express Company, needed a mail contract to subsidize its operation and was willing to pay a premium to purchase Hockaday's stagecoach line and mail contract.

It is difficult to see how this purchase benefited Russell and Jones. Having rushed to set up a stagecoach line prematurely, they then went even deeper into debt to purchase a line they didn't need, which was only available because the government hadn't paid money it owed and had reduced the line's mail subsidy to an unsupportably low level. Moreover, because Hockaday's mail contract specified the Emigrant Trail as the route, Russell and Jones had no choice but to abandon the route they had just rushed to survey and stock, and relocate all of their stations and equipment north, which of course incurred even more expense.

Which brings us back to Julesburg, Colorado.

Starting in late spring 1859, Russell and Jones were running a stagecoach line with two western termini: Denver City, Kansas Territory, and Salt Lake City, Utah Territory. They sent out their route superintendent, Beverley Williams, to review the lines and establish more stations as needed. Hockaday's stagecoaches had crossed the South Platte at the California Crossing near Brule, Nebraska. Williams moved the crossing west to Julesburg, Colorado.

Julesburg started as a small trading post run by Jules Beni near the point where Lodgepole Creek empties into the South Platte River. There was a shallow ford across the South Platte nearby, making it a popular crossing for the local Cheyenne, and a good place for Jules, often called "Old Jules," to trade. Stagecoach lines sometimes located stations at existing ranches along the road. By 1859, when Williams was scouting the route for station locations for the newly relocated Leavenworth and Pike's Peak Company, Jules's trading post seemed a perfect spot: It was strategically located at a good ford across the South Platte River, which made it a logical point to split the route, and Jules's small settlement had ready-made buildings and facilities. It may not have been much—"a small trading post and a large sodhouse that served as saloon, restaurant, hotel, store, and anything else that might accommodate travelers' needs"—but it was far more expedient than starting from nothing.

Williams had a station built near Jules's trading post, designated it as a home station, and hired Jules as stationmaster. Word reached the overland emigrants, who started preferring the nearby ford across the South Platte River. Jules improved the road to make it more attractive, and the area grew into the little town of Julesburg, a "dirty little settlement that looked like a wart on the bare face of nature," but due to its location, one of the most important stations on the Emigrant Trail.

A few months after Russell and Jones's Leavenworth and Pike's Peak Express failed, Russell set up a successor company: the Central Overland California and Pike's Peak Express. This is the company that ran the Pony Express, and as the Pony Express used the same stations as the stagecoach line, the Pony Express Trail crossed the South Platte at Julesburg rather than back by Brule, Nebraska. Which is why, back near Brule, I continued west into Julesburg rather than turning north to Ash Hollow.

The present location of Julesburg is its fourth. The original location established by Jules Beni was south of the Platte River; raiding Lakota and Cheyenne burned it down in 1865. The town was rebuilt a couple of miles away but died when the railroad tracks were laid on the other (northern) side of the South Platte River. The town moved to the railroad and was a tent city of the Hell-on-Wheels kind until the leading edge of railroad construction moved further west. The fourth and current town sprang up at the intersection of the transcontinental railroad and the Denver branch of the Union Pacific Railroad.

Once in town, I had a Hobbit-worthy second breakfast at D&J Café and drank way too much coffee just because it felt good to sit inside awhile, protected from the wind and the heat. After lunch I rolled over to the Holiday Motel on the western edge of town. The owner, Susan, asked about my itinerary for the next day, and in light of the forecast (100 degrees), suggested I see the local historic sites later that afternoon when the day cooled off and take a more direct route the next morning to beat the heat.

It sounded like a smart plan, so after I rested a bit, I jumped on my bike—without the trailer, which was a treat—and raced around to see the sites south of Julesburg. I ended up putting in another dozen windy miles visiting sites and reading interpretive signs. As things turned out, I ended up retracing this exact route the next day anyway. Unlike viewing the ruts on California Hill or locating the (probably unmarked) Pony Express station sites near O'Fallon's Bluff, I couldn't skip seeing the original site of Julesburg regardless of the weather. It was the first place west of St. Joseph, Missouri, that had any real significance to the history of the Pony Express. More importantly, it was where Old Jules Beni shot Jack Slade.

CHAPTER FOURTEEN

Jules and Jack

NOT MUCH HAPPENED IN THE WAY OF PONY EXPRESS HISTORY BETWEEN St. Joseph, Missouri, and Julesburg, Colorado. That is, as to the drama, as for connecting *this* station with *that* event, there's not a lot to write about: Pony Express riders delivered mail from one home station to the next where they ate, slept, and (with the probable exception of the Mormon boys) played cards, drank, smoked, and likely even cussed until it was time to ride back with a new load of mail.

Suggesting that Pony Express riders cussed, drank, or gambled is tantamount to blasphemy. It is a bedrock tenet of Pony Express lore that Alexander Majors, who held "stern Calvinistic Presbyterian sentiments," required all employees to sign an oath "before the Great and Living God" promising under threat of dismissal they would not drink, swear, quarrel, or fight. Majors also reportedly gave small bibles to all of his employees. These factoids are recited—religiously intoned, one might say—throughout the literature, seemingly meant to float a halo of rectitude over Alexander Majors and the Pony Express, to make the riders seem to sit a little taller in the saddle, if you will.

I suppose it's possible that Majors personally saw to it that each of the thousands of Russell, Majors & Waddell employees—hired by different supervisors over the course of a half-dozen years at multiple locations across two thousand miles of largely unpopulated country between St. Joseph and San Francisco—signed and obeyed his oath. Nevertheless, contemporary observers noted Majors's employees swearing as much as any other bullwhacker or stagecoach driver. Excavations of Pony Express stations in Nevada unearthed liquor bottles. Drunken Pony Express riders were reportedly observed falling off their horses. As for promising not to fight, two 1860 shootings involving employees of the firm took place at Smith Creek Station. Near the end of his life, even Alexander Majors reportedly lamented that his oath was not successful.

As for bibles, historian Joe Nardone believes "few, if any, Pony Express riders got one." Even if they had, do we really suppose the riders, who sacrificed all to lighten their load as much as possible, made an exception to carry bibles on their runs? Well, possibly. Majors's bibles were popular with his bullwhackers because the leaves were the right size to use as rolling papers.

Issues of rectitude aside, Julesburg stands apart from most Pony Express stations because the two most maligned people associated with the Pony Express, Jack Slade and Jules Beni, engaged in a violent feud here. The short version goes like this: Slade was a division superintendent for the Pony Express. Jules Beni was the stationmaster at Julesburg, a home station on the line under Slade's supervision. Slade and Old Jules did not get along. In March 1860, just weeks before the Pony Express started its first run, Old Jules emptied a pistol and both barrels of a shotgun into Slade, who was unarmed, at close range. Incredibly, Slade didn't die, and though his friends strung Jules up, they let him down, banishing him from the area under penalty of death. Slade healed and within months returned to his superintendent post; a couple of years later, Jules apparently forgot what it felt like to be hung and returned from exile. After being goaded for some months by Jules, Slade tracked Jules down, killed him, cut off his ears, and carried one of them in his vest pocket the rest of his short life.

The longer version is more interesting.

Joseph Alfred "Jack" Slade has been cited as the prototype for the western gunman. In *Roughing It*, Mark Twain tells of narrowly escaping death at Slade's hand just for accepting the last cup of coffee at supper. Richard Burton describes Slade as "having killed his three men." Slade was known as "The Law West of Kearny," and Wild Bill Hickok was once known as "The Slade of Kansas." Ben Ficklin, route superintendent for the Pony Express, hired Slade as division superintendent for the roughest part of the stagecoach line based on Slade's reputation.

Jack Slade is nearly always characterized as a "great desperado," the "most stunning example" that Russell, Majors & Waddell hired men who were "plainly outlaws." Slade reportedly lived in "unexplained luxury with a sour-countenanced, heavy-haunched wife, [and] ran a tight, fear-struck division, exercising ruthless control with a quickly-riled temper and a ready gun." One freighter tells of stories around a campfire: "[One old bullwhacker] would tell about the noted stage company boss, Jack Slade, who caught one of his stage tenders listening at a door and who whipped out his bowie knife and cut the listener's ear off, telling him if he ever caught him doing it again, he would cut his heart out."

Slade's assailant, Jules Beni, fares worse in the literature. At first blush, he seemed a perfect candidate to run an important home station like Julesburg. "Because [Jules] knew his prairie and his Indians and seemed to make money for himself, it was thought he would do equally well for the company." This proved not to be the case. At a minimum, he was inattentive to his duties. As stated earlier, Julesburg, Colorado, was where Russell, Majors & Waddell's stagecoach line split. Accordingly, mail needed to be sorted here, and due to his negligence or incompetence, often mail addressed to Denver would end up in Salt Lake.

Jules also had this game he liked to play. One of the main functions of a station was to keep and have ready the livestock for stagecoaches and Pony Express riders. Jules traded with Native Americans who lived in the area, and like most traders, was married to a woman from a local tribe. Every so often, Jules would ask his in-laws and friends to run off the livestock, leaving the stagecoaches and Pony Express riders in a bind because neither could continue without fresh livestock. He would then go to the local representative, and for a fee, offer to search for and negotiate the recovery of the livestock. After he collected the money, the "thieves" would "find" the livestock and run it back to town.

The company tired of Jules's apparent incompetence and thievery. At Ficklin's direction, Slade fired Jules as stationmaster. Jules appeared to take the news well, but friction between the two men continued. For example, Jules was reported to have company horses on his ranch, and occasionally he would steal company hay to feed them. Whether this was true or not, Slade would round up horses on Jules's ranch and claim they were stolen. Another source of friction was an employee of Jules who left, complaining that Jules never paid him, and went to work for Slade. Jules felt that Slade lured the employee away. At the same time, Julesburg was Jules Beni's fiefdom. He founded, built, and ran it, and did not take to being told what he could and could not do. One day, when Slade was unarmed, Jules let him have it with both barrels, plus the pistol.

By coincidence, very soon after the shooting a stagecoach pulled in and Ben Ficklin, the route supervisor who had hired Slade, was on it. He ordered a couple of men to tend to Slade's wounds while he and a couple of others tended to Old Jules. They threw a rope over something high and hung Jules on the spot. But Ficklin let Jules down before he was dead because he had a dilemma: Jack Slade was still alive. Ficklin couldn't kill Jules because Jules hadn't killed Slade.

There are other versions of how Jules escaped death that day. One is that the rope broke and he ran away; another variation holds that his Native American friends cut him down. I find the moral dilemma scenario the most plausible and the most interesting.

Between the Missouri River and Salt Lake City, there were no conventional legal authorities other than the military, which was only authorized to protect emigrants from the Native Americans. It had no jurisdiction over disputes between US citizens. In the absence of this authority, a principal of order developed: The Code of the West, a set of norms based on the concept of "fair play." That meant, for example, not shooting an opponent in the back or shooting an opponent who was unarmed.

In shooting Slade, Jules violated both proscriptions, which may be one reason Jules Beni is the only person in Pony Express lore more vilified than Jack Slade. Another reason Old Jules is nearly universally vilified may be that Jules was French Canadian, and possibly multiracial; both were abhorred by white Americans.

Along the Emigrant Trail, many of the road ranches east of South Pass were run by traders, many French Canadian. It was common practice among traders to marry into local tribes: the trader gained closer ties to the Native Americans he traded with; the tribe benefited by having ready access to trade goods and someone they could expect to speak for their interests. The arrangement was honorable among the people involved—among the men, anyway; I have yet to come across a discussion of how Native American women felt—but interracial marriage did not sit well with the wider society of white Americans. Any white man married to a Native American woman was referred to by the doubly derogatory term "squaw man." Emigrants were grateful for the conveniences offered by these ranches. Their prevailing attitude toward the proprietors, however, is summed up in one emigrant's diary: "What a shame and disgrace to our country."

But back to Jules, who somehow escaped death by hanging. If in fact Ben Ficklin and his pals did not kill Jules because Jules had not succeeded in killing Slade—even though everyone assumed it was just a matter of time before Slade died from his wounds—"fair play" seems to incorporate the notion of talion, or reciprocal punishment in kind. In other words, "eye for eye, tooth for tooth." Not in the sense of vengeful retribution, but rather in a limiting sense, holding that the punishment cannot exceed the transgression. As violent as this episode is, I would like to believe that some sense of morality stayed these impromptu vigilantes' hand.

Not that Ficklin was done with Jules. He hoisted Jules off the ground by the neck once or twice more. Slade yet breathed. So finally, Ficklin told Jules they'd let him live if he left town that day and never came back. Jules complied—for a time.

Meanwhile, Slade languished, first in Julesburg, then at Horseshoe Station, where he lived with his wife, Maria Virginia. When he was strong enough, Ben Ficklin had him taken by stagecoach to St. Louis where a surgeon removed some, though not all, of the two dozen or so bullets and shot from his body. By midsummer 1860, two months later, Slade was back on the job.

The following year, in the summer of 1861, Jules reappeared on the periphery of Slade's division. Evidently, he was vocal about killing Slade if they met. Slade, however, seemed to go out of his way to avoid a confrontation as long as he could. At some point, he deemed it unavoidable. Before going off to hunt down Old Jules, Slade went to Fort Laramie and informed the army officers of his intention. The officers told Slade they would not intervene, and in fact rather encouraged him because "there would be no peace on Slade's division while Jules lived." Slade and some of his employees went about tracking Jules down. Within days, Jules was dead.

The unsolvable question is, did Slade kill him? And if so, did he torture Jules first? Most accounts lay the killing to Slade and support some variation of a torture scenario, with Jules tied to a post and Slade shooting one part of him or another, going into the bar for drink, then coming out to shoot some other body part. A different version holds that a couple of Slade's employees found Jules and sent word for Slade; that Jules got wise and tried to escape; that the employees shot him, then tied him to a post to keep him from escaping; and that by the time Slade arrived, Jules had already died.

The detail everyone agrees on is that Slade cut Jules's ears off and carried one around in his fob pocket for the rest of his life, which, as it turned out, lasted only a few more years. Before then, and as long as he was employed by a stagecoach operator, Slade effectively maintained order on his section of the line. But even Slade's friends admitted he was a violent, destructive drunk. In 1862, he lost his job with the stagecoach company after shooting up the sutler's store at Fort Halleck, Wyoming. He and Maria Virginia ended up in the gold rush town of Virginia City, Montana. Slade saved the town during the winter of 1863 by captaining a wagon train under exceedingly harsh conditions to the Milk River to retrieve desperately needed supplies. He returned a hero, but just four months later, was hung by Montana vigilantes after he terrorized the town during a particularly destructive bender. He was thirty-three-years old.

Just a few years earlier Ben Ficklin had refused to hang Jules Beni for attempting to murder Jack Slade. The Montana vigilantes, on the other hand, seemed to have had no problem lynching Slade; not because he had murdered anyone, but for being a violent drunk. Maybe there was no such thing as the Code of the West. Or maybe Slade's hanging illustrates the injustice of vigilantism, the difference between individual conscience and ochlocracy.

Over time, a number of atrocities have been attributed to Jack Slade, including twenty-six murders, starting with his alleged killing of a man when only thirteen years old. Like most stories about the Pony

Express, most stories about Slade appear to range from exaggerations to outright fabrications. No question: Jack Slade could be bad news if you were on his bad side—or even if you were on his good side and he was drunk—but he does not seem to have been the evil man as he is nearly always portrayed. Of course, it's just as possible the same could be said for Old Jules, but no one has volunteered to come forward on his behalf other than Adeline Cayou Beckstead, who was married as a teenager to a much older Jules.

Jack Slade came on the scene as the prototypical gunslinger; he went out as the quintessential pioneer of the American West: the man who'd outlived his purpose and overstayed his welcome.

The day I left Julesburg, Colorado, the temperature was forecast to rise to nearly one hundred degrees. I had a fifty-five-mile ride to make and did not want to spend the last couple of hours in the full heat, so I rose at 5:30 a.m. and was off by 6:20. Another guest at the motel was loading up his large, loudly idling pickup. He watched as I put my bike helmet on and said, "It's going to be a hot one." I agreed, then set off.

I probably should have ridden straight west to beat the heat, as I had planned. Instead I retraced my route from the afternoon before, riding south to rejoin the Pony Express Route, which takes the South Platte Trail Scenic and Historic Byway, a gravel road just north of I-76, to visit the first site of Julesburg.

A few miles west I stopped at a cluster of stone monuments. One commemorated the first site of Julesburg. Another was a Pony Express station monument, though the station name on it was not "Julesburg," but rather, "Overland City." Ben Holladay, who took ownership of the stagecoach company after Russell, Majors & Waddell went under, changed the name due to Julesburg's bad reputation. It didn't take. By 1862, the station was again known as Julesburg. In addition to the granite monuments, the pullout had newer interpretive signs, replete with dad-joke level puns: "A Moving Story" (about the four locations of Julesburg); "The 'Earie' Tale of Jules Beni." Apart from the corny humor, anyone who took the time to exit the interstate to drive this little stretch could learn a lot about the old town.

Before moving on, I took a moment to gaze north across a wide empty field to where the original Julesburg stood in 1860. I knew there would be nothing to see—there wasn't anything to see even back in the 1930s when Irene Paden was here. But of all the stories and biographies related to the Pony Express, I'd found Jack Slade's the most interesting. After riding hundreds of miles, it was fulfilling, somehow, to stand near a place I'd read so much about, even one erased by time and circumstance. Because, really, what is the point of riding a historical route unless you feel some personal connection, however tenuous, with something about the route's history?

CHAPTER FIFTEEN

Jules Stretch

NOT FAR PAST THE MONUMENTS TO THE FIRST SITE OF JULESBURG, I turned north toward Ovid, Colorado, and crossed the South Platte River. I'd crossed and recrossed the Platte and South Platte rivers a few times by this point. The crossings were all bridged, and as such, effortless. When Richard Burton crossed here in 1860, the process was more involved: Luggage from the stagecoach was unloaded into an oxcart and carried over separately; a "youth" had to accompany the coach across, "shouting and swinging his arms to keep [the mules] from turning their heads down stream." The stagecoach crossing took half an hour or more, compared to less than a minute for me.

From here I detoured east off the Pony Express Route a mile or so. I'd read somewhere that stakes had been planted near Lodgepole Creek to mark the old trail of the Julesburg Crossing where it emerged from the north bank of the South Platte River. I found the creek but didn't find any white stakes. Maybe I'd been misinformed. More likely, given the other landmarks I couldn't find along the trail, I'd gotten the details wrong.

In addition to the town of Julesburg, Jules Beni had a ranch on Lodgepole Creek about twenty-five miles west of his town (the ranch, you'll recall, where Old Jules kept livestock stolen from the stagecoach company and fed with purloined stagecoach company hay). In Pony Express days, the road that followed Lodgepole Creek between Julesburg and Jules's ranch became known as Jules Stretch. I spent most of the day retracing Jules Stretch, and all of it following Lodgepole Creek into Sidney, Nebraska, my stop for the night.

From Ovid, I rode in light breeze under a nacre sky, thin cumulus that seemed to shimmer under the sun. The farmland all around was irrigated, but the area still felt dry. Past Ovid, the road lifted, then turned north along the edge of a divide. Near the top of the divide, I passed a battered galvanized mailbox sitting on a wooden post at an empty intersection miles from anything. The clouds dissipated, and I rode alongside a bright yellow-green field under the deepening blue sky. At some point along this stretch, I passed out of Colorado and crossed back into the Nebraska Panhandle.

Around twenty miles in, I dropped off the divide and into the Lodgepole Creek Valley at the town of Chappell, Nebraska. I stopped at a small grocery store for some water to top off my supply (in case the day got long) and coffee (because I hadn't had any yet). No brewed coffee, so I settled for a bottled Frappuccino instead. The clerk rang it up and bagged it and by way of closing the transaction said, "It's going to be a hot one today." As if I needed reminding.

From Chapelle, Lodgepole Creek bends in a wide arc from north to west, and the Pony Express Trail turned with it. I passed a little coffee house, which I would much rather have gone to had I known it was there, hesitated, wondering if I had time to ride back and get a hot cup of joe, and decided, no. Why? Because, obviously, it was going to be a hot one and I needed to skedaddle.

Then the sweetest thing happened. I passed the last building west of town and was swept along for the next thirty-seven miles by a howling tailwind. It was wonderful. I didn't realize how wonderful until later, when I arrived in Sidney, Nebraska, tried to ride against the wind on an uphill, and came to a dead stop. I was track standing—the bike frozen in place with my feet still on the pedals. I had to drop into first to get moving again. That's a strong wind. Burton described the breeze along Jules Stretch as a "sirocco," and noted that the wind "at this season blows a gale between 10:00 a.m. and 3:00 p.m." On the basis of that day's ride, I'd attest to both descriptions.

Before my impromptu track stand, in between Chappell and Sidney, I passed a couple of Pony Express station sites. The first was just east of the town of Lodgepole, Nebraska. Lodgepole Creek finishes its bend to the west here, and just before town was a turnoff to Pole Creek No. 2 Station. I thought about skipping it because it was a few miles off the Pony Express Route. But with the wind howling behind me and the valley floor laid out flat as a carpet, I was making great time. Plus, I'd skipped so many other station sites, I decided it was worth the detour.

There were nasty crosswinds getting out to the monument and back. I had to ride with the bike heeled to windward to stay upright. And for all the effort, there wasn't anything to see at the site other than the nice granite marker in a dusty pullout just the other side of Lodgepole Creek. Fortunately, plenty of tailwind waited to whisk me along as soon as I got back on the route.

Somewhere along in here I felt my arm getting wet and realized the mouthpiece of the water tube from my hydration pack had fallen off. I had a few minutes of near panic while I retraced my route on foot, wondering how I'd be able to carry enough water and manage to drink while riding, until at last I found the mouthpiece in the weeds. I had no idea why it fell out, and that was the only time it did. Just a reminder, I suppose, of how tenuous my systems were. Everything was solid and working and holding up well—including the tire I had to reinflate every morning and the hand pump I used to inflate it—but it wouldn't have taken all that much to throw a wrench in the works.

Staying Hydrated

I wore a hydration pack with a 2.5-liter water bladder, which I emptied every day. I didn't like carrying the weight on my back but found I didn't drink enough water if it was any less convenient than sucking from a tube without breaking pace. I carried a separate water bottle on the bike frame, which I thought of as my reserve tank, and had another four liters of capacity in bottles mounted on my forks (though I did not fill them for every ride). By this point in the ride, I was also buying a couple of liters of cold electrolyte drink every day to carry in the trailer. I drank steadily throughout my rides, and still felt less hydrated than I should have been most days.

A couple of miles east of Sidney, Nebraska, I came to a marker for the Pole Creek Pony Express Station, or Pole Creek No. 3 Station (as it was the third Pony Express station along Lodgepole Creek). Also known as "French Louie's," after its proprietor, Louie Rilliet (also spelled Rouliette), Pole Creek No. 3 was reportedly one of the less glamorous stations, consisting partly of a dugout into the bank of the creek. The dugout was lined with stone and topped with cedar logs, which, like the wood used to construct buildings in Julesburg, had to be hauled from Cottonwood Creek, a hundred miles east. It seemed that if someone had put that much effort into constructing the building it probably wasn't such a bad place. Nevertheless, the sole description of the station comes from Richard Burton's *The City of the Saints*. The entry for this station in the index carries the subclassification, "squalor and wretchedness of," which gives an idea of Burton's assessment. Then again, with rare exceptions, Burton did not have anything good to say about any of the stations he passed through. Which raises a couple of issues.

Most accounts of the Pony Express extensively quote Richard Burton, as well as Mark Twain, as primary sources for conditions along the route. Both men rode Russell, Majors & Waddell's stagecoaches (Burton in 1860, Twain in 1861) and described their experiences in detail. In many cases, I found Burton's pointedly acerbic remarks, like Mark Twain's comedic embellishments, hyperbolic, and to that extent, largely undependable. In this case, for instance, I could find no corroborating testimony as to the putative squalor of Pole Creek No. 3 Station. I, like others, just had to take Burton's word for it.

What also struck me about Burton's account, moreover, was his overt racism. Without jumping into a debate over Presentism versus Moral Relativism, it seemed wrong that only two authors I'd read mentioned Burton's racist point of view, or cautioned one to take Burton's strong biases into account when relying on his cultural observations. As Wallace Stegner points out, "French Canadian, American, Mormon—all struck [Burton] as lazy or sullen or uncouth, and all were shudderingly dirty." Burton disparaged French Canadians (such as the owner of Pole Creek No. 3 Station) as much as he did Native Americans, African

Americans, the Irish, multiracial children, and others. It is advisable to keep Burton's virulent sense of racial superiority in mind when reading his descriptions of other people's habits and habitations. Whereas Burton saw Pole Creek No. 3 Station as squalid, for instance, another writer noted the station's use of two-foot-thick stone dug partially into the riverbank was well suited to withstand "Indians, prairie fires, cyclones, and weather much more easily than log structures." Facing south, the structure would be braced against the strong winter winds. This information strikes me as much more informative than the Burton's often-noted comment that the walls were papered with magazine pages.

I stopped at the monument for the maligned Pole Creek No. 3 Station to snap a couple of pics. When I remounted the bike to go, I found my tires riddled with goatheads. This nasty, invasive plant, also known, appropriately, as "puncture vine," produces a hard thorn that resembles the COVID molecule, with spikes on every plane. The thorns are like miniature land mines for pneumatic tires. I got off the bike and started plucking them out. With each thorn plucked a small bead of blue sealant appeared, instantly sealing the hole. If there was one time in the ride I was glad to have tubeless tires, this was it. I'd still be out there patching tubes.

At the same time, I had to shake my head. My minor tire crisis was nothing compared with tire issues the emigrants and freighters had to deal with. The tires on wagons were iron and were mounted on wooden wheels. By this point in the overland trip, the dry plains air caused the wooden wheels to shrink; once they did, the iron tires came loose and fell off. A common remedy was to remove the wheel and soak it in the river overnight so it would re-expand. Other times, more drastic measures were needed, some requiring a blacksmith and a forge.

Take a moment and think about that phrase, "iron tire," then picture yourself sitting on a wooden bench, secured to a wooden frame, and rolling along, without springs, on wooden wheels banded by iron tires across ungraded roads for thousands of miles. Imagine an evening after a long day of walking in the dust alongside one of these wagons, marshaling oxen with a bullwhip, and rather than resting, having to place the wagon on jacks, remove one or more wheels, take them down to the river to soak, and probably helping someone else with their shrunken wheels as well. Often on my ride I thought about emigrants—pregnant women, for example, or cholera-addled men—riding in a rigid wagon made from iron and wood while I rode on air—pneumatic tires, adjustable suspension; about having to ford a river instead of being able to cross a modern bridge; about having to wait for days in camp for a swollen stream to subside, or for the return of the men who'd ridden off to round up stampeded or stolen animals; about delaying the day's start long enough to bury a child, and having to do so more than once in the months it took to cross. Bearing scenes like that in mind, a few minutes' delay plucking thorns out of a tire did not seem like such a big deal.

I reached Sidney, Nebraska ("Exit 59! We're travel with you in mind."), in the early afternoon. Sydney was a railroad town that sprang up in the late 1860s. According to an interpretive sign at the north end of 10th Avenue, "Sinful Sidney" was the "Scourge of the 'Old West'" from 1871 to 1888. At the time, "Over eighty licensed saloons, gambling halls and brothels were located on historic Front Street. Over 1,000 criminal cases and fifty-six known murders or attempted murders were prosecuted between 1876–1881." The town has even restored Boot Hill, "The Bad Man's Cemetery," as a point of interest for tourists. The old downtown was very sedate during my stay; you'd never guess it had such a storied past.

I found my motel easily enough, but thanks to the tailwind, was ninety minutes early to check in. Sidney didn't exist in Pony Express days—the Pony Express Trail left Lodgepole Creek a few miles back at Pole Creek No. 3 Station to head north to the North Platte River—but I'd booked a motel in town because I had decided to sit out the next day to avoid the peak of the heat wave. As things turned out, I had somehow managed to tear the seat out of a pair of riding shorts. So I had the additional excuse of waiting for a replacement pair being shipped overnight (as if to underscore the difference between traveling through this area in 1860 and 2021).

I ended up at a place called Brand New Items and Coffee Shop. One half was home decor (presumably brand-new) and the other was, well, a coffee shop. Truth in advertising. I sat in their air-conditioned shop and drank coffee for sustenance and something very refreshing with watermelon and lemon and ice for my thirst. I took my time because I had nothing to do for forty or so hours other than to relax in Sinful Sidney while the hottest day of the heat wave passed and hope the northwesterly wind predictions for the day after would turn out to be wrong. Because even though the worst of the heat would be over, you know, it looked like it was going to be a hot one.

PART THREE

THE NORTH PLATTE— JULESBURG, COLORADO, TO CASPER, WYOMING

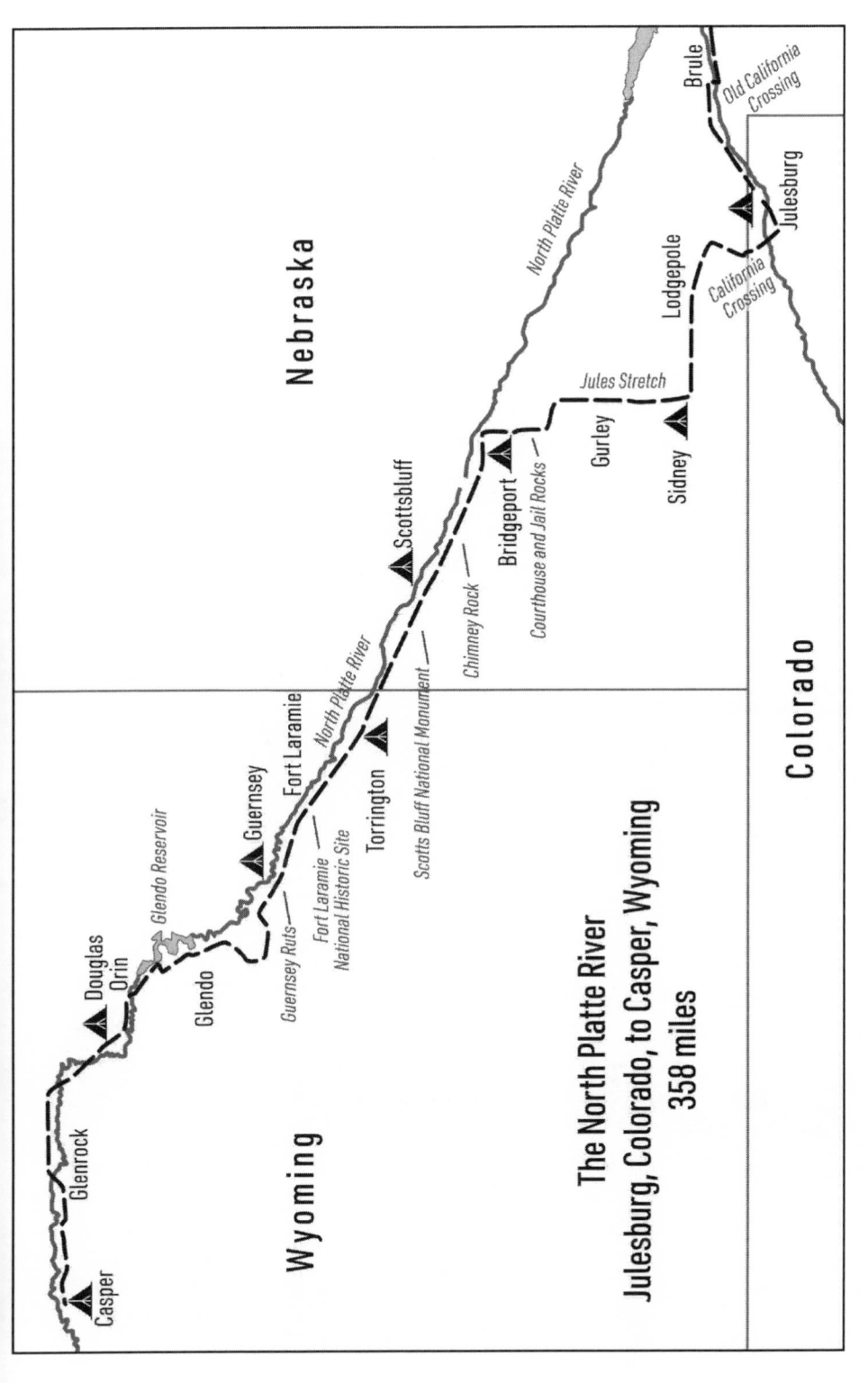

The North Platte River
Julesburg, Colorado, to Casper, Wyoming
358 miles

Wyoming

Nebraska

Colorado

Casper
Glenrock
Douglas
Orin
Glendo
Glendo Reservoir
Guernsey
Fort Laramie
Guernsey Ruts
Fort Laramie National Historic Site
Torrington
North Platte River
Scotts Bluff National Monument
Scottsbluff
Chimney Rock
Bridgeport
Courthouse and Jail Rocks
North Platte River
Jules Stretch
Gurley
Lodgepole
Sidney
California Crossing
Brule
Old California Crossing
Julesburg

CHAPTER SIXTEEN

Thirty-Mile Stretch

TWO DAYS LATER THE FORECAST DROPPED TO THE MIDNINETIES. MY course was due north nearly the entire ride. Winds were forecast to blow from the north, in my face, at around seven knots. I didn't know how much climbing I had, how bad the roads would be, how hot it would actually get, or how strong the headwinds might actually blow. I just knew I didn't want to be on the road when I found out. So, I rose at 5:00 a.m. and was on the road by 6:00 a.m.

The first part of the ride out of Sidney was a steepish climb on pavement past Camp Lookout, an 1860s fort built to protect workers on the Transcontinental Railroad. The pavement gave way to gravel after a few miles, but nicely compacted gravel, nearly as fast as the pavement, but with less traffic. In fact, none. In either direction.

During Pony Express days, this part of the route—from Pole Creek No. 3 Station (the dugout on the banks of Lodgepole Creek) to Mud Springs Station—was known as "Thirty-Mile Stretch," which denoted the waterless thirty miles between the two points. In addition to being waterless, it was barren. Passing through here in 1864, Eugene Ware wrote, "There was not a tree or a bush in sight. The valley was as smooth and polished as if it had been sand-papered and varnished. There was not a riding-switch that could be cut between us and Julesburg."

In July 1861, Deep Well Station was added in between the two existing stations because the distance between Pole Creek No. 3 and Mud Springs stations was too great for both the stagecoach and the Pony Express. Despite naming the station Deep Well, no one ever found water here no matter how deep they dug. The stagecoach company freighted water in from the stations on either end of this dry stretch.

The Deep Well Station monument was set next to the state highway, a mile east of the Pony Express Route, which kept to the gravel road. I detoured and backtracked a little to stop by the station monument. Like the Texas Station monument back on Lodgepole Creek, there was nothing to see but the monument itself. But what the heck.

Rather than return to the Pony Express Route, I kept to the paved highway and rode north to the microdot town of Gurley, Nebraska, and Outlaws Café. The cracker-box restaurant had a low ceiling and was as small as the town: six counter stools, a few booths, and a couple of tables. No social distancing here. A couple of locals sat in separate booths, talking to one another and to the owners across the small space. (Is there a single diner in the entire world that doesn't feature middle-aged men nursing coffee and passing the time?) On the low counter sat two well-used baking pans, one with maybe two dozen donuts and another of cinnamon rolls, all handmade, imperfectly formed, and looking all the more delicious for their lack of uniformity. The couple running the café made them fresh every morning. I had only planned to get a cup of coffee, but the donuts looked so good I couldn't resist buying one. And it *was* good. Probably the best I've ever had. I didn't even want to know what it was cooked in, but it was an epic donut.

On a different type of day, I could easily have sat in my booth and listened to the Nebraskan farmers talk about the weather while I stared at the mammoth white grain silos looming across the highway and ate those delicious donuts and drank coffee until I had indigestion and acid reflux. The donut and the coffee were that kind of satisfying, the place that kind of homey. But I needed to go. The day was heating up and the headwind would only get stronger. A little reluctantly, I went to the counter to pay. Coffee and a donut? Two dollars.

From here I could have made my way back to the Pony Express Route, but the route rejoined the highway up at the next town anyway, so I saved the east-west miles and kept straight north. It's one thing to sit at your computer and look at routes and say, "I want to ride off-road as much as possible." It's quite another to be on those roads and to look at the time you're making, or not making, and second-guess that commitment. More often than not, so long as I wasn't bypassing any Pony Express stations or historical landmarks, I bagged the gravel when I could to go for the better time and easier ride.

The next town, Dalton, Nebraska, had a welcome sign that seemed to pay tribute to every June honoree and holiday, save Juneteenth and Gay Pride:

> *Pray Honor Our*
> *Grads Moms Dads Vets*
> *Past Now Future*

It was still early, so the town market wasn't open. Neither was the town's Prairie Schooner Museum. I got off the bike and took a few pictures of a Pony Express medallion and an 1860s-vintage log cabin nearby while a woman across the street patiently held her dogs for my protection.

Some miles up the highway I saw someone walking ahead, which seemed strange. I slowed to go around, rang my bell, and announced I was passing so I wouldn't startle them. It was a woman who looked to be in her twenties. She was dressed for a night out—artfully torn jeans and colorful shirt showing a bare midriff—but was now walking in her socks with hiking boots slung over one shoulder by the laces. I asked if she was okay, she said she was fine. I asked if she needed anything, she said water. So I stopped and handed her my water bottle. She gulped some down and handed it back. She seemed fine. She was lucid, introduced herself and shook my hand. I couldn't really give her a ride on my trailer, so I handed my water bottle back to her instead and told her to keep it. I asked if she needed anything else. She smiled and said no, so I moved on.

A couple of miles further I turned onto a gravel road that would take me by the first two of the natural landmarks overland emigrants saw along this portion of the trail: Courthouse Rock and Jail Rock. This was a low-maintenance road, as in it seemed to receive the minimum maintenance necessary to keep it passable in good weather. Rutted in places, lots of powdery sand to get stuck in. I had mapped the Mud Springs Pony Express Station off this road, so I followed the GPS to that location. The turnoff was onto even less of a road than the one I was on, which was still okay. From there it turned onto a faint two-track (marked by a small hand-painted sign that said "Monument" with an arrow, thankfully). Finally, it faded to mere tire impressions overgrown with grass that climbed a small rise. I hesitated because I was getting pretty far off the main track. But I leveled the rise and there it was: the Mud Springs Station monument, erected in 1931. There were horses and cattle wandering through the area, but they didn't seem to mind my presence. Nearby was a small pond surrounded by trees, which I assumed was Mud Springs. It was a nice little spot, quiet and shaded, unlike the rest of my ride that day. I took a short break to eat a snack, keeping an eye out for snakes while wondering how many people had actually gone to see this monument in the ninety years since it had been placed there. Maybe a lot, but I didn't get that impression.

Back to the sandy, powdery, gravel road. A large road-construction scraper was driving along in the other direction, shaving the side of the road at a steep enough angle that I was afraid if I fell into it I might not get out again. A few miles later, as I was crawling up a hill, the scraper approached from behind. I guess the driver had finished whatever he was doing because he was moving fast. I moved to the side to let him pass and came to an immediate stop in the deep powder. He barreled by, waving through the dust kicked up by his tires as he passed. I ended up walking my bike and trailer the remaining fifty feet or so up the hill until I found solid enough ground to get going again.

More rolling miles past more rolling miles of corn than you've ever seen in your life, and finally, to the turnoff for Courthouse and Jail Rocks. I rode out to the base of the rocks. It was a little further and a bit more of a climb than I had counted on, but by the time I figured that out, I was halfway there.

Courthouse and Jail Rocks (I always read "Jail Rock" as "Jailhouse Rock") were the first of the great natural landmarks on the Emigrant Trail. They anchor the southeast end of the Wildcat Range, which includes Chimney Rock (the most noted monument on the Emigrant Trail), and ends at Scotts Bluff (the largest). It was easy to see how these formations must have impressed overlanders who'd traveled for weeks across the relatively monotonous prairie and plains.

In addition to being large, the monuments were intriguing. Courthouse Rock's aspect, for example, changed as the traveler approached it; emigrants "became more and more fascinated, to the point [they] felt magnetically drawn to the rock itself." It stood near the junction of the old Emigrant Trail (which crossed the South Platte by Brule, Nebraska) and the newer trail (which crossed the South Platte near Julesburg, Colorado). A great number of emigrants on both roads crossed the open country to climb Courthouse Rock and, of course, carve their names.

The Pony Express Trail deviated from the Emigrant Trail south of Courthouse Rock to take a shorter, steeper, road to the North Platte River. This road now crosses private land, so the bikepacking route stuck to the Emigrant Trail. There were GPS coordinates for a Pony Express station location next to Courthouse Rock, but no monument, at least as far as I could see.

More interesting than locating another Pony Express monument, perhaps, was imagining Courthouse Rock as a "prairie post office." All along the trail, emigrants left messages for those traveling behind, a system that came to be known as the "prairie" or "roadside telegraph." Messages might warn of trouble ahead with Native Americans, for instance, or poisoned or brackish water. Other notices might give details of accidents and the progress of the injured person's recovery. The messages were usually written on a piece of paper, then inserted into the notched end of a stick, pinned to trees or bushes or even grave markers. Sometimes, emigrants would skin the bark off trees to carve their names. If paper or trees weren't available, they would scratch messages on rocks and animal bones, including human skulls, a particularly effective medium. "Bone express" became another name for this trailside message system.

"Emigrant" or "prairie post offices" were places where greater numbers of these notes accumulated. Courthouse Rock was such a place. Someone even carved the words "Post-office" on a rocky ledge near Courthouse Rock.

At the base of Courthouse and Jail Rocks is a large gravel cul-de-sac. No marked parking, no interpretive signs, no warnings, no water, no restrooms—nothing other than a trash receptacle and a couple of benches placed for people to contemplate the landscape. I was surprised. These rocks were important landmarks on the Emigrant Trail. I'd expected them to be more tourist oriented, with signage, if not some facilities. At the same time, part of me appreciated that there wasn't anything to tell people what they were looking at, nothing to keep them from hiking the rattlesnake-infested trails so they could risk breaking their necks trying to scale the rocks. The site was not as unimproved as it was in 1860, but it felt closer than most landmarks nowadays.

I took one of the benches to enjoy the quiet and the chance to contemplate the monuments while I caught my breath from the climb. While I was resting quiescent, an SUV roared up the hill and parked at the far corner of the lot near the entrance to the trails. Five people piled out, three men and two women in their late thirties. They capered around and took a lot of selfies of themselves and each other, then headed up the path (a couple in sandals and flip-flops) to climb Courthouse Rock, stopping every so often along the way to caper around and take more selfies. They were still up there when I left, the men climbing higher, the women seeming to lose interest. I presumed everybody made it down safely.

It was interesting, while I sat there, to juxtapose this cavorting quintet against the awe these formations inspired in overland emigrants. The snail pace of a wagon train was probably about the right speed to get a feel for Courthouse Rock's grandeur. I would like to have stayed in the area to see it at different times during the day and witness its changing moods. Maybe even try to climb it. But I felt an urge to keep on the move.

From Courthouse Rock to my destination in Bridgeport, Nebraska ("Trail City, USA"), was a quick five or six miles. I arrived by 11:30. My precautions turned out to be unnecessary. The wind never backed further than east, the temperature was still in the eighties, and the climbing and the roads, all things considered, were not too bad. All in all, I had made a good ride plan for the day, but under the circumstances, it may have been under-ambitious. I had booked a night in a hotel after a half-hearted search didn't turn up an attractive camping option in the area. But now here I was with a nonrefundable hotel room and three and a half hours before I could check in. Which meant I had a lot of time to fill before I could take a shower.

I remembered passing a shop on the way into town named Call Me Cupcake. Who could resist an invitation like that? I went back to cool my heels indoors while the day heated up. The shop smelled like cotton candy. The bakery had all kinds of pastries and, of course, cupcakes. I settled for a cold smoothie and a hot coffee and took a seat. Well, not quite so quickly. Kathy, the owner's mother-in-law (who was working the counter joyously, if not efficiently) was having a great deal of fun explaining all the food and drink items to me and recommending sizes and giving the history of the place. I think she was a little bored. The café was large and empty except for a table of three adolescent girls who left shortly after. I kept trying to pay, but Kathy refused to take money until I was ready to leave in case I decided I wanted anything else. Which, eventually, I did.

I took a nice table by the window with a view of the main drag and, more importantly, my bike and equipment. It was cool in there, and quiet. Even the piped-in music was playing at a low volume. It was some streaming service playing 1970s Easy Listening. When I walked in Carole King was playing ("So Far Away," which felt appropriate), then Harry Chapin came on ("Cat's in the Cradle," which I have not been able to listen to without tearing up since my son, Kazu, started kindergarten). James Taylor, Neil Diamond—so many songs from so long ago. I sat there for close to two hours. No one else in the place. It was very restful. More than that, it was somehow rejuvenating.

And that's one of the funny things about traveling. You can't plan a feeling like this; it just happens. When was the last time you were thankful you had to wait for something, whether to check in to a hotel, or for some other thing that had to happen, and you had no choice but to wait? Or maybe I should say, when was the last time you felt rewarded for waiting, like maybe this moment was waiting for you? That's how this early afternoon felt. For the first time on my ride, I felt like I belonged, that what I was doing was okay, and even more, that I had every reason to be out on the road for six weeks. For the first time I felt it wasn't crazy to want to bikepack the Pony Express Trail, that I hadn't taken on something I had no business attempting.

While the music played quietly in the background, I uploaded photos and wrote postcards and worked on my journal and generally just enjoyed the vibe until, finally, I couldn't sit any longer. I stopped by a grocery store for a couple more energy bars for the next day's ride. Every time I was near my bike, locking up or getting ready to go, everyone who passed made a comment. "Hot enough for you?" "Isn't it a little hot to be riding a bike?" "Where are you headed?" Sometimes people would stop and talk and those who did seemed genuinely interested in what I was doing out there on a bike in the heat. All wished me safe travels. It made the town feel more welcoming than say, Sidney, where I'd spent the previous two days and didn't exchange a word to anyone unless we were engaged in some kind of transaction.

At some point, I recalled that there was a Prairie Trails Museum in Bridgeport. I looked it up on my map and headed over. The museum sat on the other side of the North Platte River. The volunteer working this hot afternoon was Jim. He looked elderly, frail, and a little surprised to see someone wander in. He showed me around, enough to see this museum was not nearly so much about the emigrant trails as about Bridgeport, Nebraska. It even had a blow-up of senior portraits from the Bridgeport High Class of 1965. But it was nice in there. I found the obligatory Pony Express display and some interesting maps and such. Eventually, Jim got to talking.

"How could you stand it out there in California with all the rules about COVID?"

"It isn't bad," I said, "we're kind of homebodies anyway."

"I'm a little rebellious," he said, "I refused to wear a mask."

I nodded.

"How'd you get so much time away from your family to take a trip like this?" he asked.

"Well, to tell you the truth, Jim, I think my wife was a little tired of having me around the house all the time."

"That's like my wife," he said. "When I retired, she told me she was afraid I was going to drive her crazy. I told her she didn't have far to go; she could walk there."

CHAPTER SEVENTEEN

The Eighth Wonder of the World

THE NEXT MORNING IN BRIDGEPORT STARTED OUT FINE. THE HOTEL put out a surprisingly good breakfast spread. It was overcast outside, which kept the temperature down most of the morning. I had a fifty-mile ride to a campground in Scottsbluff, Nebraska, that promised views of Scotts Bluff National Monument (and a "primitive" option for us tenters). The wind was forecast to be out of the east. Instead, it was west, so I had a headwind all morning. But it started out light, and probably did more to keep me cool than to hinder my progress.

After an uneventful dozen miles, I made it to Chimney Rock, the most popular landmark of the entire Emigrant Trail. More emigrants noted it in their diaries than any other. "In covered wagon days this was the ultimate in natural curiosities, the zenith of sight-seeing goals . . . the eighth wonder of the world."

Chimney Rock is not famous for anything beyond being famous. Nothing of serious historical import occurred here. It is simply that the specter of the pillar of rock seems to have impressed everyone who came this way. It has been described prosaically as an inverted funnel. The local Native Americans called it Elk Penis. Emigrants likened it to exotic images such as "towering clouds, necks of ostriches, mosque minarets." It is also a cenotaph, "Nature's own monument" to the graves of emigrants who died during the cholera epidemics of 1849 and 1850.

I enjoyed watching for the chimney's tower as I rode, finally seeing it edge over the hills, watching it grow as I came closer. But I felt let down once I reached the visitor center. It was the complete opposite of the parking area at Courthouse and Jail Rocks. Instead of a dusty climb up to an empty gravel cul-de-sac, Chimney Rock had a deluxe visitor center right off a nicely paved road that led from the highway. Next to the center sat a grassy area set behind a split-rail fence, posted with multiple warnings in multiple languages announcing that "Rattlesnakes have been observed" and admonishing all to keep to the sidewalks. A sign by the visitor center entrance stated it cost $8.00 to go inside. Lower down it dutifully warned off freeloaders like me that while the gift shop was open to all, restrooms were only available to "paying visitors."

That struck me as rude, and I was momentarily taken by the idea of urinating on one of the rattlesnake warning signs right off the beautifully paved parking lot. I was entertaining this puerile impulse while getting ready to leave (in part to find an appropriately out-of-sight bush along the gravel backroads nearby), when I noticed a man about my age leaning on a cane by a car in the handicapped parking area, looking at me. This happened quite often, probably because my orange bike and orange helmet and the trailer loaded with gear tended to attract attention. I nodded and said "Hi," and he asked where I was headed, so I wheeled my bike over and talked to him for a moment.

"I rode across the country twenty-six years ago," he told me. From the way he held his head and leaned on his cane, I assume he'd since suffered some sort of neurological damage, but I didn't ask. He repeated that number, "Twenty-six years," and the way he said it made it clear that the ride was a particularly special memory for him. He rode with a tour and told me that when they passed through this area it was 107 degrees, so they rode at night.

We talked about riding at night, how great it felt to stay in a hotel every so often to shower and get a good meal, and the more we talked the more animated he became, as if it had been so long since he'd talked to someone who understood what a long ride felt like, who *got it* the way he did. It was really a wonderful few minutes, and I left Chimney Rock in a much lighter mood.

From there, I came to a crossroads of sorts: I could follow the Pony Express Route and zigzag on gravel and dirt roads, or I could jump on the highway and make a straighter course for Scottsbluff, Nebraska. I had been making good time, the weather was fine, and there was no reason not to take the dirt roads. On the other hand, they were slower, longer, and the wind was steadily rising. There was also a Pony Express station monument on the highway I would miss if I stuck to the Pony Express Route. I decided to take the highway.

Soon enough I arrived in Gering, Nebraska, a few miles south of the town of Scottsbluff. Entering town from the east was a bit of a let-down because the section I rode through was industrial, and all views of Scotts Bluff National Monument were blocked by telephone poles, wires, overpasses, signs, etc. I came to the Gering Convention Center and saw some spectacularly tricked out thirties vehicles on a trailer. A sign out front advertised the Father's Day Weekend classic car show. I hadn't been keeping a close eye on the calendar, so this was the first time I realized it was the Friday of Father's Day weekend.

After a break, I rode north from Gering to Scottsbluff. Down-town Gering was cool in a forties downtown kind of way (neon signs, Art Deco movie theater), but the no-man's land between there and Scottsbluff was harrowing. The streets were four-lane, no-shoulder, curb-to-curb roadway. No one in Scottsbluff had apparently heard that bikes share the road with cars. Least of all the city engineers. It was a nerve-wracking ride the entire way.

The campground sat on the north bank of the North Platte River, and as advertised, offered a nice view of Scotts Bluff looking southwest. I made it there a couple of hours before I could check in, so I spoke with the camp host to confirm my reservation, then went off to find a laundromat.

This time I stuck to sidewalks. No pedestrians were using them, and they were my best bet to keep from getting run over, so long as I kept an eye out for the right hook (getting hit by a vehicle making a right-hand turn). It took me forty-five minutes and three tries, but I finally found an open laundromat.

Clothes washed, I endured another hot (midnineties), sketchy ride back to the campground. By this time, I was starting to dislike Scotts-bluff. I knew it was the stress of riding the untamed roads compounded by fatigue, discomfort, stickiness, heat, sweat, and wind. But I was already looking forward to leaving the next morning, putting Scottsbluff behind me, and getting back on the quiet gravel roads.

I checked in and found my campsite. It sat in full sun, with not even a bush for shade. I went back to the camp host and asked if I could switch spots. While she went into her trailer to get her reservation lists, a man wearing a T-shirt with a mountain bike logo stopped and looked at my rig approvingly. We started talking about my trip, and he told me he was there from Omaha for a gravel bike race taking place in the nearby Wildcat Hills on Sunday. And as we talked, he expressed a sort of admiration about my trip, that he thought it was just great that I would do something like that on my own. Meanwhile, the host returned and said, "Take Number 5, they're checking in tomorrow." Cool.

I rolled over to Number 5 (huge cottonwood, lots of shade), pulled some things off the trailer, then went back to the check-in area where the Wi-Fi signal was stronger to search for a place to stay the next night. Some time later a couple showed up, complaining. It turned out that they had booked Number 5, and contrary to the camp host's notes, had reserved it for that night. After some negotiations, they agreed to allow me to share their site so I could stay out of the sun.

Campsite issues settled, I started planning my ride for the next day. My goal was Torrington, Wyoming, about forty-five miles away. The town had a municipal camping area, with ten first-come, first-served spaces. The city didn't take camping reservations, so I started worrying: What if it was full when I got there? It would be Saturday night. How many people were already there because they planned to spend the weekend? There was no way to know, which meant I needed a backup plan.

I should mention that on my way back from doing laundry I had hit a Starbucks, so I may have been a little extra edgy.

I started checking motels. There were three in Torrington. All full. It turned out that Father's Day weekend in the Scottsbluff area meant lots of tourist-drawing events: the classic car show in Gering; the gravel-grinder race in the Wildcat Hills; plus, there was a huge statewide Little League tournament. Between those events and whatever else might be going on, everything was booked for fifty miles around.

Now, a real bikepacker would have had no problem with this. Riders roll out a sleeping bag wherever they can. They might pitch a tent beside a barn, for example, or behind a gas station, or set up a lean-to in a clump of bushes. Bikepackers do that as a matter of course because, well, that's bikepacking. Unfortunately, I took up the activity way too late in life to adopt wholeheartedly its minimalist ethos. If I'd learned anything in my three weeks on the road, it was that not knowing I'd have someplace to stay was a deal-breaker. Not being able to reserve a spot in the next town meant I needed to stay another night in Scottsbluff, because even though I didn't like the town, at least I had a place to sleep. Or did I?

I went back to the camp host and asked, prepared to beg, for a spot the next night. She said something to the effect that any empty camp-site that night would also be empty the next, so I could take any one of those. The more I thought about that statement, the less sense it made, especially in light of the double booking of the campsite I was staying in. I went back to the online reservation system for the campground and checked. Sure enough, the entire campground was sold out.

Meanwhile, I was texting and calling my friend Rick, who had built up a replacement front wheel for my slow-leaky one and was driving it out from California. He was on this third day of driving out in his Tesla and we were trying to figure out a location where we could meet that wasn't too far off my course, but also where he could reach me. That is, his car could hold enough charge to reach me anywhere, but there might not be a charging station close enough to give him enough power to get back to the charger.

I was calling motels, searching Google Maps and hotel websites, all while texting and talking to Rick while he searched for recharge stations within range, and to my partner, Lisa, who was helping me search for a place to stay, and nothing was working. No campsites, no hotels, every-thing sold out, no chargers in range—it was nuts. I finally managed to grab a room nearby at double the going rate, and despite myself, felt thankful for it.

By then it was coming on evening. I took a shower and started set-ting up the tent and thinking about dinner. And again, I know it was only a nasty combination of fatigue and post-caffeine hangover, but after the stress of the afternoon, I was seriously questioning my fitness for the trip. It struck me that I had become too accustomed to comforts, that I had already stayed in motels more often than I had planned, had eaten out more than I had ever thought I would. That I was on a bike tour, not a bikepacking trip, dependent on finding these oases of comfort, whether motels, bakeries for snacks, cafés for coffee, restaurants for dinner, or anyplace for air conditioning. What would I do west of Casper, where there was nothing but open land? No restaurants, no cafés, no shade, and no campgrounds, no motels. It struck me that for all my preparations and stubbornness, I may not be cut out to be a bikepacker, and it might be time to call it quits. Maybe I could drive back to Davis with Rick when we met up.

I was going about my business, as I said, brooding a little while setting up camp, trying to figure out how to deal with the disappointment of quitting and the logistics of getting back home, when up walked a man and a woman. It was Steve, the mountain biker from earlier, and Ann, his wife. They said they had cooked too much food, and asked if I was hungry and did I want to come hang out at their spot for a while?

It was like the afternoon Dale and Marilyn invited me to dinner back at Rock Springs, Nebraska. How was it that when I was at my lowest these incredibly kind people seemed to appear out of nowhere and offer me solace? Why did this keep happening just when I was ready to throw in the towel? I started to tear up again. "Of course," I said, "I'd love to."

Over at their campsite I wolfed down a meal while Steve apologized for taking seconds when he should have left them for me. We spent a pleasant hour or so while the brash afternoon light faded and lightning silently flashed over the Wildcat Hills. At one point, we were talking about the town of Scottsbluff. I let drop that I didn't really care for it very much, at which point Steve pointed to Ann. It turned out she had lived there for five years, long ago, when her first husband transferred to Scottsbluff for a job. She said she cried when she saw it, then cried when she left because of all the friends she had made.

And it occurred to me that the thought I'd had at the start of my ride, that the sites and the history at points along the way were like pearls strung together by the Pony Express Trail, was wrong. The pearls, the real treasures of the ride, were the people I'd met, especially the remarkably kind people who saved me from myself when I was at my lowest point. I still wasn't entirely convinced I was up to riding the barren steppes of central Wyoming. But thanks to Steve and Ann's kindness, I felt it was too soon to give up.

CHAPTER EIGHTEEN

Scotts Bluff and the Great Smoke

I TOOK ADVANTAGE OF MY DAY OFF IN SCOTTSBLUFF, NEBRASKA, TO RIDE a twenty-five-mile loop around Scotts Bluff National Monument. I circled about halfway around on a multiuse path that ran down from a golf course and linked into a nature path leading to the visitors' center. From the visitors' center I continued through Mitchell Pass on Old Oregon Trail, the two-lane highway running through the middle of the monument, before taking Highway 26 back into town. It was quite a nice ride, and a treat to see the formation from different sides.

Scotts Bluff was named for a hapless trader who fell ill near Laramie River, was abandoned by his compatriots, and crawled fifty miles before dying in this area where his bones were found the following year. Though the part about the fifty-mile crawl may be an embellishment. The story has multiple versions, and according to Merrill Mattes, "there is every variation imaginable, with no two versions the same."

In emigrant days, the North Platte River washed against the base of the bluffs, so emigrants had to leave the river and continue west from the present town of Gering, Nebraska, over Robidoux Pass. The Emigrant Trail didn't cross northwest through Scotts Bluff until Mitchell Pass was cut in 1850. It wasn't until sometime later I realized this was the first named pass I'd ridden on the Emigrant Trail. I'd climbed steeper hills in east Kansas and had ridden longer grades throughout Nebraska. But gentle as it was, Mitchell Pass formed something of a threshold. It was the halfway point between Courthouse Rock and Fort Laramie, the 120-mile transition zone between the Great Plains and the Rocky Mountains. I'd be climbing and descending passes for the rest of my ride.

Like Courthouse Rock and Chimney Rock, overlanders climbed all over themselves to find more expressive ways to convey the grandeur of Scotts Bluff and the surrounding area. One emigrant likened it to Tadmor of the Desert and sketched ruined cities and defeated armies. Another writer saw in the bluffs the "ruins of some vast city erected by a race of giants, contemporaries of the Megatherii and the Icthyosaurii."

Historian Merrill Mattes laments that the "jaded traveler of today" is not moved to express such levels of evocative appreciation. But it's worth noting that there might be something more at work in these grandiloquent descriptions. To the overlanders, the West was larger than life, and consequently, they tended to describe the scenery in superlatives. In the words of historian Jess Unruh, "The scenery was the grandest they had ever seen, the trees the tallest, the natural roads the finest, the water the best, the grass the most luxuriant . . . the list is as endless as there were phenomena to describe."

Back in the town of Scottsbluff, I took the afternoon to work on my journal in a common area off the lobby of my overpriced hotel. Toward evening an extended family armed with boxes of pizza invaded the area. I spoke with the clan matriarch, who explained that the family had converged on Scottsbluff to visit her parents who were in their nineties and lived in a nearby home. The family hadn't been able to visit them for over a year due to COVID, and she felt as though this may be the last chance to see them before they passed. I imagined hers was a common story during these troublous pandemic times.

The forecast for the next day was for high wind. I should clarify that statement. The wind was forecast to be fifteen knots out of the north. Stiff, though not too bad. But one thing I'd learned about Nebraska wind predictions was to take them with a grain of salt, the salt being that the predicted speed was the absolute minimum it would blow. To get a more realistic idea of what to expect, I needed to add 50 percent to the baseline prediction and allow for even stronger gusts. With that in mind, I took to heart something Jan Bennett (who mapped out the Pony Express Bikepacking Route) had written to me. The upshot was that some days the weather would be bad and you may ride twenty miles and just decide to quit for the day. Amen to that.

If I had stuck to the Pony Express Route, I would have had to start the day by riding five bicycle-unfriendly miles south to rejoin the route at Gering, Nebraska, and cross over Robidoux Pass, the road the emigrants took prior to 1850. Even if I were tempted to do so, there was always the matter of windblown dust. And there was 100 percent chance of rain forecast for that night. All of which said to me, *ride short, get a hotel.*

I got an early start, but the breeze was already up. I stuck to Highway 26, which just like Highway 30 back on the windy run between Lexington to Gothenburg, Nebraska, angled to the wind. If I were in a boat, I'd describe my point of sail as close-hauled, which is as high as a boat can point into the wind and still move forward. A close-hauled course is also called "beating," or "beating to windward," which is just as appropriate to the feeling of angling a bike into a stiff breeze as it is sailing a boat to weather. The course gets you there, but it takes its toll.

In an abundance of caution, I'd booked a room in Morrill, Nebraska, which seemed like a reasonable distance to ride from Scottsbluff on a blustery day. By getting an early start, I was hoping to beat the worst of the wind and be battened down well before the rain. My plan worked like a charm. In fact, it worked too well. I was in Morrill by 10:15 a.m. Somehow, I had wildly overestimated the time it would take to cover the distance. As a result, I found myself stranded in a west Nebraska fly-speck farm town five and a half hours before check-in time with no place to hang out (with the possible exception of a bar called the Rustic Tavern).

I called the motel chain's 800 number and after fifteen minutes or so got them to allow me to move my reservation to Torrington, Wyoming, another fifteen or so miles west. I purchased some water and electrolytes at a gas station c-store, then got back on my bike, prepared to fight the wind for another couple of hours.

Not far west of Morrill, Nebraska, was a highway pullout with interpretive signs commemorating one of the epic events in the US relations with Native Americans: the Great Smoke, a treaty council between the United States and most of the Plains Indian tribes along the Emigrant Trail. The council took place in September 1851 and an estimated eight to twelve thousand Native Americans attended, including Lakota, Cheyenne, Arapaho, Crows, Assiniboin, Mandan, Gros Ventres, and Arikara. The primary purpose for the United States was to ensure safe passage along the Platte River Road for Oregon- and California-bound emigrants. Native Americans wanted compensation for the ravages of the overlanders, including the vanishing game and depleted forage along the Emigrant Trail. The council was remarkable not only in size, but in that nations normally at perpetual war with one another maintained peace throughout.

The result of this treaty council was the Fort Laramie Treaty of 1851. One interpretive sign on this spot states that the treaty provided that the United States agreed to give the Native Americans $50,000 per year in goods for fifty years. In exchange, the Native Americans "would allow free passage on the emigrant trails, permit forts to be built on their land, and pledged peaceful settlement of intertribal disputes." The sign continues to state that "[w]ith few exceptions, the tribes honored the treaty until 1864."

The signage isn't exactly correct. It doesn't report, for example, that Congress failed to ratify the treaty as negotiated, reducing the period of annuity payments from fifty years to ten, with an option to extend it to fifteen years. Also, as soon as the treaty was signed, the Lakota violated its terms by invading the hunting grounds of the Crows, and over the next few years, taking over their lands by conquest. The US Army also violated the treaty three years later when it allowed Lieutenant Grattan to attack a Lakota encampment awaiting distribution of the treaty annuities, an event memorialized a little further along the road.

The Great Smoke, a treaty council so large it had to be moved thirty-five miles away from Fort Laramie to provide enough forage for all the animals, had the stated intentions of fostering goodwill, purchasing rights from the Native Americans, and reimbursing them for the losses they'd suffered due to the overland emigration. Most accounts omit the fact that it was also designed as a first step on the part of the United States to bring the Plains tribes under control. Even so, the Fort Laramie Treaty of 1851 represents the high-water mark of US relations with most of the Plains Indians. Holding council with the Plains tribes stands in stark contrast to the unbridled violence that followed soon after.

As it turned out, the interpretive signs sat about three miles from the actual council site, which was now on private land. I could only look across the fields and try to imagine what the scene might have looked like before rolling on.

A few miles west, the town of Henry, Nebraska, leaned against the eastern border of Wyoming. I crossed through town, then crossed into my fifth state since St. Joseph some 750 miles back. By this point the wind was better than twenty knots with gusts over twenty-five. Fortunately, it wasn't many more miles until I reached Torrington, Wyoming. Once there, the highway shoulder disappeared, so I rode the sidewalks into town. Like Scottsbluff, everywhere I went I felt like I was taking my life in my hands. I lost count of how many cars and trucks cut uncomfortably close in front of me even though I was running a headlight and taillights fore and aft.

I arrived too early to check in, so I searched downtown for a bakery or café to hang out in and found that Torrington, Wyoming, does not open for business on Sunday. Maybe I had so many close calls with cars because all those folks were rushing home from church. In any case, away from the highway, Torrington was a ghost town. I checked all the restaurant local listings online. Nothing was open until Monday or Tuesday.

At last, I found a family restaurant set to close within the hour and managed to get an order in just under the wire. While waiting more or less patiently for my food to arrive, I worked on my ride plan for the next day. Guernsey, Wyoming, looked like a good destination. The town was around forty-five miles away and had a park for camping.

Thinking about the park in Guernsey, I remembered my initial plan to stay in Pioneer Park in Torrington before abandoning that plan once I realized the campground might be full because there was no vacancy anywhere in the Nebraska Panhandle. Out of curiosity, I decided to go by the park and learn for myself what the city employee whom I'd spoken with couldn't tell me: That is, how many tent sites were there in the park? After lunch, I swung by to find out.

There was a very large, illustrated sign at Pioneer Park showing all the numbered spaces for the RVs. The tent ("Dry") camping area was not organized into specific sites, but rather was only as limited as space allowed. And it was a pretty large area. Had I left Scottsbluff the day before as I'd planned, I almost certainly would have had a place to camp.

While I was there, I scouted around the park some more and found not only were there no showers, but I would have had to get my water from the "basic restrooms," which were so far away from the dry camping area I never found them. All in all, Pioneer Park was not a very alluring campground. Then it struck me that the situation at my next stop, the park in Guernsey, Wyoming, might well be the same.

And in that moment I had an epiphany—a flash of insight such as we who are gifted with a profound lack of self-knowledge are fortunate enough to receive from time to time. It came to me in this moment of clarity that I didn't really like camping in these city parks. Which is to say, I loved the picture of me camping my way across the West, but found reality far less romantic.

In the early stages of planning I looked into hauling along a small Dutch oven and making biscuits from a sourdough starter every morning. I purchased a pair of moccasins because I'd read that emigrants replaced their worn-out shoes with moccasins they'd purchase from Native Americans along the trail. I'd even bought a hand mill to grind my coffee beans because overlanders had to roast green coffee beans over the fire and grind them; packaged, roasted coffee wasn't available until after the Civil War.

Happily, I was disabused of these ideas before I started my journey. In part, I was persuaded by reading about the items offloaded by emigrants all along the trail. Who was I to laugh about someone foolish enough to haul a piano across the plains when I was hauling a five-pound Dutch oven I'd probably never use? Grudgingly, I came to accept that I would be better off drinking "premium" instant coffee, wearing lightweight sneakers off the bike, and boiling instant oatmeal for breakfast.

But some part of me still held onto this notion of having to camp in city parks whenever possible. That is, until this moment of insight when I realized I didn't really enjoy camping in these showerless city parks. And what's more, that I didn't have to camp at all, at least as far as Casper, Wyoming. It finally dawned on me that I could stay in motels! And that there was no reason not to!

I booked a place in Guernsey for the following evening and instantly felt a weight lift off my shoulders. I reveled in the delight of how nice it would feel not to have to rush to secure a spot at a first-come, first-served campground; how I could spend extra time at Fort Laramie on the way if I wanted; how I could look for the Pony Express stations, walk the Guernsey ruts, study emigrant signatures on Register Rock, and breathe that much easier because I had a room and a shower waiting for me at the end of the ride.

One could argue that forgoing campgrounds to stay in motels was not true bikepacking. But by the same standard, one could also argue that overland emigrants in 1860 were tourists compared to the emigrants of just a few years earlier. Travelers in 1860 could take a stagecoach to California. Emigrants could sleep inside every night between the Missouri River and Fort Laramie. With the increased frequency of stations set up to serve stagecoaches and the Pony Express, traveling to the Pacific Coast "resembled the pioneering ventures of the early 1840s in name only." Maybe I was wimping out. But even Pony Express riders, those dauntless centaurs of Western lore, had a roof and a meal waiting for them at the end of every ride.

CHAPTER NINETEEN

Battles and Massacres

I HAD A QUICK BREAKFAST AT THE MOTEL IN TORRINGTON THE NEXT morning. The coffee was watery. Not weak, watery. So, I started in the opposite direction of the Pony Express Trail and rode north into downtown. I downed an Americano and ordered a breakfast burrito to go from a coffee place that shared a nice space with the Goshen County Information Center. I wrote a postcard home, dropped it off, and got rolling by 8:30 a.m.

For the first time since leaving St. Joseph, it was actually cool. High fifties or low sixties, maybe. It stayed cool most of the day, the sky polka-dotted with black-bottomed fair-weather cumulus. It was also a little breezy (what else is new?), and on my nose (no surprise there), but not as bad as I had feared.

South of Torrington I looked for a monument for the Cold Springs Pony Express Station, the second of three Cold Springs Stations on the Pony Express Trail. I found Cold Springs Avenue, Cold Springs Business Park, and a monument to the Oregon Trail. But alas, no Cold Springs Station monument.

Twenty or so miles along I came across a monument without a title. The top portion read, simply:

SIOUX INDIANS MASSACRED
29 SOLDIERS WITH THEIR OFFICER,
BREVET 2ND LT. L. GRATTAN,
ON AUG. 19, 1854. SITE IS
1/2 MILE NORTH-WEST

The monument commemorated a short battle known as the Grattan Massacre, or the Grattan Fight, depending on one's point of view. This was the incident where the United States violated the Fort Laramie Treaty of 1851—a violation the Great Smoke interpretive signs back by Morrill, Nebraska, failed to mention—by attacking a Lakota encampment rather than accepting their offer of restitution. The skirmish took place in August 1854 and resulted in the death of the Brulé chief Conquering Bear and the entire thirty-one-member US Army contingent under Lieutenant Grattan.

In a sense, the Fort Laramie Treaty precipitated this engagement. At the same time, the army's refusal to abide by the terms of that treaty led to this pointless loss of lives. All over the death of a lame cow.

In August 1854, three years after the Fort Laramie Treaty was signed, bands of Lakota gathered near Fort Laramie to await distribution of the annuities they were to receive under the terms of the treaty. The Lakota included bands of Brulé and Oglala, along with a few visiting Miniconjou. The Oglala and Brulé were in two separate camps near one another about eight miles east of Fort Laramie along the Emigrant Trail. The story varies according to the storyteller, but in essence, at some point a cow (possibly lame) lagged behind its owners, a group of Mormon emigrants passing by the Brulé camp. High Forehead, a Miniconjou staying at the camp, slew the cow for food, or spite, or possibly both depending on the version being told. Once the Mormons reached Fort Laramie, they reported the incident.

Under the terms of the Fort Laramie Treaty, the offending party needed to make restitution. To that end, Mahto-Ay-Ahway (Conquering Bear) went to the fort and offered the offended Mormon his pick of any horse from Conquering Bear's personal herd. The Mormon refused the offer and demanded satisfaction from the army. Under the treaty, the commander of the fort, Second Lieutenant Hugh B. Fleming, should have accepted Conquering Bear's offer and the affair should have ended there. In fact, under the treaty's terms this matter was not subject to the army's jurisdiction at all, but rather, fell under the purview of the Indian Agent, Major John Whitfield, who was on his way to Fort Laramie to oversee the distribution of the annuities.

In the event, John L. Grattan, a lieutenant at the fort, protested. Grattan "had appeared to be a rather boisterous, swash-buckling youth, anxious for a notch on his gun," and was "a firm believer in severely punishing Indians for all their mistakes." He demanded to be allowed to arrest High Forehead and hoped to engage the Lakota in the process. Conquering Bear and others with him asked Commander Fleming to put off any action until Indian Agent Whitfield arrived to negotiate a settlement, hoping the ensuing wait would cool tempers. Fleming vacillated, but in the end, gave in to Grattan's insistent demands.

The following day Grattan assembled a detail of twenty-nine volunteers and the fort interpreter, along with two pieces of field artillery, and marched toward the Lakota camps. As they passed through the Oglala camp, Grattan had a message sent to the Oglalas not to leave their camp or he would "crack it to them." Before reaching the Brulé camp, where High Forehead was staying, Grattan stopped at a trading house run by James Bordeaux and called for Conquering Bear to meet with him. Grattan told Conquering Bear and three other Brulé leaders who gathered that he was there to arrest High Forehead, and asked them to bring High Forehead to him.

What Lieutenant Grattan didn't appreciate was that Conquering Bear had no authority over High Forehead. The structure of Lakota society was different from that of the United States. There was no single chief of the Lakota, no equivalent of the Great Father in Washington to whom all others paid allegiance. The Lakota lived in more than four hundred separate political units organized into small groups that ranged over a territory wider than Texas. In fact, there was seldom any governing structure at all except during a tribal hunt or ceremony. At the Great Smoke, the 1851 treaty council that produced the Fort Laramie Treaty, the lead US negotiator, Indian Affairs Superintendent David Mitchell, insisted that the disparate bands of Lakota name one man as chief of them all. This was a violation of their tribal customs, and as such, they refused. Commissioner Mitchell arbitrarily assigned the role of "paper chief" to Conquering Bear. To American thinking, Conquering Bear should have been able to command High Forehead to surrender. But Conquering Bear was Brulé, and High Forehead, a Miniconjou, was his guest. Conquering Bear had no authority over High Forehead under these circumstances.

Nevertheless, at Grattan's demand, the Lakota sent two different parties to try to get High Forehead to cooperate. Both came back with the same message: High Forehead would rather die than give himself up, and that he was standing in front of his lodge with his bow and arrows waiting for the soldiers to come and try.

All this time, as Grattan was aware, Oglala warriors had ignored his warning to stay in camp and were preparing for battle instead by driving their ponies into camp while the women and children left the village to find cover. In the Brulé camp, warriors were massing behind plum and willow thickets nearby. Grattan's interpreter, who was drunk, was trying to anger the Lakota by riding his horse back and forth in a maneuver the Lakota used as preparation for battle. It is also possible he was intentionally misinterpreting communications, trying to stir both sides to battle.

At length, Grattan lost his patience and ordered his men to fire. One Lakota man was injured. The Lakota did not return the fire, hoping Grattan had now had his vengeance. Instead, Grattan ordered another volley, this time fatally wounding Conquering Bear. The Lakota retaliated. By the time the melee was over, they had slain Grattan's entire command, save one soldier who died later of his wounds. Lieutenant Grattan lay with twenty-four arrows in him and could only be identified by his pocket watch. Conquering Bear died of his wounds a few days later.

The Lakota raided the stores where their annuity good had been waiting for distribution and fled north of the North Platte River. Over that winter, a small band of Brulé killed three mail contractors on the Emigrant Trail in retribution for Conquering Bear's death. The peace between the US government and the Lakota was broken.

The US government felt it had to do something, so the army recalled General William S. Harney (the "iron-jawed veteran of the Mexican War with a well-deserved reputation for Puritanical severity") from leave in France to lead the retaliatory Sioux Expedition. In September 1855, one year after Conquering Bear's death, General Harney staged an early-morning attack on an encampment of Brulés under Little Thunder (Conquering Bear's successor) on Blue Water, a stream near Ash Hollow, Nebraska. This time, it was the Lakota who underestimated their enemy. This attack, known as Harney's Massacre, or the Battle of Blue Water, depending on one's point of view, resulted in the death of eighty-six Lakota, including an unspecified number of women and children, earning Harney the epithet of "Squaw Killer."

Three months later, three Brulé who'd killed the mail employees in retribution for Grattan's killing Conquering Bear surrendered themselves at Fort Laramie. Their murder of the mail coach crew was one of the justifications for General Harney's Sioux Expedition. With their surrender, open hostilities between the army and the Lakota along the trail ceased until August 1864 when some Lakota joined Cheyenne and Apahoe warriors in the raids memorialized at Plum Creek and Oak, Nebraska.

These two conflicts are known by multiple names: the Grattan Massacre and the Grattan Battle; the Battle of Blue Water and the Harney Massacre. But signs and monuments only tell one side of the stories. It is indicative of the point of view of the sign makers along the Emigrant Trail that the granite monument to the first conflict refers to the Grattan command as "massacred" by the Lakota, while the Nebraska State Historical sign at the site of the latter engagement is titled "Battle of Blue Water." Massacre is defined as "savage and indiscriminate killing," and is used commonly in reference to those not in a condition to defend themselves. It's hard to see how the term "massacre" applies to the annihilation of Lieutenant Grattan's fully armed contingent after it shot two volleys into a Brulé village. On the other hand, General Harney's early-morning attack directly on Little Thunder's camp and the resulting deaths of women and children seems more a massacre. Calling the destruction of this village a "battle" hardly seems to convey the reality. Then again, maybe that's the point.

CHAPTER TWENTY

Greatest Hits of the Emigrant Trail

I HAD A RELATIVELY EASY RIDE FROM THE GRATTAN MONUMENT TO the town of Fort Laramie ("250 Good People and 6 Soreheads"). East of town I caught my first view of Laramie Peak. At a little over ten thousand feet, it was the first mountain I'd seen since leaving St. Joe. Emigrants would see the peak from as far back as Scotts Bluff, and had I been paying attention, maybe I would have, too.

I stopped by the Fort Laramie National Historic Site to have lunch and spend a little time soaking in the history. This was where Jack Slade checked in to get permission to kill Jules Beni. It's where Spotted Tail and two other Brulé warriors surrendered themselves in 1855 for killing three mail coach employees the year before. The name Laramie dates from 1818, when a trapper named Jacques La Ramie built a cabin, and courtesy of the locals, "left his bones to bleach" four years later at the confluence of the North Platte and the Laramie Rivers. Subsequent traders built trading forts in the area. In 1849, the US government bought a cluster of adobe buildings from the American Fur Company to turn the fort into a military base to protect and support overland emigrants.

When the government purchased the fort, however, it only acquired title to the buildings. Under the Doctrine of Discovery, the land on which the buildings sat belonged to the Lakota, Arapaho, and Cheyenne. Obtaining clear title was one of the reasons for the Great Smoke, the treaty council that led to the Fort Laramie Treaty of 1851.

The Doctrine of Discovery, which has roots dating back to the Crusades, granted property, commercial, and sovereign rights to the

European nation that "discovered" lands previously unknown to other European nations. Under this doctrine, indigenous peoples' claims to the land were reduced to "native title." That is, a right to occupy the land or to sell it to the nation that "discovered" it. In exchange, the discovering nation's gift of "civilization and Christianity" were thought to be ample compensation to the indigenous population for unknowingly forfeiting their previous independence.

One way for the United States to obtain title to the land was to purchase it from the Native Americans. Another, equally valid means of acquiring title under the doctrine was by conquering the indigenous owners and taking it. While it might be nice to report that the United States had enough respect for the Plains Tribes' rights to deem it appropriate to make a treaty with them rather than fight for title, the truth is that it was the tribes' military might that the United States respected. Thomas "Broken Hand" Fitzpatrick, the Indian Agent for the tribes of the Arkansas, Platte, and Kansas Rivers, had interacted with Native Americans for decades as a trapper, guide, and as one of the past owners of Fort Laramie when it was a trading post. He warned the government that the local tribes could wipe out Fort Laramie or any other station along the Emigrant Trail any day they might be so disposed. Under the circumstances, a treaty of friendship seemed the better option. Hence, the Great Smoke and the Fort Laramie Treaty of 1851.

Fort Laramie represented many things to overlanders. Like Fort Kearny, it was a remote outpost of civilization, the last outpost holding any semblance of life back in the States. It was the last place until Fort Bridger, four hundred miles west, where migrants could lay over, buy supplies, and have repairs made. Fort Laramie sat about one-third of the way between St. Joseph, Missouri, and Sacramento, California, and passing this point was akin to crossing the equator on an ocean voyage. "Seeing the Elephant" was an idiom for the difficulties of the overland journey. Making it to Fort Laramie entitled an overlander to "spit in the Elephant's eye."

A Pony Express plaque mounted on an obelisk on the Fort Laramie grounds states that Fort Laramie was a "major post on the Pony Express Route." Nothing in the record, however, supports that claim. There was a Pony Express station in this area, but no one knows exactly where. The sutler's store in the fort housed a US post office, but as the Pony Express was a private enterprise, the station most likely would not have been allowed on the fort grounds.

Far more interesting than the undocumented Pony Express "major post" at Fort Laramie are a couple of earlier overland mail services that relied on the fort.

The first overland US Mail service west of the Missouri River started in 1849. It was run by Almond Babbitt and operated between Kanesville, Iowa, and the Great Salt Lake City. Travel time was about thirty days in each direction. The US government didn't pay Babbitt. He delivered mail at his own expense, earning money only by collecting whatever postal fees he could recover.

Two things are notable about Babbitt's service. First, there were only three stations along the 1,200-mile route between the Missouri River and Salt Lake: Fort Kearny, Fort Laramie, and Fort Bridger (in extreme southwest Wyoming). Second was the extreme effort it took for Babbitt to deliver the mail, especially at river crossings. Two or three times in one trip he had to construct a rude raft with logs tied together by lariats, load the mail wagon onto it, then pole the raft into the stream. Once the water became too deep, he had to jump in and swim the rest of the way, towing the raft by a rope clenched in his teeth while being swept downstream.

In 1850, the US government decided to pay for mail service to Utah. It awarded a contract to Samuel Woodson to deliver mail between Independence, Missouri, and Salt Lake City. A year later Woodson subcontracted with Feramorz Little to deliver mail on the western part of the route, between Fort Laramie and Salt Lake City, thereby dividing the mail route into two halves. Ideally, the mail would leave from Independence and Salt Lake City on the first of each month, the parties would meet at Fort Laramie on the 15th, exchange loads, then return to their respective starting points.

Little worked primarily with two brothers-in-law, Ephraim Hanks and Charles Decker, as well as a man only identified as "an Indian called Yodes." These mail carriers made a thousand-mile round-trip journey every thirty days and had only one station on their route, Fort Bridger, which lay around 110 miles north of Salt Lake and four hundred miles south of Fort Laramie. Sometimes other travelers joined them for safety.

By the time Little and Hanks reached Fort Laramie on their first trip, their mules were too exhausted to make the return trip to Salt Lake. They bought five unbroken mules from a nearby rancher. To manage the mules, they had to wrestle them to the ground, bind them, and tie on blindfolds. They harnessed four and saddled the fifth, which Ephraim Hanks then tried to ride. Hilarity ensued.

In November 1852, Little and Yodes had to wait twenty days for the mail to arrive from Independence, which was delayed due to bad weather. During this time, Little injured his leg. The fort surgeon told Little that between the winter weather and his injury, he could die if he attempted to return to Salt Lake City. Little left anyway, primarily because his wife was expecting a baby. The party got lost in a snowstorm near South Pass, but eventually made their way to a trading post on Green River (where Little discarded his crutches) and from there to Fort Bridger where they joined with another group that had been holed up due to bad weather.

They all left together for Salt Lake, but made it only five miles due to the deep snow. The next day they returned to the fort to purchase two Flathead horses, which were bred to work in deep snow, to lead the teams. It took them twelve days to reach the mouth of Echo Canyon, a distance of about seventy miles. At this point the country became too difficult for the horses, so they turned them loose to fend for themselves until they could be rounded up again the following spring. But there was still the problem of getting the mail to Salt Lake City. The postmaster at Fort Laramie had divided the mail into two sacks of roughly seventy pounds each. One held letters and the other held the rest of the mail. Little cached the mail bag in an iron kettle for later retrieval. He put the letters into a parfleche—a waterproof container made of buffalo skin—and the party took turns dragging the mail over the snow to Salt Lake City. Exhausted, and with supplies running short, they cached the letters at the foot of Big Mountain and hiked the final seventeen miles.

On a trip in 1857, the best mules of the outfit either strayed away or were stolen. The loss slowed Little and Hank's progress so much their provisions gave out and they lived for five days on parched corn. On yet another winter mail run they were treated to warm hospitality and more food than they could eat by Old Smoke, an Oglala chief, who expressed his admiration for men who would try to travel in that weather. On a different trip they were surrounded by a group of Crow Indians. Badly outnumbered, they could do nothing but wait to see what would happen. At some predetermined signal, the Crows started to raid the party's stores. Only the surprise appearance of another party of Euro-American travelers stopped the Crows from taking everything.

According to historian LeRoy Hafen, these and other experiences and other experiences recorded by Feramorz Little aren't extraordinary, but rather were typical during the early period of overland mail. Reading these accounts, I couldn't help but thinking that compared to these mail carriers, Pony Express riders were the prima donnas of the overland mail. Compared to the jackass mail carriers (as mule-powered mail services were called), Pony Express riders had it easy.

Where Little and his companions had to take time to purchase and break mules, station keepers led out saddled horses for the Pony Express riders. Instead of setting up and breaking camp day after day, feeding themselves and sometimes nearly starving, Pony riders were fed and housed. Whereas Pony riders were instructed to avoid confrontations with Native Americans by speeding away, mail carriers lumbering along with mule-drawn carts had no choice but to face whoever and whatever came their way. If a Pony's horse was somehow lamed or died, the farthest a rider had to walk was fifteen miles, and even less if he could flag down a stagecoach. The mochila, which held the Pony Express mail, lay across the saddle and carried only ten pounds, twenty at most. A rider could sling it over his shoulder if he had to carry it any distance. Little and his companions dragged their seventy-pound mailbag with a lariat through the snow over Big Mountain in Utah, which I can tell you after riding it, was no mean task.

Was riding for the Pony Express difficult work? Absolutely. Did it take a measure of bravery and resourcefulness? No question. I do not mean to belittle the Pony riders. The point I'm trying to make is that they were no braver, tougher, more resourceful, less fearless, or unquestionably loyal than just about every other trans-Mississippi mail contractor of the period. Pony Express riders' performance record is a credit to their effort. But this is one area in which Pony Express mythmaking goes a step too far, because in lionizing Pony Express riders, others who are equally deserving of such praise have been eclipsed rather than highlighted. It seems a disservice to those who risked at least as much and suffered more to see the mail through.

On some level, I suppose it comes down to that Pony Express image of the dashing figure barely hanging on to the racing horse. Poking along on a mule, however admirable, could never be as sexy.

Fort Laramie marks the end of the high plains and the beginning of the approach to the Rocky Mountains. Statements like that sound arbitrary. How can this side of the fort be plains and that side be foothills? But that's actually how it felt. As soon as I got back on the Pony Express Route I started climbing. There were still stretches that ran for miles of cropland, rangeland, and feed lots, but the terrain was rougher, rockier. The sky, if possible, seemed even larger. Overland emigrants jettisoned a lot of equipment and even food along this tougher stretch of road to lighten the load for their oxen. Notably, the first items to go were domestic goods such as cook stoves and furniture, books and chinaware, items that gave the camps a sense of home. Many of the items were heavy and were not essential to making a successful trip. At the same time, the items tended to be more important to women emigrants who already felt displaced.

In emigrant days, this area was referred to as the Black Hills for the dark stands of pine, spruce, and cedar trees. Today these hills, which are not part of the more famous Black Hills of South Dakota, comprise part of the Laramie Mountains. The Pony Express Trail crossed the lower portions of this range all the way to Casper, Wyoming.

Fort Laramie also marks the place where the Mormon Pioneer Trail crosses the North Platte River to join the three national historic trails that run along the south bank of the river: the Oregon, California, and Pony Express Trails. Though Mormons traveled from the Missouri River along the north bank of the Platte River and kept to the north bank of North Platte River after it branched off near North Platte, Nebraska, it was thought that the north bank was impassable for wagons past Fort

Laramie. For the first few years of their emigration to Utah, Mormons crossed the North Platte near the Laramie River and joined the other emigrants along the more established trail up the south bank. This wasn't easy for them—not because the river crossing was particularly difficult, but because after suffering so much violence in the past, they were afraid the emigrants would attack them on the trail. Non-Mormon emigrants, fed stories of the avenging angels of Mormons, were just as afraid Mormons would attack them. As it turned out, neither side attacked the other and all got along well. The Mormons even ferried emigrants across the North Platte River by present-day Casper, Wyoming—for a fee.

In 1850, overlander Andrew Childs blazed a trail along the north bank. This became known as Child's Cutoff. The going was equally difficult on both sides of the river, but by keeping to the north bank, Mormons and other overlanders could avoid two crossings of the North Platte River: once to cross to Fort Laramie, and a second time where the trail leaves the river near Casper, Wyoming.

As the Pony Express Trail stayed south of the river, so did I. At first I tried to capture some aspect of the scenery, but the camera lens was too narrow. Not far past Fort Laramie I pretty much stopped taking landscape pictures at all because everything looked familiar. The striated rocks, the yuccas, the open ranges, and yes, even the wide, wide sky did not look much different from places I knew in central California. The North Platte ran deep and swift through this area, but the land carried the same dry feel of California in summer; the colors had the same faded look, as if bleached by the summer sun.

Though it was not an easy ride, this windy, dusty, hilly stretch between Fort Laramie and Guernsey, Wyoming, turned out to be unexpectedly rich in trail history. You can see more artifacts of the overland emigration in these twelve miles than just about anywhere else between the Missouri River and the Pacific Coast: the most impressive wagon ruts, the most accessible emigrant carvings, a couple of marked graves, and a Pony Express station marker. It's like a twelve-mile stretch of Emigrant Trail Highlights, two thousand miles of trail legacy packed into a dozen miles of gravel road.

The first stop was Mary Homsley's grave. As Fort Laramie marked the end of the plains, it also marked the western end of cholera territory, though it was the beginning of a different malady: mountain fever, which caused nausea, headaches, and dysentery. Ironically, Mary Homsley died in 1852, not from cholera or mountain fever, but from measles. She'd given birth earlier in the trip. Sadly, her newborn child died just weeks later.

Just past Mary Homsley's grave I came to the Bedlam Ruts, an area of ruts (wagon tracks) and swales (depressions caused by wagon traffic). I rode the short cutoff to view the ruts, but though the area is open to walk, I stayed near the interpretive signs. I wasn't sure about rattlesnakes, and I was also fatigued from riding about forty miles to that point. I wasn't sure I could walk carefully enough over the uneven ground and worried about twisting an ankle.

Back on the road after leaving the ruts I came to a type of roadblock I'd see here and there for the rest of the trip: cattle. There were about fifteen scattered across the road, and as I approached, not one gave any ground. All turned instead to stare at me in that silent cowlike way. I don't know much about cattle—how they act, what might set them off—but I'd read a lot of accounts of stampedes during the overland emigration. They didn't sound like fun. These cattle seemed complacent enough, but a cow is a large animal. Standing next to one, or passing through a crowd of them, it was easy to imagine that, if they took exception to something I did, any one could stomp me and my bike and my trailer and wander off unfazed, and maybe a little happier for it. So I dismounted and approached slowly, ringing my bike bell to make sure I didn't surprise any. I also veered as far from any calves as I could. For all I know these steps were completely unnecessary, maybe even wrong, but they seemed like good sense at the time. As I came closer, the cows dispersed, some walking away, some running. That was a relief.

The oxen that pulled the overlanders' wagons and died by the thousands every year were similar to the cattle staring me down. That is, emigrants' oxen were domestic cattle, *Bos taurus*, which could be found on any farm. According to National Park Service archeologist Lee Kreutzer, what made them oxen was that they were "educated," trained to understand commands and to pull under yoke. Emigrants often bought oxen at the jumping-off towns along the Missouri River. More often than not the oxen weren't as well educated as they should have been, leading to some exciting experiences the first few days. Freighters often used untrained steers as well. Before getting underway they might have to brand hundreds of steers and break them to yoke, which was an experience every inexperienced freighter seemed to enjoy writing about.

Steers (castrated males) were preferred because they grew larger and stronger, but any cattle could do the work. Even the milch cows some emigrants brought along for their milk (as well as the cream and butter their milk provided, produced by hanging a covered pail of milk to swing behind the wagon all day) would sometimes be yoked up to pull the wagons. Oxen were the slowest but most economical means of locomotion on the Emigrant Trail. They were the least expensive draft animals and were the easiest to feed from forage along the trail. Plains Indians didn't steal them as they did horses. Overlanders also liked cow meat, making the oxen useful in life and in death.

Safely through the cattle gauntlet, I topped a rise and dropped down to two better-known Emigrant Trail sites, Register Cliff and the Guernsey Ruts. Both are just across the North Platte River from Guernsey, Wyoming, and US 26, so they are visited more frequently than the Bedlam Ruts and Mary Homsley's grave. My first stop, Register Cliff, was a wall of easily gouged soft Arikaree limestone. Reportedly there are more than seven hundred visible names. The oldest date back to the eighteenth century; the newest were from the 2000s. In emigrant days Native American petroglyphs covered the cliffs, but they were lost under the overlanders' carvings well before the twenty-first-century scrawlers.

Register Cliff is part of a river flat known as Sand Point. It was often the first camp for emigrants west of Fort Laramie, and also served as the site of the Centre Star Pony Express Station. There is nothing left of the station but a concrete monument and a steel pole. The site is on a nice flat alongside the river. It looked like it would be a welcome place to camp after a long day of humping oxen over the hills.

From there I rode a short distance to the Guernsey Ruts. If you've seen any pictures of wagon ruts along the Oregon Trail, chances are they were these. Impassable terrain next to the North Platte River forced overlanders to climb over an eighty-foot-high limestone bluff. They followed in the same narrow path and over the years wore down a five-foot-deep trench in the soft rock. The area features a nice, paved loop that shows off the ruts to advantage and has well-placed interpretive signs. About halfway into taking this short hike, I realized I'd left my iPhone on my handlebars and raced back down the hill. That phone was my pilot, my primary means of navigation. As it turned out I needn't have bothered. It was still there, as was all my gear, but I was tired. It was time to finish the day's ride.

I headed into town, paying my respects along the way at the nearby Lucindy Rawlins grave. The simple monument at her site is dedicated to the pioneer women of Wyoming, a marking I hadn't seen elsewhere. Not much is known about Ms. Rawlins (whose name is sometimes spelled Lucinda) other than she died in 1849. For all her anonymity, she is one of the few emigrants whose resting site is still acknowledged today.

A national historic site, two emigrant graves, two areas of swales and ruts, and a Pony Express station—four stations, actually, though not all had monuments, at least that I was able to find. I'd left the Great Plains and had crossed into the Rocky Mountain foothills, all in the span of about fifty miles. Not a bad day of sightseeing on the Pony Express Trail.

CHAPTER TWENTY-ONE

Sisyphus in the Black Hills

I WENT FROM HAVING THE MOST HISTORICALLY SPECTACULAR RIDE TO the toughest so far.

My next layover spot was Casper, Wyoming. The distance from Guernsey (where I'd spent the night) to Casper along the Pony Express Bikepacking Route was about 160 miles. Most of that lay along the quieter, more remote roads of the Laramie Mountains, which looked like a nice area to ride and camp. At the pace I was averaging, it would take me three hard days to ride that stretch, four if I wanted to do so comfortably.

On the other hand, the weather forecast called for increasing heat, rising from ninety-four degrees the day I left Guernsey to ninety-eight degrees the day after. More worrisome were thunderstorms due to hit the area three days out. A little research showed I could reduce the distance to Casper to 120 miles if I abandoned the Pony Express Route and stuck to frontage roads. The Pony Express Trail between Glendo and Glenrock, Wyoming, promised to be particularly scenic, but I wasn't in the mood for scenic. I had heat and distance and bolts of lightning to worry about, so I decided to power through two sixty-mile days on the more prosaic frontage roads rather than four forty-mile days along the loopier bucolic ones.

I left Guernsey at 7:00 a.m. Like the day before, the morning was cool. A few miles west of town I turned off the highway onto Wendover Road. It was a gravel road that was quite a climb to a ridge, followed by an equally steep decline on the far side. The road dead-ended into railroad tracks and Cottonwood Creek. There was a Pony Express station marker at the base of the hill, but I had failed to note it when mapping this route, so I missed the opportunity to stop by.

I was relying on Google Maps through this area. I had found out on previous rides that Google Maps doesn't always distinguish between public roads and private. In this case, the app tried to direct me onto a road through a ranch clearly marked "No Trespassing." While I was consulting the map, by which I mean staring at it hoping the road would magically change from private to public, a white Ford truck came bouncing down from the ranch. The driver pulled over, rolled down the window, and asked, "Where are you trying to go?"

For the first time on the trip, I felt uncomfortably grubby. The rancher was about my age, but unlike me, very tidy, with rectangular glasses, neatly trimmed mustache and beard, and a closely shaved neck. Had I leaned into the cab I probably would have caught a whiff of aftershave. I, on the other hand, was covered in a layer of gravel dust caked onto sweat over a foundation of sunblock. I had decided not to bother shaving on this trip, so my beard was unkempt. I looked and probably smelled this way every day on the trip. But for the most part, I was alone, so I didn't notice. Despite my appearance, the rancher was polite and helpful. After assuring me the road to his ranch was private, he gave me directions to Glendo, Wyoming, the next town.

I was uncertain throughout the next part of the ride, not sure whether I was on track or had maybe strayed. Over the previous weeks I had become accustomed to each turn being dictated to me by my navigation app ("In a quarter of a mile, turn left"), and it was unnerving not to be reassured I was on the right course. The rancher's directions were easy to follow. And as it turned out, I was still on the Pony Express Bike-packing Route. In my haste to abandon the longer, hillier route section through the mountains, I mistakenly thought I had to reroute entirely from Guernsey west, when in fact I was only detouring between Glendo and Douglas, Wyoming. Had I been a little less careless, I could have saved some time navigating this section.

The climbs through here were relatively short, but as steep as anything I'd ridden yet. The scenery was gorgeous. Wyoming ranchland. It was like California (because everything looks like some place in California), only multiplied by ten. Go out to the largest field you can find and imagine that ten times larger. Go to a place with the most unobstructed view of the sky and multiply that by ten. That's how it felt out there. Limitless.

At length, after a lot more climbing, I came to a frontage road. It turned out to be the old highway between Guernsey and Glendo, Wyoming, and wound through some more lovely country. I was not, however, too crazy about the winding part. It wasn't hot yet, but it would be, and I still had a long way to go. I wanted the route to be more direct and questioned whether I should have just ridden the noisy shoulder on the even more direct interstate instead.

I made Glendo at close to forty miles, about ten more than I had mapped thanks to the detour around private land. Still, I needed a break, so I stopped for lunch. A few days earlier I had been reflecting on my trip up to that point, and for some reason, felt I had not stopped in enough towns to have pie in the local diner. Kind of a random thought. I don't know why it hit me. But here I was, given an opportunity to remedy that oversight, so I took it.

I sat at the counter of Micke's Family Diner and drank water and coffee and ordered the only nonmeat item on the menu: grilled cheese. Then had strawberry rhubarb pie a la mode. It was wonderful. One upside of riding all day is that it's just about impossible to eat enough to make up for all the calories you burn. Welcome news to those of us who otherwise have to forego desert.

While I ate, I talked to a guy sitting next to me at the counter who worked for a local utility. He and his work partner had passed me on the road a little earlier, so he asked about my trip. Somehow the question of my age came up. He was surprised when I told him. He said he wasn't into auras or anything like that, but thought I had a much younger air about me. Immediately after he assured me he wasn't trying to pick me up. As if to underscore the fact, he started talking about his wife, a Wyoming state trooper.

Back on the road, well fed, duly caffeinated, I rolled past Glendo Reservoir and was having a nice time of it. The pavement was red, the shoulder pink, and the lake and sky wonderfully blue. The sun was still benign, not oppressive. The wind had been light all day, playful. There was barely any breeze blowing across the surface of the languid lake below. I pictured my son, Kazu, down there trying to coax the wind into the sails of his Laser.

I passed a marker for the Horseshoe Creek Station. I was particularly interested in this spot because it was Jack Slade's home station when supervising this part of the Pony Express and COC&PP stagecoach line. Sir Richard Burton stayed here and did not like it. More particularly, he did not like having to sleep on the floor with the other men, and thought Maria Virginia Slade, Jack's wife, and her friend weren't very feminine (referring to her disparagingly as a "Bloomer"). Well, I thought, Sir Richard can stick it up his English arse. I took a couple of pictures, then moved on.

An hour or so later I came to a turnoff to the little burg of Orin, and my day went straight to hell. The road past Glendo had trended northwest, and the wind had been steadily building off my port forward quarter. As I approached the junction with Highway 18, it had risen more quickly and was then in the midtwenties. I turned west at the highway to ride to Orin, Wyoming, and it was as if someone had opened the door and let loose the full force of the wind. From that point on I had better than twenty-five knots, with gusts into the midthirties, right on my nose for the rest of my ride. I again experienced that phenomenon where if I stopped pedaling, the bike stopped moving forward. Progress was painfully slow, excruciatingly slow. The last mile into Orin probably took fifteen minutes, but it felt much longer.

I stopped at a gas station convenience store just before the highway crossed I-25 and bought Gatorade and V-8 and a bottle of water as a backup in case I sucked down the last of the water in my pack. It was hot now, upper eighties, and the wind was screaming. I had fought some strong winds earlier in the trip, but this wind was different. It felt antagonistic, vengeful. Every book I've read about traveling through Wyoming commented on the wind, and I soon discovered why. This was my first head-on collision with Wyoming wind. I soon came to see it as the defining characteristic of the landscape, a force of nature I'd have to contend with for hundreds of miles.

I left the convenience store, crossed over the interstate, and began the last fifteen miles of the day to my motel in Douglas, Wyoming. Naturally, it started out as a climb. And here's the thing about hill climbs in the Laramie Mountains: You don't climb up one side of a hill then descend down the other. I'd noticed this the day before, as soon as I entered the hills west of Fort Laramie. Climbs here are Sisyphean. You climb, level off, then climb some more. It feels as if the uphills are endless, as if no matter how much you've worked, you're starting over again after any level. You get to the part that from down below looked like the top of the hill only to find that the steepness of the grade blocked your view of the next part of the climb, which is even steeper. So, climb, climb, climb; *oh, there's more, okay*; pedal, pedal, pedal; *that curve ahead has to be the top*; climb, climb, climb; *it's not the top?*; spin, spin, spin. . . . That's the profile of a Laramie Mountain hill climb.

But this climb out of Orin, in the full heat of the sun and against the force of the wind, was the worst. It felt like that scene in *National Lampoons' Animal House*: I thought I might as well drop my shorts, bend over, and get whacked on the butt by a wooden paddle, at which point I'd say, "Thank you sir, may I please have another?" That's what climbing these hills felt like. *Why yes, of course I'd love another hill to climb. Steeper? Yes, please. Thank you!*

These last two days drove home the fact that I was no longer riding over hills and ridges. I was working my way up the eastern slope of the Rocky Mountains. Orin sat at around 4,700 feet. I still needed to gain another three thousand feet over the next two hundred-plus miles to reach the Continental Divide at South Pass. There would be a few descents along the way, but there would be a lot more climbing in the short-term fore-cast. In a sense, getting slapped by the wind at Orin was just added insult. Wind so strong I had to pedal to keep moving *downhill*. Forget coasting, stretching, relaxing. If I stopped peddling, the bike would roll to a stop within a few feet.

I don't know how long it took to make the last ten miles into Doug-las, Wyoming ("Home of the Jackalope"). Whatever joy I had felt in the grandeur of the morning, whatever delight in the ride after lunch in Glendo, was gone. It had all been sucked dry by the demon Wyoming wind. It was now past three o'clock. I had been riding for eight hours, had covered sixty-six miles, the last twelve into gale-force gusts, climbed about three thousand feet, and the temps were officially in the lower nineties. I was fried.

I reached my motel on the east end of town, which was beyond funky. The compound was a labor of love someone put together from "historic" (which I felt pretty sure really meant "condemned") buildings in the area. But it was a room. It was out of the sun and wind and heat. As funky as it was, this room was my home until I would leave at 6:00 a.m. to get an even earlier start on the next day's ride. Then, if all worked out, a few days off in Casper, Wyoming, to evaluate the next part of the trip.

CHAPTER TWENTY-TWO

Thalassa, Thalassa

WIND HAS BEEN CALLED THE "TYRANT KING OF WYOMING," AND HAS been blamed for driving people to murderous insanity. To be fair, the same has been said about winds on the Great Plains. Nevertheless, after my next day's ride to Casper, I could attest to the tyrannical nature of Wyoming wind. It was my second day riding straight into headwinds and it tore at my nerves. Like the day before, the ride was long (sixty miles), hot (ninety-four degrees), and Casper sat at 5,100-foot elevation. No doubt these factors added to the strain of the ride. But still. I crawled the last fifteen miles into Casper, and it shouldn't have been that hard. It wouldn't have been that hard, except for the incessant, brutal, and yes, tyrannical Wyoming headwind.

I was out the door by 6:00 a.m., hoping to beat the higher temperature and praying that the wind forecast would turn out to be wrong. There was a twenty-four-hour restaurant attached to my motel, which was convenient, but it allowed inside smoking and seemed ridiculously overpriced. I opted for Egg McMuffins and coffee outdoors at McDonald's instead. By the time I rode there and ate and drank, it was about 6:45 a.m.

The first ten miles led north toward historic Fort Fetterman. I didn't know what the fort was historic for, but it wasn't the Pony Express, and anyway it wasn't yet open for visiting, so I passed it by. These first miles were on nice pavement, with little traffic, and much to my surprise, normal hills. That is, hills where you ride up one side, go over a small pass, then down the other. Not the Laramie Mountains torture chambers of endless climbs as on the previous days' rides. I didn't mind these climbs so much.

They slowed me down, of course, but they weren't punishing. Plus, I was able to coast down the backside when it suited me. What a concept!

Just after the fort the road crossed the North Platte River and I turned west onto Tank Farm Road. The gravel roadbed was damp and looked as if a water truck had passed recently to keep down the dust. Not a bad ride at all. A couple of miles further I crossed onto a ranch displaying a large "No Trespassing" sign telling all travelers to stay on the county road (the one I was on) for the next five miles. This stretch, between Douglas and Glenrock, Wyoming, was the shorter, flatter detour from the Pony Express Route I had mapped out back in Guernsey. It had looked good on the screen. But about two miles into the "stay on the road for the next five miles" section, my mapped route turned left onto an overgrown two-track heading southwest to the north bank of the North Platte River. I stopped and weighed the alternatives. I'd been told that ranchers' main concern out there wasn't cyclists, but hunters, so I probably could have taken that road and had a nice, shaded ride alongside the river. On the other hand, the sign telling me to keep to the road was pretty clear. Plus, the road I'd been riding was in better condition. It might be a little longer and less shady, but would probably still be faster. I decided to keep to the main road.

It continued through the ranchland, a lovely, quiet area. I saw some jack rabbits scurry by. Also a number of pronghorns (which are often mislabeled as antelope). I had seen pronghorns on previous days, but there were a lot more in this area. They tended to stare at me for a few moments, then bound away, their furry white butts bouncing over the grasslands. It was quite a sight. Emigrants tried to shoot pronghorns on the overland trek, but more often than not failed. The animals were very fleet, and most overlanders weren't experienced hunters. Also, pronghorns are very hardy. One writer noted that pronghorns "possess a great vitality" and "will carry off more lead in proportion to their size than any other animal."

The thought of filling pronghorns with lead brought to mind those two great American pastimes, hunting and fishing. I'd been thinking about these sports the entire trip. Everywhere in Kansas, and through- out Nebraska and Wyoming, were signs posted, "Walk in hunting only." Along the North Platte River, wherever there was access to water there was also a symbol showing access to fishing. I've never been fond of either activity. I've never gone hunting. And whatever fantasy I might have held about fishing was drummed out of me by the sight of a crewmate on a sailboat in the Sea of Cortez trying to kill a dorado he had landed by beating the crap out of it with a winch handle while it splattered fish blood all over the cockpit of our boat. Neither activity is something I condemn in principle. They just hold no interest for me. Seeing so many references to hunting and fishing out on the road those past few weeks somehow made me feel even more out of place. They underscored the fact that I was out of my element.

But at least I recognized I was out of my element. As I mentioned earlier, hunting was a huge part of the mythos for the men of the westward emigration. They used the justification of bagging animals to supplement their diet as a means of measuring themselves against an earlier, more heroic generation of men who actually did have to hunt for food. In reality, most emigrant men were as unfamiliar with using firearms as I was. As a result, death by gunshot was the second largest cause of accidental death for emigrants behind drownings. Accidents became less common further along the trail as emigrant companies tightened up the rules on firearms storage and use in response to the self-inflicted mayhem earlier in the trip. But in the meantime, it seems emigrant men shot at anything that moved, including themselves, each other, and even prairie dogs, which were neither good sport nor a source of food.

About thirty-five miles into the ride I came to Glenrock, Wyoming ("Big Enough to Enjoy. Small Enough to Care."). Glenrock (not to be confused with Glendo, Wyoming, some sixty-five miles back) sits where Deer Creek joins the North Platte River. In the late 1850s there was an Indian Agency office here run by Thomas Twiss, as well as a trading post (about which Richard Burton, typically, had nothing good to say) run by a man named Bissonette. The town had a stagecoach and a Pony Express station. There was also a rickety ferry across the North Platte, though Deer Creek does not seem like an ideal place to cross. The river flowed swiftly here. One emigrant in 1849 witnessed twelve drownings in a single day of men trying to cross stock nearby. Perhaps due to the difficulty of crossing here, the first known billboard on the Emigrant Trail was posted close by. In June 1847, the Mormons established a ferry across the North Platte River near present-day Casper and planted a billboard near Deer Creek, which read, "To the ferry 28 ms the ferry good and safe, maned by experienced men, black smithing, horse and ox shoeing done all so a wheel right."

Ten years later, in 1857, the Mormons started a small settlement at Deer Creek to support their own mail service, known as the Brigham Young Express (BYX). In late 1856, the US postmaster general awarded a Mormon named Hiram Kimball the contract to deliver mail to Salt Lake. Whether Kimball was acting on his own or on behalf of Brigham Young, the church soon took over his operation. It planned a string of settlements that would not only support a mail service but would also provide way stations to support the ongoing Mormon emigration to Salt Lake City. The stations were substantial. BYX station at Deer Creek, for instance, included a 320-foot square blockade enclosing forty-two buildings, a 150-foot square corral, and fifteen acres of gardens. The church reportedly spent upward of $200,000 to start the service, but it never went into full operation. The postmaster general canceled Kimball's contract in June 1857, just six months after awarding it. The Utah Expedition was on its way to Salt Lake to chastise the Mormons. The Mormons abandoned the settlements they had started all across the West, including the one at Deer Creek, and returned to Salt Lake to prepare for the American invasion.

I took a picture of the Deer Creek Station memorial and went looking for something to eat. Nothing open, so I went to the grocery store and loaded up on fluids and a donut and breakfast burrito to go. From there I went to the post office and dashed off a quick postcard home saying I wished I were spending the day (my birthday) there—as if I had someone else to blame.

While I was walking out of the post office, a young woman held the door for me. I alternated shirts every day on my ride, both screened with a Pony Express logo I'd designed after the original Pony Express stamp, but with my mountain bike in place of the prancing pony. She saw my shirt and told me she'd just ridden in the Pony Express re-ride, which went through that area the night before. The National Pony Express Association stages annual re-rides of the Pony Express trail each summer.

It accepts mail and delivers it in ten days by running relays similar to the fashion of the original Pony Express, though the format has adapted to modern times. Rather than remote outposts, the riders are supported by a small mobile army of volunteers and vehicles. Their runs are also far shorter than the original riders', largely I suspect because more than 750 riders participate in each re-ride. The re-ride alternates every year between westbound and eastbound routes. As it happened, the year I was riding west, the re-ride was headed east. It had passed through Douglas, Wyoming, sometime the night before, while I was sound asleep.

Back out on the road, I was once again on the Pony Express Route, which takes Old Glenrock Highway (US 20/26) into Casper. This stretch was wide-open road with a steady stream of seventy-miles-per-hour traffic whizzing by in both directions. Wyoming highways had very generous shoulders separated from the driving lane by a rumble strip. In theory, the rumble strip would warn a driver if they wandered too far to the right. But that was a small consolation. I am accustomed to cars and trucks speeding past just a few feet away, but never comfortable. Every cyclist rides knowing they could be killed by only a few seconds of malice or inattention on the part of any driver.

It was now late morning and the wind was building. True to the fore-cast, it was from the west at about twelve knots, gusting around eighteen. I was riding directly west, dead into it, and I still had twenty-five miles to go. I had fewer feet to climb than the previous days, but that was probably the only good thing I could say about this ride. These were river valley hills, benign, not endless, malicious hill climbs, but they still wore me down. Like the previous day, the wind was so strong I had to pedal to move the bike downhill. The closer I came to Casper, the more the wind built, until the gusts, again, blew well over twenty knots.

Pedaling for hours into a stiff headwind is torpefying. It dulls your senses to everything other than physical pain, which I felt from my neck to my thighs. The driving wind saps the life out of the ride—the joy of it, the essence of what causes you to want to ride in the first place—because you are riding head-down, not up, focusing on the task at hand rather than taking in the scenery. Fighting instead of flowing. I doubt any-thing could have made this ride pleasant. My only reward for struggling through these two long days was that I wouldn't be riding in rain.

Finally, I reached the eastern outskirts of Casper. For the past few days I'd been holding a romantic notion of making it here. I had planned to spend a few rest days in Casper, and in that sense, I saw it as a city of respite. It was the largest city I'd pass through between St. Joseph, Missouri, and Salt Lake City, Utah, and the last town of any size I'd see for the next few hundred miles. I pictured it all small-town charm, walkable, friendly. In the back of my mind I even whispered the incantation of joy at reaching a place of refuge, "Thalassa! Thalassa!"

But the Casper I saw was all industrial, ragged, truck depots and RV storage lots. The road into town from the east, which had been a highway, downgraded itself to a narrow four-lane with narrower shoulders. Like in Scottsbluff, the drivers were antipathetic to bicycles. Further on I came to a bike path of sorts. It looked like a trails-to-rails conversion, elevated like train tracks would have been. It was unpaved, unevenly graded, and had hoof prints, I assumed from the Pony Express re-ride that had passed in the other direction the day before. A couple of miles further the bike path dead-ended abruptly, despite the markings on the map, falling victim to off-ramp construction for a freeway running through the middle of town.

All the time the sky threatened rain. It was hot outside, and muggy. And, of course, the wind still blew in my face. I made it across town, mostly on sidewalks, and ended up in downtown Casper (where, like Seneca, Kansas, they play music over speakers along the Main Street) at a coffee house called Bourgeois Pig. The barista asked about my bike, so I explained my ride, and he excitedly held forth on trail history for the benefit of everyone within earshot. It was the most bizarre mis-telling of American history I've ever heard. He started by explaining that Alexander Frémont was called the Pathfinder because he led emigrants to the West, then how Frémont issued an Emancipation Proclamation in Missouri before Lincoln issued his national proclamation, and how Lincoln wanted Frémont to rescind his proclamation and sent an agent to tell Frémont he was fired. He went on and on in this vein, covering a range of subjects as long as I sat there. None of it was true (including everything he'd said about Frémont, whose Christian name was John, not Alexander), but it was wonderfully entertaining. Every time he opened his mouth it was a tour de force of historical gibberish. I wish I had recorded him.

153

After I felt rested, I rode the last few miles to my hotel, checking into a place a step or two up from the roadside motels where I'd been staying. I was glad I did, because as I passed all the less expensive motels I'd considered, I saw they were all in the noisier, busier sections of town. Perfectly adequate, and closer to restaurants maybe, but in my frazzled state of mind, not attractive at all. And after all, it was my birthday.

Making Casper meant I had ridden roughly two-thirds of the route between St. Joseph and Salt Lake. I had something over nine hundred miles behind me and something under five hundred miles to go. The next three hundred miles would be the most remote country I would cross. In that sense, if I wanted to stop, Casper was my Pony Express Rubicon, the point beyond which there was no turning back.

Not that Casper was a convenient place from which to get back home. Though the route to South Pass was the primary overland road from the 1840s to the early 1860s, there was a better transportation route further south. In 1862, just two years after the Pony Express went belly up, Ben Holladay's Overland Stage Line, which had bought up the Central California Overland and Pike's Peak Express from the bankrupt Russell, Majors & Waddell, abandoned the South Pass route for the Cherokee Trail and Bridger's Pass. This route continued west from Julesburg, Colorado (rather than turning north, like the Emigrant Trail), and ran through northern Colorado and southern Wyoming. The move was ostensibly made to avoid disruptions along the Emigrant Trail caused by Native Americans. More to the point perhaps, the new route saved the stagecoach line some money because it offered a lower and more direct route across the Continental Divide to Salt Lake City.

The Transcontinental Railroad, Lincoln Highway, and I-80 followed this same route, which was at least three or four days' ride south for me. If I were to abandon my ride, the time to do so was before I left this major transportation corridor back in Sidney, Nebraska.

On the other hand, I had received an offer of help from an unexpected source. Over the previous couple of days my mother had started texting me:

"R U ok?"

"Brutal ride. I think it would be easier going the other way like the horses."

"Sharon standing by if you need her."

First of all, when did MJ (my eighty-ish-year-old mom) learn texting shorthand like "R U?" Second, Sharon was my sister who lived in Denver, a five-hour drive from Casper. Did she know MJ had put her on call? MJ offered to fly out to Casper and sit in a hotel room to stand by in case I had any trouble crossing Wyoming. Failing that, she offered to send food. She all but flew to Denver to make Sharon and her husband, Gary, drive up and force me to go back home with them. All of which was very sweet, but worrisome. MJ is a lot of things, but "motherly" and "sweet" are not among them. I don't mean that in a negative way. She is a very strong-willed, highly intelligent, fiercely independent woman who still worked and was an active horseback rider (trail and dressage) on a huge, strong brute of a horse named Cisco. If she was so concerned, maybe I needed to reevaluate whatever reservations I still held.

Eventually I talked her down by laying out all of my contingency plans for the ride across Wyoming, including the fact that I'd have Mormons and Buddhists looking out for me. I don't know that I allayed all of her concerns, but in doing so, I put to rest some of mine. I decided to see the ride through to Salt Lake City.

Later that afternoon I watched the thunderstorm I had raced to beat from the shelter of my hotel. It was everything I'd hoped to avoid, whipping winds and profuse, fat drops of water crashing down. I only wished it lasted longer to justify the torture of what I'd put myself through to beat it. More storms were forecast for the next few afternoons. As Don Weinell, a cyclist who'd ridden the Oregon Trail before noted, the road west of Casper lacked any buildings, houses, bridges, or any other structure that might offer shelter from a storm. I had no interest in riding or camping in rain and mud. Even if I could beat the rain into camp every day, there was the lighting to consider, and the unpaved roads would be sloppy, slow riding if not impassable. It looked like I would have a few more days' rest than I had planned, which was not necessarily bad news. The steppes of Wyoming were out there and I'd ride them soon enough. In the meantime, it felt nice to watch the storm rage outside while staying warm and dry indoors.

CHAPTER TWENTY-THREE

The Last Crossing

I SPENT A RESTFUL COUPLE OF DAYS PUTTERING AROUND CASPER, Wyoming. I thought I would be hunkered inside, sheltering in place, as it were, from thunderstorms. They were stacked up for the next three days, but all forecast to hit in the late afternoon, which gave me time to get around during the day. Portions along the North Platte River are part of the Platte River Trails, a system of multiuse paths in the area, so I could get most places I wanted to go around town without having to brave too much local traffic.

On my first morning, the wind was very light, and in fact never rose above a gentle breeze until a squall whipped it into a frenzy in the late afternoon. First thing I did was head out to a self-serve car wash to blast the sand and grit out of my bike. My daily maintenance routine (in addition to pumping up the front tire) included lubing the bike chain and suspension O-rings to keep them from drying out. I flushed out the finer particles whenever convenient to help prevent either system from breaking down at some inopportune time.

Wagons crossing the plains had similar maintenance requirements, though less refined lubricants. The early freight wagons on the Santa Fe Trail had wooden axles that had to be greased daily with a mixture of tar, resin, and tallow. The emigrants' prairie schooners required liberal applications of grease. After they ran out of store-bought lubricant, they would use boiled buffalo or wolf grease instead. Stagecoach axles had to be greased every twenty-five to thirty miles. In one instance, when a stagecoach failed to get greased at a stop and the axle seized, the stagecoach driver stuffed clumps of grass and pieces of cheese to "dope" the frozen axle and get the coach to the next station. With these stories in mind, squirting a little lubricant out of a plastic container once a day didn't seem such a tedious chore.

After washing the bike and trailer, I went to breakfast at a restaurant downtown called Sherrie's Place. There were a few tables outside. All full. I stepped inside, opening a screen door with a hand-written sign that read like two-thirds of a haiku: "Hold on door. Wind grab it." I wondered how many times the door had been blown off its hinges.

The place was packed inside as well. A server told me that a woman sitting at one of the tables outside was waiting to sit inside so I could have her table when she moved if I wanted it. I approached the woman from across the table to maintain space between us, told her what the waitress told me, then asked if she'd mind if I sat as it seemed she was going to be seated inside in a moment. She said no problem, then stood abruptly and backed away. I apologized and said I didn't mean to steal her table. She said it was okay, no worries. So, I set my pack down on the chair and we stood at opposite ends of the table and talked for a brief moment until she was seated inside.

While I ate, a few people asked me about my bike and about the ride. I had a long discussion with an older rancher seated at the table next to mine. He did not have a particularly high opinion of California—no one I talked to on the entire trip had anything good to say about Californian politics—but we had a nice chat. When I told him I would be riding over South Pass to Farson, Wyoming, his expression became grave.

"That's the Red Desert." He shook his head slowly while fixing me with his clear blue eyes. "There's nothing out there," he said solemnly. "Nothing."

At one point a woman came out to look at my bike, saying she'd noticed it from inside. She asked how the ride was going, and I told her okay, except for the wind. She nodded and smiled—everyone to whom I mentioned the wind in Casper had the same reaction, the knowing smile—then she said, "You can always tell someone's from Wyoming because they walk like this," and she pantomimed a person blown back on their heels, arms reaching out in front to keep from falling over backward.

As I was finishing up, the server picked up my bill. It turns out that the woman I'd unintentionally evicted from her table paid for my breakfast. I was shocked. By rights I should have bought *her* breakfast. The server told me it happened all the time there, and that in fact someone had paid for the woman's breakfast, too. The old rancher said, "I'll bet that never happens in California."

I felt so good after that huge meal and the random Casper goodwill that I rode back to the hotel and took a nap, a luxury I never indulged in on a ride day. After I woke, I walked up the hill to the National Historic Trails Interpretive Center and poked around. It was a beautiful facility run by the Bureau of Land Management full of well-researched interactive exhibits. It sits on a rise and offers a sweeping view of the valley and eight-thousand-foot Casper Mountain to the south. I came here every afternoon to scan the sky and gauge the weather. Mostly what I saw were magnificent storm clouds sweeping in from the west. Grumbling thunderheads with bellies full of rain. There may be nothing more beautiful than watching an approaching storm—at least, so long as you know you're safe from it.

After lunch I rode from the National Trails Center to the Fort Caspar Museum. Fort Casper is confusing, starting with the fact that the fort (and the city which took its name) go by the misspelled word "Casper" with an *e*, whereas Fort Caspar Museum is spelled with an *a*. The fort was named after Second Lieutenant Caspar Collins, a US Army officer killed in the 1865 Battle of the Platte Bridge Station. The army got his name wrong when they renamed the fort in Collins's honor; the museum thought it appropriate to get it right.

Similarly, sorting out the different names of the historical sites in the area and their relation to the overland emigration can be confusing, even to historians. In fact, when Fort Casper was rebuilt in the 1930s, the drafters of the interpretive signs misidentified locations and dates. Fort Caspar Museum later corrected these misstatements. More impressively, the museum went a step further to use the opportunity to amend the prior historians' derogatory depictions of local Native Americans as well.

This area was known to trappers as the Crossing of the Platte or the Last Crossing, as in the last crossing of the North Platte River. The

North Platte took westbound travelers on the four major overland trails (Oregon, California, Mormon Pioneer, and Pony Express) from the forks of the Platte (near North Platte, Nebraska) to this area. Before Child's Cutoff was blazed in 1850, everyone traveled along the south bank of the North Platte River. Casper sits at the northernmost point of the Pony Express Trail. South Pass, the only wagon route over the Continental Divide, is a little south of west from there. Not far past the site of the current city of Casper, however, the North Platte turns sharply southwest, away from South Pass, forcing overlanders to follow a different source of water and forage toward South Pass. The Sweetwater River provided just such a natural road. To reach the Sweetwater, however, overlanders had to leave the North Platte River at some point near Casper and travel fifty (mostly) waterless miles of high desert. The only question was where to cross. Hence the Crossing of the Platte, or for those who had crossed from the north bank to the south bank back at Fort Laramie, the Last Crossing of the Platte.

I spent some time along the North Platte River during my few days in Casper, and I have to say, it looked like it moved pretty swiftly through this area. It was not a river I'd like to have had to swim across, let alone try to get oxen, wagons, kids, and whatever else across safely. In the 1850s the North Platte was not dammed, making it much wider and wilder than the river I saw. People kayak the river today, and there are stations all along the bike path with PFDs (personal floatation devices) for the public, so maybe it wasn't as dangerous as it seemed. But I was still apprehensive.

Apparently, many overlanders felt the same. A number of ferries and bridges popped up to get the emigrants across the North Platte, starting with the ferry run by Mormons in 1847. With this service, the Last Crossing acquired a new name: Mormon Ferry.

Brigham Young and the lead group of Mormon pioneers came to this crossing in June of that year. Though they had traveled from the Missouri River along the north bank of the Platte and North Platte Rivers, they, like everyone, thought the north bank impassible west of the Laramie River. So they had crossed to the south bank at Fort Laramie and now had to recross the river to get to the Sweetwater. The pioneer group was around 150 people who traveled with 72 wagons. The North Platte was in flood—150 yards wide and 12 to 15 feet deep—and the wind (not surprisingly) was strong. After two days they had only managed to get half of their wagons across. They decided to construct a ferry for the remainder. By the time they finally had everybody and everything across, a week had passed. In the meantime, a group of Missourians had reached the crossing and were willing to pay the Mormons to ferry them across. Brigham Young appointed nine men to stay behind to operate the ferry through the season to make money from the overlanders and to help ferry other Mormon groups headed out later that season.

The Mormons subsequently moved their ferry a little downstream of Mormon Ferry and operated until 1852. By then Louis Richard had built the first successful bridge across the North Platte about five miles east, near the present site of Evansville, Wyoming. It was known as Reshaw's Bridge based on overlanders' phoneticization of Richard's French-Canadian name. In 1858 the US Army set up the Post at Platte Bridge nearby Reshaw's Bridge to protect supply lines for the Utah Expedition. The camp became known as the Post at Platte Bridge.

In 1859, Louis Guinard built a second bridge near the site of the original Mormon Ferry. Guinard maintained a trading post at this location that also acted as a stagecoach and Pony Express station. In 1862, Lakota and Cheyenne were disrupting travel, mail delivery, and the telegraph line along the Emigrant Trail. The US Army took over Guinard's post and established a camp known as Platte Bridge Station to help protect communications and travelers on the Emigrant Trail. It was Platte Bridge Station that the army renamed Fort Casper in 1865 after the death of Lieutenant Caspar Collins in the Battle of Platte Bridge Station.

This litany of facts becomes even more confusing because the names are inaccurate. Though many overlanders crossed the North Platte at Crossing of the Platte, people crossed the river from as far back as Glenrock, Wyoming (where Deer Creek joins the North Platte), to Bessemer Bend, a low ford in the North Platte River about twelve miles west of Casper, Wyoming. Any of the spots used along this forty-mile stretch of river were viable crossings, with only Bessemer Bend accurately described as the last. After 1850, travelers who took Child's Cutoff stayed on the north bank and never crossed the North Platte River, so in a sense, they never reached any Crossing of the Platte, last or otherwise. Even Mormon Ferry was the site of the Mormon ferry for only two years, until it was moved further downstream.

Most confusing, however, were the identities of the two bridges and their attendant army posts: Platte Bridge Station (by Guinard's Bridge) and Post at Platte Bridge (by Reshaw's Bridge). The original interpretive sign for Old Fort Casper confused the building of Guinard's bridge (also known as Upper Crossing of the Platte) in 1859 with the establishment of the Post at Platte Bridge at Reshaw's Bridge (also known as the Lower Crossing of the Platte) in 1858. The original sign also stated that the fort was attacked by "hordes of Indians" in 1865, and that Indians burned the fort buildings and bridge after they were abandoned in 1867.

Fort Caspar Museum has mounted the original Old Fort Casper sign inside the museum along with an accompanying sign titled "Reinterpreting History." The new sign clarifies the Old Fort Casper sign's mistakes concerning the post names and dates. It goes further to note that Fort Casper was cannibalized by the army and repurposed to establish Fort Fetterman and to note that there is no archeological evidence that the site was ever burned by Native Americans or anyone else. Finally, the new interpretive sign, in very carefully crafted language, states that the old sign's use of the descriptor "hordes" of Indians, like the contemporary reference to Native Americans as "savages," was inappropriate.

The new sign distinguishes between reinterpreting history and revisionist history. It is perhaps some measure of the state of the cultural divide rending our country that the museum felt it had to defend corrections to historical inaccuracies couched in racist terms and ideology as a reinterpretation rather than a revision. Nevertheless, this was the only time I came across a sign acknowledging the racism of older signs. Looking back on the un-reinterpreted signs elsewhere along the Emigrant Trail, I thought it bold of Fort Caspar Museum to do so.

On my last full day in Casper, a friend drove up from Colorado. We took a driving tour of the area, heading out to Bessemer Bend. The area is also known from emigrant days as Red Buttes for the surrounding sandstone formations. There was a stagecoach and Pony Express station here. The ford located here across the North Platte River was used primarily during the early years of the overland emigration. It remained in use despite the hazard of fording even after bridges and ferries were established near present-day Casper. During the peak of the emigration season, in June and July, wagon trains were backed up for miles and sometimes had to wait days to be ferried or to take a bridge across the river. Some didn't want to pay the tolls. Others didn't want to wait.

Along the way out and back to Bessemer Bend we stopped at some of the pullouts along the highways in the area to read the interpretive signs and take in the views. My route west led over a different route, so I would have missed these spots otherwise. I also took advantage of being driven around to do some final provisioning for the rest of the trip—which maybe was not such a boon. I ended up buying far more food than I could ever eat and purchased other just-in-case items I never used. Had I gone shopping on my own, riding and having to pack everything as I went, I might have shopped more intelligently. I ended up hauling a lot of extra weight to Salt Lake City.

Finally, the weather outlook improved. The temperature was forecast to climb over ninety degrees, but the wind was moderate and the chance of rain was down to 24 percent. My clothes were washed and my bike was clean. I was probably over-rested, definitely over-provisioned, and was spending far too much money on my nice hotel room. It was time to move on.

PART FOUR

THE STEPPES OF CENTRAL WYOMING— CASPER, WYOMING, TO GRANGER, WYOMING

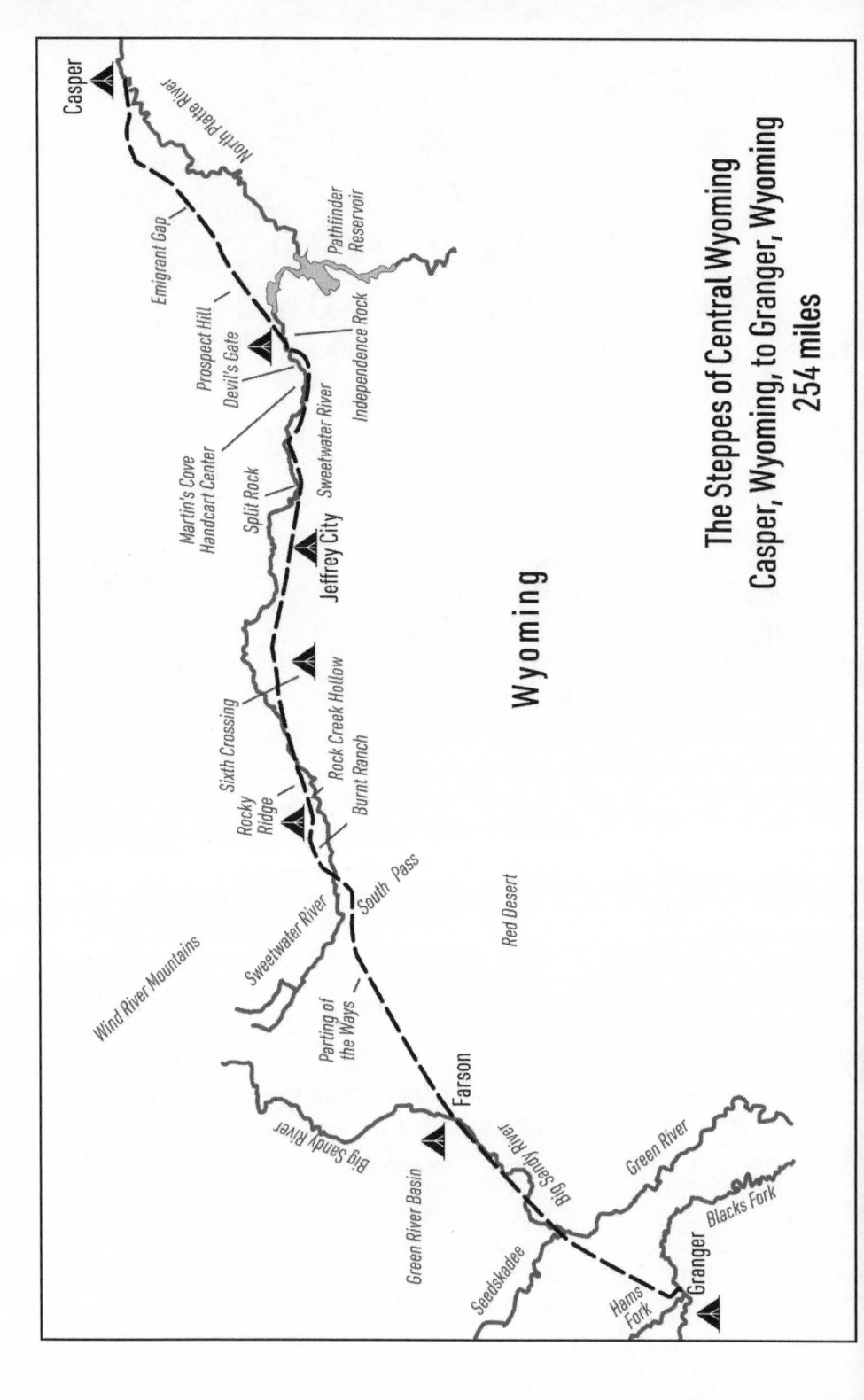

The Steppes of Central Wyoming
Casper, Wyoming, to Granger, Wyoming
254 miles

Wyoming

Casper

North Platte River

Pathfinder Reservoir

Emigrant Gap

Prospect Hill
Devil's Gate
Independence Rock

Martin's Cove
Handcart Center

Split Rock

Sweetwater River

Jeffrey City

Sixth Crossing

Rock Creek Hollow

Rocky Ridge

Burnt Ranch

Wind River Mountains

Sweetwater River

South Pass

Red Desert

Parting of
the Ways

Big Sandy River

Farson

Big Sandy River

Green River Basin

Green River

Seedskadee

Green River

Blacks Fork

Hams Fork

Granger

CHAPTER TWENTY-FOUR

The Poison Spider Route

I GOT OFF TO A DECENT START THE NEXT DAY. THE FIRST FEW MILES were on the multiuse path alongside the North Platte River, which I must have ridden a dozen times or more over the previous few days. Starting with this familiar path was a comfortable sendoff into the wilds of Wyoming.

My destination for the day was Independence Rock, another of the often-noted landmarks in emigrant diaries. Independence Rock sits on the Sweetwater River, which "points like an arrow" west toward South Pass. But between Casper and Independence Rock lay fifty hazardous miles. As if to underscore the nature of the land, the route I followed most of the day was Poison Spider Road.

Poison Spider Road was named after the Poison Spider Creek. There are different versions of how the creek got its name usually ending in death by poison. The crossing from the North Platte River to the Sweetwater would take emigrants two or three days. There was some good water between the two rivers, most notably at Willow Springs. But there was also a lot of heat and dust, and the trail was dotted by alkali lakes—shallow, temporary pools of rainwater containing saleratus and salt—which were fatal to livestock. Thirsty oxen tried to drink in these alkali pools every chance they could, to the point where the owners had to club the oxen to keep them from drinking the poisonous water. They were not always successful, and during the gold rush emigration of 1849 this stretch became "all but impossible to travel through because of the stench from the 2,000 dead oxen."

Wallace Stegner calls this crossing the "worst stretch of trail between the Missouri and the Salt Lake Valley," fifty miles that killed more cattle, sickened more people, and where emigrants abandoned more equipment than any comparable section of the trail east of Salt Lake City. But it wasn't all bad. Kit Carson reportedly found an oil seep by the creek. Emigrants mixed the oil with flour to lubricate their wagon axles.

What struck me as I left Casper was how quickly the landscape changed. The terrain seemed to morph from a broad riparian plain into high desert as soon as I crossed the city limits. Twelve miles out I came to Emigrant Gap, a pass through Emigrant Ridge. By this point I was well out of the Laramie Mountains, but not finished with hill climbs. The ride up to Emigrant Gap wasn't bad, but enough to encourage me to stop at the top to catch my breath and take in the interpretive sign and the view. By this point the land was wide open, largely sagebrush and wild grass. The only trees were scattered pines on hillsides and those planted around farmhouses and Poison Spider School ("Caught in the Web of Learning").

Emigrant Ridge marked the edge of the North Platte River Valley. From the gap I descended to Poison Spider Creek, and from there, started a fifteen-mile uphill slog that culminated in a gut-wrenching climb up Prospect Hill. Along the way I passed the dilapidated Oregon Trail Pet Cemetery, named after the road I was on, not from the era of the pets interred there. The road was mostly dry except at cattle guards, parallel steel bars across the width of the road. Twenty or so feet before and after each were still dark with mud from the previous days' rains and deeply rutted from vehicles that had passed through them—signs that maybe it was prudent not to have tried to cross this area sooner. There was no way around some of these muddy patches, so I had to pick my way through. But this was normal mud, not East Kansas glue-clay, so no problem. The bike and my shins got splattered, but the tires kept rolling.

Somewhere along here I passed the site of Willow Springs. In addition to being a noted emigrant camping spot, the springs also had a Pony Express and stagecoach station. I might have tried to find a marker, but the station site was somewhere along the ten-mile unbroken climb leading to the top of Prospect Hill and I didn't want to lose what little momentum I had. Unlike the Laramie Mountains, where the grade and twists of the road prevented me from seeing the top, I could see the final pitch to the top of Prospect Hill for miles. It was not a happy sight.

There is no worse feeling on a bike than when you're bogging down on a climb and you go to downshift only to find you are already in your lowest gear. Nothing is more disheartening than listening to your derailleur struggle and fail to find that nonexistent cog I hit that point two miles below the summit. Even worse, the grade was steepest on the final pitch to the top. At that point a lesser man probably would have rested. But my experience is that once I stop to take a break it is too hard to get the bike rolling again, and this was not a hill I wanted to push a bike and trailer over. I had also felt sprinkles on and off through the morning and didn't want to risk being out in the late afternoon when storms seemed to occur most often. So I soldiered on.

It took a lot more than leg power to get over the top. I was out of the saddle, stepping as if I were treading a StairMaster rather than spinning the pedals on a bike. I felt the pull through my abdomen throughout that final pitch. By the time I topped the rise I felt nauseous. It nearly wiped me out, and I still had more than twenty miles to ride that day. I pulled over to rest.

A Footbed of Nails

Nearly all serious cyclists ride with their shoes clipped to the pedals. This allows a rider to maintain power through the entire pedal stroke, facilitating a more circular, even movement and enabling them to have more power on hills. I clip in when riding road bikes, but not on the mountain bike. I never felt comfortable with my feet locked in place riding over sketchy terrain like rocks and sand. My pedals had little spikes, a footbed of nails you might say, that dug into the thick soles of my heavier mountain bike shoes. These helped me to pull upward and keep some of the better, more circular pedaling form. But on hills like this there was no way to pull all the way through the backstroke and use the pedals as efficiently as I could had I been clipped in.

Prospect Hill is officially Ryan Hill. The emigrants named it Prospect Hill because it showed them what lay ahead, giving them "a superb view of the desolation on all sides." Which is not to say the prospect was bleak. From here the Sweetwater River was less than a day's journey. Emigrants would find fresh water and forage and a good place to camp that evening. And far from desolation, emigrants were so excited to see the mountains ahead they would recite poetry, shout, and even break into song. All Prospect Hill got from me was a lot of cussing.

The Bureau of Land Management (BLM) maintains an interpretive site at the top. Trail ruts are visible along the top of the ridge. I roamed the area, walking the ruts while I ate and drank, noting ruefully that the Emigrant Trail over this summit passed through a saddle somewhat lower than the peak the road and I had climbed.

I don't mean to be disrespectful to the many devotees of the National Historic Trails, but trail ruts are not always all that impressive to look at. Areas like Prospect Hill, where you can walk in the footsteps of the pioneers are the sine qua non of the trail experience. After all, what is the point of following a nearly two-hundred-year-old trail unless you can see the actual trail? And how much better can it get than to be able to walk the ruts and swales rather than just know they're somewhere nearby? One of the primary reasons I chose to ride this route was that over 85 percent of it was off-road, as close as possible to the trail and to the experience of struggling over the same terrain at roughly the same speed as the Pony Express riders.

Nevertheless, visually speaking, ruts aren't all that exciting. Faint tracks across the largely trackless land of Central Wyoming. That they are so old and still visible speaks at least as much to the undeveloped, unpeopled remoteness of the area as it does to historical preservation. The attraction of seeing trail ruts is not the visual spectacle so much as it is the knowledge of how those tracks were made, who made them, what they went through, what changes they wrought, what they created, and in doing so, how much they destroyed, the words and images they left behind. Those silent tracks on top of that windblown hill don't tell that history; they evoke it, and in that sense require the viewer to see more than what was etched into the ground all those years ago. It's worth the effort, but I could only conjure so much history. After fifteen minutes I was ready to remount and move on.

I had to stop at the bottom of Prospect Hill to work my way through another gauntlet of grazing cattle blocking the road. Ninety minutes or so later I came to the junction of Highway 220, the paved road out of Casper I could have taken instead of the Poison Spider route. I turned west to follow it for a mile and a half to the entrance to Pathfinder Ranch, where I stopped to make a decision. My destination at Independence Rock was a dozen miles or so further along the highway. The Emigrant Trail, however, cut straight southwest across the ranch. I had contacted the good people at Pathfinder Ranch before my trip and was granted permission to cross. So now I had to decide which route to take. The question really came down to how committed I was to sticking to my stated aspiration to ride the trail as nearly as I could. It would likely take me twice as long to cross the ranchland than to ride the highway and would take a lot more physical effort. On the other hand, I had plenty of daylight and the clouds were dissipating, not gathering. As I sat, drinking and thinking, cars and trucks sped by. It struck me that none of them could do what I had the option of doing just then. The closest they would get to the Emigrant Trail along this stretch was to imagine it somewhere over there while they whistled past at seventy miles per hour. I opted to cross the ranch.

And immediately regretted it. It took me ten minutes of wandering back and forth off the ranch driveway to find the trailhead. Even then I had to follow the track on my GPS because I couldn't see the actual trail under the grass. A little further on the trail became more exposed and easier to follow and I was graced with a classic view of the American West: a thin trail winding through sagebrush and sand for miles toward distant, rocky hills. No concrete or asphalt in sight, no buildings or cell towers, not even a contrail streaking across the sky. Though I was surrounded by life, everything seemed still. The only sound was the wind, which at times fell silent. I felt that at last, after nearly a thousand miles, I had finally reached the trail I had hoped to find. The emptiness, the quiet. The solitude.

But while I could appreciate my surroundings, I still had to focus on the mundane. In this case, the ground just ahead. Over the course of the day, I noticed prickly pear cactus growing more frequently at the edges of the trail. The trail itself was rough, a two-track jeep trail (not unlike wagon ruts, a philistine might observe) over ungraded ground. The Emigrant Trail was just off to my right, marked at regular intervals by white Carsonite posts placed by the Oregon-California Trails Association. I would glance over at the trail occasionally, but dodging between patches of deep sand, clumps of sagebrush large enough to stop my trailer wheel, and prickly pear thorns, all the while swatting at bugs that were swarming around my face kept my attention largely focused on the road ten feet in front of me at any given time.

At one point the trail opened into a large area near a watering tank. The ground had been well trodden by large animals, cattle I assumed, and was not especially pleasant. Worse, the cattle had obliterated the trail. I got off the bike and wandered in a large semicircle but never did find exactly where the trail recommenced. Eventually I headed cross-country in the general direction of Independence Rock, dodging obstructions, swatting bugs, and slogging through sand until I picked the trail up again. From this point on, I came across a new obstacle, the alkali pools I'd read so much about. In some stretches they completely filled the tracks I was following, forcing me to ride through the slower sandy sections off to the side. Further on, the trail virtually disappeared again, only marked by grass that was barely a shade lighter than the grass surrounding it.

I suppose I didn't have to follow the trail. I probably could have followed a ley line straight to Independence Rock and ridden cross-country. But I didn't know what kind of soil I would cross, whether there would be even larger pools of water along the way. I also worried about crossing the Emigrant Trail tracks, so well preserved here. In the end I decided to meander along the trail as best as I could.

Eventually, the trail showed itself again, as did Independence Rock. It is a curious rock, shaped like a whaleback in one writer's apt description. I appreciated approaching it from the northeast as the emigrants did, rather than circling around it to the north as the highway did.

As I neared the rock, I had to pass through a livestock gate. These are generally three strands of barbed wire attached to a post, which is stretched across the road and held in place by a loop of wire over a fencepost fixed at the far side. To open the gate, you have to lean into the loose post to create enough slack in the wire loop to lift the loop off the post, then let the barbed wire gate drop to the roadbed. You repeat the process on the other side, of course, to resecure the gate. I'd become accustomed to these gates in my scouting rides through Nevada, but this was the first time I'd come across one on this ride.

Finally, I reached my penultimate destination for the day, the Wyoming State Rest Area adjacent to the Independence Rock Historic Site. Penultimate because it was illegal to camp at the rest area or on the historic site. I still needed to find a place to camp for the night. Pathfinder owns all of the land in the area. I had received permission to camp anywhere I chose on the ranch, "depending on shade, river view, cow turds or rattlesnakes." But before I set off to choose a spot, I needed to rest and eat.

I took over one of the "picnic arbors," concrete pads partitioned to provide some shelter from the wind, each with a table and barbecue grill. There was no electricity, but water was available in the restrooms. I washed off the first layer of dust, then ate and drank and wandered around reading the interpretive signs, all the while glancing at Independence Rock.

The rock sits on the Sweetwater River. It is over 2.6 billion years old, more than half the age of Earth. In addition to signaling the end of the poisonous crossing from the North Platte, it also signaled the beginning of South Pass even though the Continental Divide was still a hundred miles away. Tradition held that reaching Independence Rock by Independence Day, the Fourth of July, meant emigrants headed to the coast were on track to reach their West Coast destination ahead of the first blizzards in the mountains.

Being large and stationary, overlanders, starting with the fur traders who named the rock in 1830, carved, scratched, or painted their names anyplace they could find room among the others already inscribed. It's possible to climb the rock, and I saw some travelers wandering back and forth in that direction. But I was preoccupied, uncertain where I would camp, wondering how long it would take to find a suitable spot. And like California Hill back in Nebraska, Independence Rock is easily accessible by car. I decided to leave climbing to another day.

I found an access road to the ranch just across Highway 220 from the rest stop. Had I more energy, I might have scouted in a wider circle and found something closer to the river, or maybe further from the road. But I'd ridden nearly sixty miles over seven hours that day and even after resting I still felt beat. The spot I'd found was convenient. It would be easy to cross the highway in the morning and reoccupy a picnic arbor for breakfast, refill water, use the restroom—all the little conveniences that would give me a good start on the next day's ride. I set up camp and settled in to watch the late-afternoon light play over the sagebrush and the myriad facets of the famous, ancient rock.

CHAPTER TWENTY-FIVE

Handcart Anabasis

I HAD AN INTERESTING NIGHT ON PATHFINDER RANCH. THE HIGHWAY was raised, blocking my view of the rest area on the other side, but not of the bright lights on top of tall lampposts that lit up one side of my tent all night. A truck driver who spent the night there was apparently hauling pigs. Every so often one or more of them would make known its or their objection to confinement by squealing loudly for a prolonged period of time. Also, cattle graze on both sides of the highway. Occasionally they sounded as if they were communicating to one another across the road. Do cows do that? I don't know, but I fell asleep to the sound of lowing, which wasn't entirely unpleasant. I was concerned they might object to this green blob of tent that had appeared in their range—maybe the lowing was my temporary ranchmates complaining to the cattle across the highway—but they left me alone.

The next morning, I loosely packed everything, rode back across the highway to a picnic arbor in the rest area to cook breakfast (no fires allowed on the ranch's property), and spread the tent fly out to dry. I'd hoped to get on the road by 8:00 a.m., but didn't make it until 8:30 a.m. No biggie. I had planned a shorter ride to Jefferey City, Wyoming, that day, only forty miles, and the forecast was favorable: clear skies, moderate temperatures, and moderate winds.

I started along Highway 220, which was easy riding but not very pleasant. After a few miles I turned off to take the old highway, which crossed through the Granite Mountains via Rattlesnake Pass. Just at the turnoff, a sign warned that the bridge was out. The Pony Express

Bikepacking Route notes stated it was probably okay for bikes, so I took a chance and continued on. Along the side of the road were more white Carsonite posts placed by the Oregon-California Trails Association to mark ruts through the pass. I passed a protected grave in the pass for an emigrant named Frederick Richard Fulkerson, who died in 1847 at the age of eighteen, the same age as my son at the time.

A macabre theme seemed to be emerging these past two days. Rattlesnake Pass that morning, Poison Spider Road the day before. A lonely grave in the Granite Hills. I was riding on the patchwork pavement of an abandoned highway toward a condemned bridge, following signs marking the Emigrant Trail that historians estimate cost the lives of thirty thousand persons to cross between 1842 and 1860, an average of fifteen deaths per mile. It was a good thing I was about be delivered into the hands of the Mormons near Devil's Gate, where I was welcomed with open arms. Let me explain.

Months earlier, when I was researching the route, I had the most trouble planning out the section from Casper to Fort Bridger, Wyoming. Not only were there few towns in between, there were fewer motels, and even fewer public campgrounds. In fact, there were none along the trail. There was a lot of federal land managed by the Bureau of Land Management on which I could camp ("dispersed camping"). But that meant finding a suitable spot every night, and if there was one thing I'd learned about myself on my scouting rides, it was that I *really* liked knowing where I was going to spend the next night. I also wasn't sure I would be able to identify public land and not inadvertently camp on private, didn't know what rivers or creeks I could count on to have water, and had no idea what resupply options there might be. In short, there was a lot of uncertainty.

There are historical sites in the one hundred miles between Independence Rock and Farson, Wyoming—the most remote stretch between St. Joseph and Salt Lake—run by the LDS (the Church of Jesus Christ of Latter-Day Saints, or Mormons). From east to west they are the Mormon Handcart Visitor Center near Devil's Gate and Martin's Cove, Sixth Crossing Visitor Center, and Rock Creek Hollow. I came across a reference suggesting it might be possible to stay at the last two of these sites. Eventually, I tracked down a church member through the internet,

Elder Cook, who ran one of the centers and was able to ask him about camping at the Mormon sites. When we spoke on the phone, I learned his name, Keith, and that he and his wife, Ann, were cyclists who used to live about an hour from where I lived in California. It turned out we knew some of the same riders. Then we discovered we had ridden some of the same events, and in fact, ten years earlier the three of us had actually spent twenty-four hours together riding on a long-distance ride known as a flèche as part of a five-tandem team.

Flèche

Flèche is the French word for "arrow." A flèche is a twenty-four-hour, point-to-point ride (as opposed to a round trip) of at least 360 kilometers (224 miles). Teams of participants start from different locations and ride a one-way route of their design, subject to approval by the Flèche Coordinator. The routes all end at the same destination, like arrows pointed toward a central target. Traditionally, flèches are held over Easter weekend, and there is a large breakfast feast for all the riders at the end.

A flèche is a type of *randonnée*, and as such, has very specific requirements. For example, teams must have between three and five bikes and at least three riders must finish together; cyclists have to check in at preapproved points along the route to prove the team didn't take any shortcuts; and the maximum break period at any one time is two hours. The team Ann, Keith, and I rode in broke the mold somewhat in that instead of five people, we had five bikes, each with two people. A flèche is about as much fun as a person could have in twenty-four hours on a bike. Admittedly, that's not everyone's idea of a great time.

Even so, I had no personal memory of Keith or Ann, until he told me their tandem was the white Da Vinci, and I instantly recalled the bike. It's like when your kids are in grade school and you know all the other adults as so-and-so's mom or dad, but not the mom or dad's name. Same with cyclists. It's much easier to identify someone by their bike than by any other trait. Likewise, Keith recognized my tandem. It was a Tango, designed and built by my good friend Rick Jorgensen. (Remember Rick? He drove all the way to Nebraska to bring me a new wheel only to get within two hundred miles and have to turn around.)

To make the coincidence even more striking, Keith and Ann didn't live in Wyoming. They were there temporarily to help run the Mormon sites at Sixth Crossing and Rock Creek Hollow as part of their church service. They would be returning home by the end of that summer.

I took our conversation as a sign that as remote as this part of the world seemed to me, as difficult as it had been to plan my trip across the emptiness of Wyoming, everything would be okay. Knowing I knew someone in Wyoming convinced me that riding from Casper to Salt Lake City was doable. That was what I meant earlier when I assured MJ that the Mormons and Buddhists in Wyoming would be looking out for me (though I will have to explain the Buddhist connection later).

Not that I thought the Mormons would actually look out for me. I'd really just meant to assuage MJ's concern. Keith told me he and Ann would host me at the Sixth Crossing Visitor Center, but I assumed that would be the extent of my contact with Mormons in Wyoming. When I rode up to the Mormon Handcart Visitor Center that morning, however, one of the elders greeted me and said they'd had people posted at the entrance since 8:00 a.m. awaiting my arrival. He and I spoke for a few minutes, and soon we were joined by what I have to believe was the entire volunteer staff of the site. It was very sweet. We were a group of about ten. They welcomed me with a bottle of Gatorade and we formed a loose circle while they asked questions about my bike and the ride until it became clear that I was to be handed off to another elder, at which point everyone else filtered away back to whatever they were doing before, wishing me a safe journey.

While the LDS church owns the land the Handcart Visitors' Center sits on, it does not own Devil's Gate or Martin's Cove. That land belongs to the United States and is managed by the Mormons under a lease from the BLM. It seems indicative of the bifurcated management of the area that the National Park Service refers to the area as "Devil's Gate-Mormon Handcart Visitor Center," and the Mormon website calls it the "Martin's Cove: Mormon Trail Site."

When the Mormons first bought the property, the only access to the federally owned sites was through the visitor center, and the lease allowed church authorities to decide, in consultation with the bureau, who may be denied admission for, say, improper deportment. According to historian Tom Rea, many felt that the Mormon rebranding of the area around Devil's Gate as Martin's Cove crossed the line between separation of church and state, allowing the Mormons to use federal lands for prosletyzing. Non-Mormons were also concerned that enshrining the deaths of Mormons at Martin's Cove to the exclusion of countless non-Mormons who'd also died in the area crossed the line from reinterpretation to historical revisionism. Not long after the Mormons started operating the visitor center, the American Civil Liberties Union sued the government. The case settled in 2006. The parties agreed the Mormons would remove religious signs from public areas and to allow anyone to visit the federal sites without having to go through the Handcart Visitors' Center.

I didn't feel I had that choice. It seemed apparent that Keith had called ahead, and the volunteers here had planned my visit for me. Not that I minded. I rather appreciated my guided tour. The elder escorted me through the visitor center, housed in an old ranch house from the Sun Ranch, which sold this property to the church. The visitor center features a history of the Mormon handcart emigration, a central event in Mormon history and the primary reason Mormons have purchased and leased so much land along the Sweetwater between Devil's Gate and South Pass.

As I mentioned in the introduction, Mormons had been run out of every town they tried to settle in between 1830 and 1846. In 1831, Joseph Smith first tried to establish the Church of the West in Kirtland, Ohio; the following year, the people of that town tarred and feathered him and one of his counselors. During this same period, there was another Mormon colony being established in Independence, Missouri, which was driven out by mobs in 1833. Over the next five years Mormons were run out of seven counties of western Missouri. In 1838, the governor of Missouri, Lilburn Boggs, issued his Extermination Order to the general of his militia: "The Mormons must be treated as enemies and must be exterminated or driven from the State if necessary for the public peace—their outrages are beyond description."

The Mormons left Missouri to resettle in Illinois on the banks of the Mississippi River. Joseph Smith named the town Nauvoo, which he said meant "beautiful plantation" in Hebrew. At first, Illinois greeted the Mormons. But as in Ohio and Missouri, things turned bad. Joseph and his brother Hyrum were killed by Illinois militiamen while jailed in June 1844. In January 1845, the Illinois legislature revoked Nauvoo's charter. Nine months later, in light of ongoing violence between Mormons and Illini, the Mormons agreed to leave Illinois the following spring, "as soon as the grass grows and the water runs." The violence continued, so they started in February 1846, beginning their trek across Iowa in the dead of winter.

Given this history, it's easy to see why Brigham Young wanted to take the Mormons as far from American settlements as possible. Once there, he and the leadership sought to grow the colony, doubling it every year if possible. Spiritually, it was the leadership's duty to gather the faithful for the second coming of Christ, which they believed was imminent. Temporally, a larger population would bolster Utah Territory's chances for statehood and give the Mormons more autonomy over political affairs. On entering Salt Lake Valley in 1847, Brigham Young reportedly said if left alone for ten years, the Mormons would be able to stand up to anyone. In 1856, he said, "we are bound to become a sovereign State in the Union, or an independent nation by ourselves." Rapidly increasing the Mormon population was an essential part of gaining that strength.

To that end, the Mormons set up the Perpetual Emigration Fund in 1849, a plan to use voluntary donations to help pay the expenses of Mormon emigrants to Salt Lake from the United States and from abroad. Joseph Smith had sent the first Mormon missionaries to England in 1838. In 1850, the first wagon train of English converts arrived in Deseret, the name the Mormons chose for their home at Salt Lake. Dubbed the "Poor Company," they were the first European paupers to migrate under the fund. By 1854, more than fifteen thousand English Mormons had emigrated, along with some Scandinavians and Germans. But there were an estimated thirty to forty thousand more. The problem was how to afford to get them all to Utah. The Mormons were short on cash. In 1855, a grasshopper plague and drought destroyed most of the Mormon crops. This was followed by a hard winter that killed two-thirds of their livestock. The Perpetual Emigration Fund was over $100,000 in debt.

The church decided the solution was to replace ox-drawn wagons with human-powered handcarts. Handcarts cost a fraction as much as a wagon and team. Also, the Mormon leadership was keen to test the faithful and the followers were equally keen to be tested. "Do you not like this method of traveling?" the Mormon First Presidency wrote in an epistle. "Do you think salvation costs too much? If so, it is not worth having." A later epistle stated that "If any apostatize in consequence of this regulation, so much the better, for it is far better that they deny the faith before the start than to do so, for a more trifling cause, after they get here." European Mormons not only accepted the handcart proposal, they "clamored to be included in it."

The carts were similar to wheelbarrows, though much larger. Brigham Young, who'd had training as a carpenter, roughed out the design. The wheels were five feet in diameter, the bed three feet by four, and it had poles extending in front with a crossbar so someone could push or pull the cart. The church gathered members with extensive travel experience across the prairie to specify the type and amount of provisions each cart would carry. The load came to 450 pounds, and there would be a cow for each two carts and a wagon with three yoke of oxen for every ten. Resupply would be made available at the Upper Crossing (near Casper, Wyoming) or Devil's Gate (just a half-mile from the Mormon Handcart Visitors' Center). Emigrants would be organized and escorted every step of the way from Liverpool until they entered Great Salt Lake City. The plan worked great—on paper.

Anyone tempted to try the experience can pull a virtual handcart at the National Historic Trails Center in Casper, or they could try their hand at the real thing, though unloaded, at the Mormon Handcart Visitors' Center where I was visiting that morning. I passed on both opportunities. After riding my bike for a thousand miles, I didn't need to tug on a cart to know it was difficult. It was already incomprehensible to me how anyone could have hauled a fully loaded, wooden handcart that distance, not to mention still having 450 miles to go. Even more so when the cart included the emotional and physical weight of a sick or injured loved one too weak to walk. Then again, Mormon emigrants had a lot riding on their hejira. The Mormon emigrants were seeking nothing less than sanctuary from their enemies and salvation for their souls. They weren't just emigrating to Utah; they were traveling to the Kingdom of God on Earth. It was an honor to be chosen to prove their devotion through trial and labor.

Five handcart companies were organized and emigrated in 1856. The first two reached the Salt Lake Valley by the end of September, and the third just one week later. The official church line was that for the first three companies the crossing was flawless, a demonstration of the efficacy of the idea and the power of faith. Unofficially, the crossing had taken a terrible physical toll on the emigrants. They made it but were much worse for the wear.

Even so, their trials paled compared to the experience of the last two companies, the Willie and Martin Handcart Companies. By the time the last of the handcart emigrants trailed into Salt Lake in November 1856, more than two hundred had died, representing 14 percent of the Willie Company and nearly a quarter of the Martin Company.

Like many such tragedies, the cause of the disaster wasn't one large mistake so much as a series of compounding incidents. Bad weather delayed the ships carrying the emigrants from England. The first group didn't reach Iowa City, the staging area for the trip across the plains, until mid-May when most emigrants were already crossing the Missouri River three hundred miles west. Once there the handcart emigrants found that the carts, which should have been waiting for them, had not yet been assembled. Due to the lateness of the season, the best wood had already been used. Instead of seasoned hickory and oak, the carts were assembled using whatever wood could be found, most of it green. Once the Mormons crossed out of the prairie and into the Great Plains, the drier climate shrunk the wood, warping the beds and loosening the spokes, causing breakdowns and more delays for repairs.

And there were the emigrants themselves. These weren't people used to the outdoor life on the American frontier. Most had never pitched a tent, slept on the ground, cooked outdoors, or built a campfire. They were "millhands and miners . . . the industrially dispossessed, the chronically unemployed, the widowed, the orphaned." They exhibited "starved cheeks, pale skins, bad teeth, thin chests, all the stigmata of unhealthy work and inadequate diet." It was the church's belief that life on the road would toughen them up, build their strength. That happened to some extent, but some children died in Iowa City while the handcarts were being built.

The Willie Handcart Company of five hundred emigrants started from Iowa City on July 15, nearly two weeks after overlanders strove to be at Independence Rock in order to beat the winter snow. The Martin Handcart Company set off a few days later, and both finally left Florence, Nebraska, on the west bank of the Platte River, by the end of August.

At Wood River, Nebraska, bison stampeded the Willie Company camp and took most of their cattle with them, leaving them without enough cattle to reserve for butchering, nor enough to pull all the wagons. They reached Fort Laramie, a popular reprovisioning post, on October 1, 1856. The emigration season had passed and the fort had no provisions to sell other than two barrels of crackers. Captain Willie cut rations. The emigrants, growing weaker, discarded many belongings here, including bedding and heavy clothing.

When they reached the next reprovisioning point at Independence Rock, all they found was a note from Franklin Richards, the organizer of the English migration, reporting that there would be no resupply until South Pass, another 150 miles away. Captain Willie further reduced rations down to an average of ten ounces of flour per day. At this point, the stronger members of the emigration, those who had been pulling the carts, started to die from exhaustion and malnutrition.

A couple of days later a carriage rode up to them from the east. It carried Joseph Young, Brigham's brother, who told the emigrants to take heart because supply wagons were on the way. Nevertheless, the Willie company stalled soon after, at the Sixth Crossing of the Sweetwater, unable to move any further. They ran out of flour that day. Captain Willie rode ahead to search for the rescue wagons. He found them about twenty-five miles west and guided them to the camp. Once again on the move, the Willie company crossed Rocky Ridge, a steep exposed climb, in a snowstorm. The next day at Willow Creek the company buried fifteen people who had died. By the time they finally made Salt Lake, the company had lost more than sixty people.

The Martin company suffered even more. At Deer Creek (near present-day Glenrock, Wyoming), they discarded excess clothing and bedding to save weight. Two days later, on October 19, 1856—the day the Willie company ran out of flour at Sixth Crossing—the Martin company forded the North Platte River at Bessemer Bend (twelve miles past the Last Crossing, near Casper, Wyoming) in flurries of snow and sleet, with floating mats of slush. Weather conditions then stalled them for nine days somewhere between Bessemer Bend and Independence Rock, during which fifty-six people died before rescuers could reach them.

In addition to the Willie and Martin companies, there were two ox trains with 385 more European emigrants bringing up the rear. By November 2, 1856, rescuers had them all gathered around a trader's cabin near Devil's Gate. Two days later, they moved to a circular wall of granite fronting the Sweetwater that provided some shelter and waited five days in temperatures as low as eighteen degrees below zero before pushing on. This area became known as Martin's Cove. The last of the handcart emigrants were brought into Salt Lake on November 30, 1856.

At the end of my tour, my guide pointed to a name on a plaque of those in the Martin Company who died and told me the woman was one of his ancestors. He talked about how people who came across in the handcart emigration had grit, then turned to me and said that taking on a ride like I was, I had grit, too. I corrected him. "No," I said, "I'm just stubborn."

I'd mentioned I wanted to see Devil's Gate, so he led me outside and pointed the way. Devil's Gate was one of the wonders of the trail for emigrants. It is a narrow, three-hundred-foot-deep chasm through a granite ridge. Emigrants wondered why the Sweetwater River worked its way through the rock instead of just going around. It didn't. About five million years ago the Sweetwater used to flow above the ridge on a bed of gravel and sand. Around that time, the rivers started washing away the gravel and sand to reveal the buried mountain ranges, slicing down through rock in the process during a geological event known as the Exhumation. Wagons could not negotiate through the cleft, and there was no reason to. There was a fine road around the south of the ridge. At fourteen miles, it was a day's travel from Independence Rock for the overlanders, and many camped here. As the two sides of the rift are stationary objects, overlanders carved their names in the rock. Others climbed to the top of the cleft to get the view from above.

The walk to view Devil's Gate was the most mosquito-infested fifteen minutes of my life to that point. The area is beautiful. The cliffs were quite striking, and the river meandered peacefully through them. But the mosquitoes were so voracious I pointed my phone, snapped a couple of pictures, then ran back toward the visitor center swatting mosquitoes off my legs and arms every step of the way. Back at the center I ran into the elder who'd greeted me that morning. When I complained about the mosquitoes, he told me they were worse at Sixth Crossing, the Mormon site where I'd meet up with Keith and Ann.

By the time I rolled out, it was approaching noon. I still had at least three hours of riding ahead of me to make Jeffery City, Wyoming. But I could hardly complain. I'd had a wonderful visit and some nice conversations with some very pleasant people. All in all, it had been a great morning.

CHAPTER TWENTY-SIX

Sixth Crossing

A FEW MILES PAST THE MORMON HANDCART VISITOR CENTER, I stopped at a monument to the Martin's Cove rescue. Soon after, the Pony Express Bikepacking Route turned off the nicely graded gravel road to cleave to the Emigrant Trail along the Sweetwater River. The markers were now concrete posts, roughly four inches square, standing about four feet high, and stamped with the names of the four National Historic trails: Oregon, California, Mormon Pioneer, and Pony Express.

The Emigrant Trail markers were sometimes close to the road, sometimes further away. In places, the swales and ruts created by the wagons were easily visible. At least I assume these were bona fide emigrant-era swales and ruts. A few days earlier, while I was in Casper, a friend had asked me how anyone could tell these tracks were *the* trail tracks. All I could suggest was that the claim was nondisconfirmable. There was no way to prove they weren't.

Up ahead was the next overland landmark, Split Rock. Like Devil's Gate, Split Rock is a cleft in the Granite Mountains, but less dramatic. It is more like a shallow "V." Some liken it to a gunsight. It was a useful landmark for the overlanders because it was easy to locate and steer by. The straight-line distance between Devil's Gate and Split Rock is about fifteen miles. The route along the trail was closer to twenty because it followed the course of the Sweetwater, partially to avoid a lot of badland in between. I would imagine a Pony Express rider could have made some time along here by cutting cross-country, one of the advantages of riding a horse as opposed to marshaling an ox team and wagon.

I passed a steel post marking Plant's (aka Plante) Pony Express Station. Nothing of note happened here during Pony Express days or during my ride, so I continued on. My pace had slowed considerably over the uneven, sandy ground, and pedaling became more taxing. Like the day before, I was constantly zigzagging across the two tracks of the path, trying to avoid the deepest sand while dodging between the Scylla of prickly pear and the Charybdis of mud and alkali pools. Multiple times I had to stop to open, pass through, then re-close a barbed-wire range fence.

But the ride wasn't unpleasant. The weather remained mild. It was wonderfully quiet. I enjoyed the solitude. Maybe my pleasant visit with the Mormons that morning had tempered my mood and tamped down my daily anxiety about making my destination by early afternoon, because as I rode along, I felt a glow of appreciation for my good fortune. It is a singular experience to ride next to a historical trail at somewhere between ox-drawn wagon speed and Pony Express horseback speed over a barely visible track through an ocean of sagebrush accompanied only by the sound of the wind in your ears and the thoughts in your head. I felt fortunate to be able to do so physically, financially, and emotionally.

The trail eventually let out onto Turkey Track Road, which was a prime example of the disparity between Wyoming's paved and unpaved roads. The paved roads are first rate. Every highway I rode had some of the smoothest pavement I've ridden anywhere and most had ample shoulders. But the graded gravel roads were rough, the surface often washboarded, as bumpy as a corrugated tin roof. They were the first roads I had to go full-squish—opening up my bike's front and rear suspension all the way—to keep my teeth from rattling out. Even with full suspension, Turkey Track Road wore on my nerves.

A Word on Suspension

My mountain bike had three suspension settings: full suspension, partial, and lock-out (or no suspension). Most of the time I rode with my rear suspension locked out and the front suspension on partial. This took care of most of the bumps in the road. My oversized, low-pressure knobby tires took care of the rest. But heavily washboarded gravel like Turkey Track Road is its own special hell. I happily traded the loss of speed and efficiency of open suspension to avoid the constant jarring of the bumpy road.

Eventually the road devolved again to sandy two-track with a median of wild grass, prickly pear, and long patches of alkali puddles filling the ruts. At one point I passed through a fence clearly marking the area as private property. I stopped and read the sign and found this was another part of the Pathfinder Ranches, which had already given me permission to cross their lands. Truthfully, I probably would have continued regardless of permission. It was miles to retrace my route to go around. And as it turned out, I didn't come across a person or a vehicle until miles later when I was back on the highway into Jeffery City.

I rounded a series of bluffs and from that point Split Rock was always in view, which meant I was nearing the end of the dirt trail. The closer I came to the highway, however, the further away it felt. A sure sign of fatigue. The air was pristine, and in the limpid light it seemed like I could make out each tiny crevice in the rocky hills. On maps and in descriptions, I'd come across three different names for the surrounding mountains: Granite Mountains, Sweetwater Rocks, and Rattlesnake Range. I don't know which is correct, but I think they all give some sense of their desolate beauty. The trail left the river and became rougher. I started climbing sandy hills and negotiating steep, rocky descents, all the time trying to take in the breathtaking desert mountain scenery. By this point I was absolutely schizophrenic. One half of my brain drank in the gorgeous solitude of the desert and mountains while the other half could not wait to reach the highway and know that this trail was not a dead end I would have to retrace.

Not long after, the trail met the highway and once again I was whistling along on smooth pavement while cars and trucks and RVs streamed past. "Whistling" might be an exaggeration. Away from the shelter of the hills, I was once again bucking a Wyoming headwind, so my progress was slow. I came across a pullout with a Split Rock memorial, which noted the landmark's importance and the existence of a Pony Express station nearby.

A couple more highway hours finally brought me to Jeffery City, Wyoming. There is not much there. In fact, it's often described as a ghost town. The town started when a couple took over an abandoned homestead in 1931 and named it Home on the Range. The little town experienced boom times from the late 1950s, when uranium was discovered nearby, until 1983 when the bottom fell out of the market. In that year, the Jeffery City National Bank closed and the *Jeffery City News* stopped publishing. There was so little life left even the ministers left town.

But reports of Jeffery City's demise are premature. Around thirty people still live there, and I saw three working businesses—Green Mountain Motel, Split Rock Café, and Monk King Bird Pottery, which occupied an abandoned gas station across the highway—and was happy to patronize two of them. I'd also read that somewhere nearby was a church that ran a cycling hostel in the basement. The highway through town, US 287, is part of the Trans-America Bicycle Trail. Though I didn't see any cyclists, a couple of people I spoke with said riders came through all the time. Many stayed at the hostel. Apparently, they also came for Split Rock Café's plate-sized pancakes.

I had planned to stay at the hostel but wasn't able to contact anyone there to make sure it was open. Instead, I stayed at the Green Mountain Motel, right off US 287. It was a very low-key motel of modular units and a gravel lot, with an owner named Lisa and a dog named Tuffy who loved to have his tummy rubbed. I may have been the only guest. While I was checking in, I told Lisa I'd like to wash some things and asked whether she'd mind if I hung some laundry outside to dry. She offered to wash them for me. Jeffrey City, Wyoming instantly became my favorite spot on the Pony Express Trail.

Actually, the town sits a mile and a half south of a section of the trail known as Three Crossings for reasons you can probably surmise. A Pony Express station was located there. Overlanders could avoid the crossings by taking the Deep Sand Route that ran south of the narrows and closer to the current site of Jeffrey City. Either route would have been a chore.

I slept in the next morning because the day's ride would be my shortest yet, about twenty miles. I was only riding as far as Sixth Crossing Visitors'

Center, where I would stay with Keith and Ann. Lisa (the motel owner) came to see me off and wished me safe travels. I told her I was going to stop by Split Rock Café for breakfast, so she said she'd notify the owner. Small town.

I finally got going around 9:00 a.m. The sky was clear, the wind moderate, and knowing I only had a two- or three-hour ride that morning, I rolled out at an easy pace on the shoulder of the highway with very light traffic. It was a pleasant start to the day.

My first hour of riding was on the highway. Just before the turnoff to the dirt trail, I came to Ice Slough (or Icy Slough), another spot heavily commented on in emigrant diaries. Emigrants found ice below the surface even in midsummer, which provided a nice diversion from the monotony of the trail. There was a stagecoach station here, though no one identifies it specifically as a Pony Express station.

Ice Slough was now private property. Also, I didn't have a spade, so I couldn't go down to check it for myself. But after riding through this area, I felt I had a better idea why spots like this were such a big deal. Plodding along at a pace of about two miles per hour, days on end, weeks on end, months on end, staring at the sky and the sagebrush and often nothing more entertaining than ox butts, you would look forward to something, *anything*, to break the monotony. It must have been such a relief from so much tedium. So yeah, take a break to dig down and find ice when it's hot outside? Absolutely.

I turned off the highway here to follow the Pony Express Route, passed through another range gate, and set off down a nice two-track running south until it disappeared into the Green Mountains. I'd followed a lot of this type of trail when scouting the route in Nevada, and every time I saw a thread of road winding off to the horizon, I got a little intimidated, but I got a little excited, too. It struck me that if a view like that doesn't excite you, then the Pony Express Bikepacking Route should probably not be your ride of choice. It may be that a healthy dose of intimidation is, well, healthy. But if that line doesn't draw you forward, you'd be better off riding somewhere else.

While I was musing on these thoughts, my GPS sounded an "off-course" alarm. I turned around and retraced my route to a point where I should have turned, wondering how I missed the trail. When I arrived, I realized I had missed the trail because there was no trail to see. My map showed the Pony Express Route running perpendicular to the two-track I was on, straight up a hill. After a few minutes of searching, I saw an unpainted concrete-post Emigrant Trail marker at the top of the rise, cleverly designed to be invisible against the gray-green ground cover.

Directions

The app I was using had the option of giving audible directions on streets and highways. But to get directions on a trail, I would have had to enter waypoints and turning directions manually ahead of time, which I did not think to do. Also, I usually ran with the screen turned off to save battery power. The off-course warning often saved me from wandering too far in the wrong direction when I rode the more remote parts of the trail.

At this point I did what I had done many times on this trip. Curse Jan Bennett, the person who mapped the Pony Express Bikepacking Route. *Why in the blankety-blank did they map the route on this blankety-blank trail when there's a blankety-blank highway right blankety-blank here?* Words to that effect anyway. Then I did what I always do next: I started on the trail thinking I'd give it a quarter mile and if it got too hard to follow, I'd turn around.

I struggled up the hill to the marker and found a more definite trail heading west from there. The trail got better and worse, as these trails do, but it continued. In time it led to a steel post marking the site of the Warm Springs Pony Express Station. The marker stood next to a marshy area, which I took to be Warm Springs.

A little before noon I arrived at the Sixth Crossing: Mormon Trail Site Visitors' Center on the eastern edge of a tiny hamlet called Sweetwater Station. The building looks like a ski chalet and at first I thought I had stumbled on the vacation home of some Californian who'd bought property here for a summer house. But no, it was the right place. Waiting inside to greet me (or anyone who wandered in through the doors), was Sister Cook, whom I knew as Ann of the Da Vinci tandem.

Prior to June 2020, this development was known as "Mormon Handcart Historic Site: Willie Center at Sixth Crossing." The LDS changed the name, along with others, ostensibly to make it clearer to non-Mormons that the renamed sites had historic significance to the greater community outside the LDS.

The Sixth Crossing of the Sweetwater was where the Willie Handcart Company stalled, and where the first rescue wagons, guided by Captain Willie who'd gone searching for them, reached the emigrants. It is now revered as something of a sacred site by the Mormons for the hardship endured by the company, the faith that sustained them, and the rescue that saved them. Every summer, fifteen to twenty thousand Mormon youths come to centers like this, including Martin's Cove behind me and Rock Creek Hollow a day's ride west, to camp and reenact the handcart migration.

The visitor center sits on a rise above a turn in the Sweetwater River and has a commanding view up the river for some distance. The Sweetwater here is a beautiful, serpentine ribbon coiling back on itself amid lush, deep green bottomlands surrounded by sand and sage. There is a camping area spread into one of the bends in the river just below the center. Normally it would be filled with teens who would have come to participate in a handcart reenactment, but as there were no reenactments that year due to COVID, it was empty. In a normal year, I might have camped there, too. At that moment, still scratching bites from mosquitoes at Devil's Gate, I was content to enjoy the view from afar and thankful not to be looking forward to facing off hordes of blood-sucking insects.

I had conflicting reactions to learning that Mormon teens in period dress push replica handcarts along portions of the Mormon Pioneer Trail. Certainly it is one way to honor one's ancestors, a way to connect with their past. To the extent the Mormon hierarchy saw handcart emigration as a test of worthiness for the European Mormon emigrants, it could also be seen as similar rite of passage for modern Mormons. At the same time, some have accused the church of covering up the fatal mismanagement of the Willie and Martin Company emigration under blankets of denial, obfuscation, and piety. Brigham Young deflected criticism of the First Presidency of the church by finding a scapegoat in Franklin Richards, the man nominally in charge of the 1856 European emigration. In this sense, reenactments could be seen as part of an effort to buttress church orthodoxy. Maybe the point is simpler. As one of the sisters explained to me, in her view the handcart reenactment teaches teens that they have the strength to overcome a daunting challenge.

I pictured myself telling my son, Kazu, I had signed him up for a handcart camp. I had to laugh because I knew his reaction would be to smile his beatific teenage smile and say, "There's no way," and that would be the end of that discussion. I guess neither of us would make good Mormons. Nevertheless, though I am sure thousands of devout Mormon teens were let down when they heard this summer's camps weren't going to happen, I have to believe there were at least some who whispered fervent prayers of thanks.

A little while later Keith made it up to the center and we shook hands and looked at each other, much as Ann and I did, with absolutely no facial recognition taking place for either of us. But the warmth of our communications since I'd reached out six or so weeks earlier was enough to preclude any awkwardness. I felt instantly, unconditionally welcome.

After lunch, we moved my bike down to the center's garage. And in a sense, this was when the fun began. There were eight volunteers (four couples) at the center that summer—normally they have fourteen couples—and all of them were cyclists to some extent. The garage area had a spotless concrete floor and a handful of high-end mountain bikes, each of which had its own stand and seemed to be perfectly maintained. There was a bike work-stand, tools, pumps, trainers—it looked like a bike shop showroom. And the words Keith had been writing finally made sense to me: Everyone is looking forward to your visit. Because, yes, they all loved riding, and with me there they would have an excuse to take a little off-road bike tour. There is nothing a cyclist likes more than to show off their local riding ground to a newbie.

My dirty bike and dusty trailer stowed, we got into a side-by-side (a high-clearance Off-Highway Vehicle, or OHV) to tour some local historic trail sites. We first went south of the emigrant trail I had come in on to a historical marker for the Seminoe Cutoff. This cutoff avoided the last four crossings of the Sweetwater, as well as the brutal climb over Rocky Ridge, and saved a day of travel. On the other hand, it left the river, so there was less water available. Freighters preferred this route because it was easier, but the lack of water kept it from becoming an important cutoff for the overland emigration. Fort Seminoe, by the way, was the trading post located near Devil's Gate where the Martin Hand-cart Company huddled before being shunted to the better protection of Martin's Cove. The fort and the cutoff were both named, in a roundabout way, for Charles Lajeunesse.

We then visited a few other sites before zipping back to the visitor center. A higher-up from the church was visiting that evening and the volunteers were going to have a meeting, so we ate dinner early and I stayed downstairs in the apartment to write while they all did their thing.

Afterward, Keith asked if I'd be willing to talk to the volunteers, so I went up to meet those whom I hadn't yet and answer their questions about my ride. The Q and A session soon segued into making plans for the next day's ride. I bowed out of that discussion because it was all about duties and who could cover for whom and what needed to be done when. They worked it out among themselves in a way that seemed very familiar to them as a group. It was fun watching them go at the work assignment issues almost playfully as they tried to figure everything out and be fair to each other. It was also interesting to listen to them address each other (even spouses) as "Elder" and "Sister."

Then came sleeping arrangements. The Cooks had a trailer I could use. But due to COVID, the church allowed only family to stay on church property. Keith came upon the idea of moving their trailer to Bureau of Land Management (BLM) land near the church property. At some point while we were enjoying root beer floats, the guys all disappeared. They'd gone to hitch up the trailer and move it to a patch of BLM land about a quarter mile from the visitor center. Issue solved. Keith ran me and my huge bag of gear out there in the side-by-side, and that was pretty much it for the day.

Except for something I skipped. At one point during the Q and A session, someone asked me about the most meaningful part of the trip so far. I told them without hesitation it was the kindness of people who had helped me along the way, including them. After which I broke down and cried in front of the entire group.

What got to me was the open-handed welcomeness I felt. The folks here seemed genuinely happy to have me there, to be honestly interested in my trip, to want to join our next-day's mountain bike ride or support it however it worked best for everyone concerned. It would be easy to write off my presence as a welcome distraction from routine—like coming across Ice Slough in the middle of the Wyoming high desert—but it felt deeper than that. I felt taken care of, and that is no small thing under any circumstances. It felt even more special in that arid, forbidding, sparsely populated section of the world that I came close to avoiding on this trip.

CHAPTER TWENTY-SEVEN

Sufficient unto the Day

SOMETIME BEFORE DAWN THE NEXT MORNING I WAS WOKEN BY WIND intense enough to rock the trailer, then the sound of rain. I thought we might have to cancel the day's ride and I would end up spending a second night there, which, all things considered, was not a bad option. A day off sounded nice, and there was a bookstore in Sweetwater Station, the tiny town near the visitor center, I wanted to check out.

But when I rose a little while later, the weather system turned out to have been more noisy than wet, just a passing squall that had already moved on. Instead of rain I was greeted by a rainbow and clearing skies in the west, auguries of the day ahead. Keith picked me up at 7:00 a.m. and we rode back to the Sixth Crossing: Mormon Trail Site Visitor Center for breakfast.

The volunteers all met at 8:30 a.m. down at the bike barn (which was how I thought of the equipment building). While they met, I went about my daily bike maintenance duties (lube, reinflating tires, visual inspection), topped off water, loaded snacks and extra clothing, etc. Our destination for the ride that day was Rock Creek Hollow, another significant area on the Mormon Emigrant Trail, and also home to another Mormon handcart reenactment camp. The volunteers had some maintenance work to do there, and still had to staff the Sixth Crossing Visitor Center that day, so they hashed out a rather complex plan for the ride involving two trucks, a lot of driving (given the paucity of roads in the area), and—be still my heart—trucking my bike trailer to the end of the day's ride so I could ride unencumbered.

Four of us (all guys; two women riders were shuttled ahead to ride the upper section) left the center on bikes. I am tempted to say that once we were rolling I felt as if my companions changed from church elders to ordinary mountain bike riders, but that isn't exactly true. One elder told me I was perfectly welcome to call him by his first name when he didn't have his name tag on, but the interactions among us didn't change. They continued to call each other "elder." Every time we came to a range gate, they took turns, usually without discussion, and worked the gate in a practiced fashion: One rider would dismount; another would hold his bike while he opened the gate; we'd ride through, everyone thanking the gatekeeper, who would then re-latch the gate and take his bike back, thanking the holder. There was nothing formal about it; this was just their routine. But it had the same air of cooperation and mutual respect that seemed to color every interaction.

I don't mean to make too much of this. After all, it was a small thing; any group of riders would work out something similar. It was the way they went about it, respectfully, without any ego, something rare in most gatherings of men. Keith is as hardcore as any rider I know. He is a California Triple Crown Hall of Fame cyclist, which means he has ridden fifty or more double centuries—two-hundred-mile rides—some, including his fiftieth, with Ann on the Da Vinci. And Barrie, another rider, was the ultimate sandbagger. He walked with a little hunch in his back and a hitch in his step and carried a perpetual "aw-shucks" smile, but he left everyone in the dust up every hill, the whole time talking about what a powerhouse rider Keith was.

Through most of my ride from Missouri to Utah I was glad to be riding alone. I wouldn't have wanted to drag someone through a lot of the territory I crossed. I also would have hated to know someone was waiting for me ahead, or have to worry about someone lagging behind. Being free of those concerns allowed me to be more present in the here and now of whatever I was experiencing. But riding with these guys made me realize how much I missed the camaraderie of riding with a group, an aspect of cycling that makes it genuinely fun.

The first part of our ride was through private land (with permission) along the Sweetwater River. At every turn I wanted to stop and take pictures. There was something so peaceful about the silent blue river swaddled in the rich bottomland of a deep green valley, especially after three days of riding across high desert. I kept saying aloud how amazingly beautiful the trail was. As if my fellow riders didn't already know.

But while the river valley was unquestionably beautiful, there was a different reason for my gushing reaction. I was looking at the Sweetwater from the perspective of the overland emigrants, and in that light it seemed to me the very idyll of emigration, the easy times, the kind of scene that would motivate someone to emigrate, the mirage that it would all be like this. The Sweetwater had an abundance of everything the emigrants hoped for in a night's camp: clear water, fodder for the animals, a gentle grade, and flat ground to sleep on. This was the emigrant trail I was expecting to see along the Little Blue River way back in Kansas, the river the emigrant diaries described in such glowing prose. Bernard De Voto summed up the fondness emigrants felt for that section of the trail by writing, "This is what the grandfathers remembered when they told us stories." But the Little Blue I saw lay in a dry, dusty country, all farmed, hidden on private land, not easily reached, and even then, nothing like the emigrants' descriptions. At the Sweetwater I felt I caught of glimpse of the enchantment I had missed earlier.

At the same time, while the Sweetwater represented such an idealistic picture for me, by the time the emigrants got this far few were laughing or singing or maybe even talking much at all. They'd been on the trail two months or more and were not yet halfway to the West Coast. They'd probably had to bury a family member and then driven their wagon over the grave to try to erase any sign of it. If they were in the Willie or Martin Handcart Companies, they were starving and freezing and hanging on for dear life. So, while there are descriptions of the Sweetwater as a good river, with drinkable water and plentiful forage, you do not hear about quilting, or debate societies, or children playing as they did back on the Little Blue. You don't really read about the good times on the Emigrant Trail in western Wyoming.

We came to a marker for St. Mary's Station, also known as Rocky Ridge Station. The marker is an unassuming, roughly hewn granite post about ten inches square and standing about three feet tall, engraved with

"Old Oregon Trail," the name of the station, and "1913," the year the monument was erected. This is where Mark Twain, on his way west with his brother as a young man, met Jack Slade, the division superintendent for the California Overland and Pike's Peak Express Company (which ran the Pony Express) in August 1861.

A short while after, we came to the most challenging part of the ride, the climb up Rocky Ridge. Overland emigrants were forced away from the Sweetwater here because the river carves an impassible gorge through the rock. It's been called the hardest pull along the 1,300-mile Mormon Pioneer Trail from Iowa City to Salt Lake City, and was "legendary as one of the most punishing climbs of the Oregon Trail." The climb is best described as "an abrupt seven-hundred-foot rise over an ascending staircase of gravel and brown shale." The elevation at the top of the ridge is 7,300 feet, just a hundred feet lower than South Pass. Emigrants sometimes had to help push their wagons over the boulders one wheel at a time.

In other words, Rocky Ridge was the kind of challenge mountain bikers live for.

Which is not to make light of the suffering of the handcart emigrants who labored up the ridge in a snowstorm. There are monuments to the handcart emigration at the bottom of the climb and the top of Rocky Ridge. The monument at the bottom, titled "Willie Rescue Site," tells how it took twenty-seven hours for the Willie Handcart Company to ascend Rocky Ridge and struggle into Rock Creek Hollow, a distance of only fifteen miles. The monument at the top of the climb calls this area the Trail of Blood. The Willie Company buried fifteen people the day after they climbed Rocky Ridge, a testament to the strain the climb had put on the exhausted, underfed, and underclothed Mormon emigrants.

I knew I was in trouble on this climb when I found myself out of breath just getting to the lower monument from the Sweetwater River. In my defense, the lower monument is close to seven thousand feet elevation, and the approach from the river had grades over 13 percent in places. But if the climb to the base of the climb was this hard, I wondered how bad the rest would be. One of the trucks from the Sixth Crossing was waiting for us there, so we took a break to refill water and get a snack.

Keith and I visited the monument plaque. After, we stood for a moment taking in the sweeping landscape around us, glorious on a bright summer day, and talked about what it must have been like to walk in the Willie Company's footsteps in a blinding snowstorm.

Break time over, three of us continued the climb to the upper monument. Keith and Barry zipped up like they were on electric bikes. Me, not so much. I would have had to walk parts of the climb if I had been pulling a trailer. As it was, Keith waited for me about halfway up. He pointed out the dirt road leading up to the lower monument and traced a dirt trail loop to the top of the ridge and back down. He told me the loop was six miles, and that it was used for the handcart reenactments. Before my comment filter could kick in, I shook my head and said, "You have a brutal religion."

Keith laughed. "Can I quote you?"

We rode on to the upper monument, which sits just below the top of the ridge. Keith was stopped there, so I stopped as well, thankful because I would have embarrassed myself trying to ride over the rocky ledges on the trail. This way, I had an excuse to walk the final few yards to the top.

Rocky Ridge surmounted, we continued on. We were rolling through rangeland now. Beautiful, open country. The Emigrant Trail did not follow the Sweetwater through this section, and in fact, only touched the river again to cross it one last time at the Ninth Crossing. We passed by Lewiston Lakes and rode by the abandoned Gillespie Ranch buildings by Radium Springs, which reportedly provided a place for "sexual favors" to local miners in the 1870s. It was a pleasant ride with pleasant company. That is, until we came to Strawberry Creek. The creek cut the trail, ballooning into a wider pool where it crossed, and for the first time on my trip, there was no bridge.

Barrie went through first. He built up a head of steam and coasted through, lifting his feet off the pedals. He almost made it, too. At the very end, he had to pedal. But it didn't look that bad. I did not get as much speed up, so I got bogged down in the middle and nearly stopped. I pedaled the rest of the way through, but my feet were soaked. We forded two more creeks and some soggy bottomland before arriving at Rock Creek Hollow. I crossed these more successfully, but by that time it didn't matter. Mountain bike shoes and wool socks stay wet for a very long time. Overnight, in fact, as I was about to learn.

Rock Creek Hollow is a large flat area surrounded by low hills, purchased by the Mormons in 1992. The campground is built on tailings from a 1930s dredging operation. Like Sixth Crossing, it is a Mormon campground that normally houses handcart reenactment camps during the summer; like Sixth Crossing, the campground at Rock Creek Hollow was closed that summer due to COVID. Both trucks were waiting when we arrived. There were seven of us total. It was around two in the afternoon, and it looked like it might rain. Someone decided lunch would be nice, so we drove over to Atlantic City, Wyoming.

Pause here and look for that town on a map. It's a tiny dot serviced by dirt roads about eight miles up Rock Creek from Rock Creek Hollow. The town has a number of historical buildings, mostly one-room cabins, many of them marked by historical plaques. The town sits on the Continental Divide Trail, so through-hikers and bikepackers who are trekking the three-thousand-mile trail from Canada to Mexico come in to eat at the Miner's Grubstake, a restaurant/bar/small general store where we ate as well. There were four young bikepackers there, two couples who looked to be in their twenties. It was hard to tell for sure because they were all face down in their plates, shoveling food into their mouths as quickly as they could. I would have asked them about their ride, but I didn't want to interrupt. I knew how they felt.

After lunch, one truck headed back to Sixth Crossing while Barrie and Keith drove me back to Rock Creek Hollow. With nothing left to do, it was time for goodbyes. We weren't particularly maudlin about it, but Keith said he felt like he was deserting me by leaving me in an empty campground. I think he felt even worse because he had no authority to give me permission to camp there. I thanked him for everything and told him not to worry, I'd be fine.

And there I was. Alone again after so much interaction, the camp seemed very, very quiet. But afternoon was fading and I had things to do.

Though I did not have permission to stay, I was, after all, standing in a campground. I decided so long as no one was around, I might as well find a quiet spot where no one would notice me. I moved my bike and trailer to the back end of a parking lot near the restrooms where I was immediately set on by the entire mosquito population of central Wyoming. In the mosquitoes' defense, they were used to hundreds of kids being shipped in every day to feed on, and they must have felt neglected. But it was bad. I sprayed myself, which kept them from landing on me, but they still hovered incessantly around me, mostly in my face. The only way to escape was to stand in the middle of the road that passed through the camp where enough breeze whisked through to keep the nano-vampires away.

Mosquitoes, like sandy roads, axle-burying mud bogs, and hills so steep they required double-teaming the oxen to get the wagons up and over, were aspects of the overland emigration about which I'd read plenty but dismissed as problems for the emigrants, not me. Wrong again. Emigrant accounts of mosquitoes are legion. A swarm was said to be able to cover an entire horse in a few minutes. My experiences at Devil's Gate and Rock Creek Hollow suggested this was not an exaggeration, then or now.

The area was beautiful. It's a small depression surrounded by low hills, with clear, willow-lined Rock Creek flowing through it. Off to the northwest was the snowcapped Wind River Range, which astounded emigrants who'd never seen snow in summer. I do not think Rock Creek Hollow would provide much shelter from winter weather, but on this warm afternoon it felt cozy, like a nook, a small oasis in the sagebrush desert.

Keith had urged me to walk the grounds to visit the gravesites and read the plaques. I thought paying heed to this part of church history that was so important to him and all the other volunteers I'd met was the least I could do to thank them. There was a monument erected in 1933 for the fifteen Willie Handcart Company emigrants who died after the climb over Rocky Ridge and were buried somewhere in this area. There was another monument to the Second Rescue, also referred to as the spiritual rescue of the Willie and Martin handcart emigrants, an effort by modern-day Mormons to complete temple work on behalf of the handcart emigrants buried along the trail so the deceased could enjoy the full benefits of the afterlife. With no one there but me, and possibly the spirits of the dead, it was a very peaceful walk.

Except for the mosquitoes. As evening fell, I cooked dinner out by the road to take advantage of the breeze, then set my tent up in record time, and once done, dove in. If I weren't already tired, I probably could have counted mosquitoes on the mesh netting in place of sheep. Instead, I listened to their humming along with the lowing of some cattle nearby.

I drifted off thinking I'd just had the best day of the trip. So much joy, it seemed, packed into such a short amount of time. I was thankful for the efforts of the Mormon missionaries who had done so much to take care of me since I'd arrived at Devil's Gate two days earlier. I felt blessed in the sense that I had done nothing to earn the blessings so freely given.

I had no idea what the next day had in store for me. The highlights were Burnt Ranch, the last crossing of the Sweetwater River, and crossing the Continental Divide at South Pass. But other than those landmarks, there was nothing but open desert between me and Farson, Wyoming, about fifty miles west. I hadn't checked the weather, or the terrain, and had no idea where I'd stay. I hadn't worried about it all day, and I tried not to let it keep me up that night. Instead, I thought about a passage from the Sermon on the Mount: "Take therefore no thought for the morrow: for the morrow shall take thought for the things of itself. Sufficient unto the day is the evil thereof." Sound wisdom. As proof, here was this perfect day that was handed to me almost in spite of all my preparation and planning and worry. Tonight, it was enough to appreciate the day I'd had. There would be plenty of time to worry about tomorrow when I awoke.

CHAPTER TWENTY-EIGHT
Burnt Ranch

I WAS RIGHT NOT TO WORRY. THE NEXT DAY HAD ITS FULL MEASURE OF evil and worrying about it the night before would have only robbed me of the rest I needed to get through it while doing nothing to ameliorate the evil thereof, biblically speaking.

Things started off on a bad foot less than one hundred yards into the day's ride when I rolled off the trail and into soft sand on the ridiculously steep climb out of Rock Creek Hollow. I had to push the bike and trailer to the top of the grade. Not the end of the world, but in retrospect, a harbinger of bad times ahead. Once out of the hollow I was into the wind. This was not a gentle morning breeze or a light stirring only to freshen later in the day. It was a thirteen-knot headwind at 8:00 a.m. and I couldn't see any reason it would drop any lower.

This first short section crossed the divide between Rock Creek and Willow Creek along the northern edge of Wyoming's Red Desert, the desolate area the rancher back in Casper had warned me about. It is a high-elevation basin with long winters, hot and dry summers, and persistent winds. The kind of area where the climate is so harsh no plant can grow more than a foot tall. Bonsai sagebrush as far as the eye could see. The steppes of central Wyoming.

Wyoming has more sagebrush than any other state. Estimates vary from 23.5 million acres to approximately 37 million acres. Sagebrush has an allure to some. Mark Twain called it "an imposing monarch of the forest in exquisite miniature," and waxed poetic about how sagebrush made "a very sociable camp-fire." His contemporary Richard Burton, on the other hand, took time out at Cottonwood Station (back near Kearney, Nebraska) to describe "this hideous growth, which is to weary our eyes as far as central valleys of the Sierra Nevada." For the early emigrants who had no actual trail to follow, sagebrush and greasewood were difficult obstacles. It tired the lead oxen to tromp over it all day to the point that teams needed to be rotated, with the lead team one day being the last on the next.

My impression of the Red Desert across this short divide was that the land was empty, which is not to say barren. It supported an abundance of life, from pronghorns and jackrabbits to sagebrush, greasewood, prickly pear, bunch grass, cheat grass, and probably a thousand other things undetected and unappreciated to my untrained eye. Rather, the divide was empty in the sense that it was featureless. There were no landmarks, nothing to entertain the eye. Sand, rock, and sagebrush blanketed a rolling terrain veined with gullies extending to the horizon in every direction.

And that was just the first mile.

When my trail crossed Riverview Cutoff a short time later, I had a decision to make. The Emigrant Trail ran straight through Burnt Ranch, which is privately owned. The Pony Express Bikepacking Route turned left to take Riverview Cutoff around the private property. I had written to the owner of the ranch and received permission to cross his land, so if I wanted, I could continue along the old Emigrant Trail. The question was, should I stick with the bikepacking route, which followed a graded gravel road around the ranch, or stay on the sketchy two-track I'd been riding and take the road less accessible? The wind was up and it was going to be a long, hot ride to Farson, Wyoming, my destination for the day. I was tempted to take the relatively faster, easier road.

On the other hand, Burnt Ranch had a lot of history centered on a cluster of buildings that lay along the Sweetwater River at the Ninth (and final) Crossing of the Sweetwater. During the overland emigration period the area included a Pony Express station, a trading post, a military fort, and a short-lived Mormon station. It was something of a privilege to visit the site; not everyone gets permission. I decided to stick to the trail.

Worst decision of the entire ride.

I crossed Riverview Cutoff and passed through a range gate on the other side. Willow Creek crossed the trail a little further on. But whereas Rock Creek ran swiftly through a well-defined channel, Willow Creek was more of the meandering type, and in its lazy wanderings had spread out to cover a wide swath of ground. The creek was not bridged, so I would have to ford it or turn around. I'd forded three creeks the day before. I was a pro. And this crossing wasn't very wide and didn't look too deep, so I moved ahead.

As I got closer, I noticed the fenced area I had entered wasn't open rangeland, but a narrow corridor maybe twenty yards wide by two hundred yards long. It was fenced on both sides, gated front and back, and filled with about two dozen cows milling about, mooing their displeasure at my presence. Now, here's the thing about cattle and water and small spaces. Water from the creek, augmented by recent rains, seeps into the surrounding ground, saturating it. Cows are heavy. When they go to the water to drink or to cross the stream, they sink into the soft, wet land. The result was a landscape of three-foot tall mounds, like bales of hay with a maze of cow tracks weaving among them. A *mauvaises terres* in miniature, accented by cow poop.

While I might have been able to negotiate the labyrinth of cow-defiled paths among the mounds if I had only my bike, it was impossible with a trailer. I unhooked the trailer, carried my bike to the last firm piece of ground before the creek, then went back and carried my gear-laden trailer and hooked it back up. In the wind, of course, because it was windy even here. I got everything lined up, then pedaled through the creek without getting anything wet, other than my wheels. Not too muddy; not so bad. Once across and on solid enough ground I unhooked the trailer again and carried the bike and trailer past the poop-besmirched maze of cow-mounds on the far bank and hooked it all up again.

Only to ride thirty feet and find that there was another branch of the creek to cross. I had not seen it earlier because this was rising ground and the undulation of the land hid what lay at the bottom of the rises. Where I expected to find a depression, I found instead another unbridged branch of the creek. At that point the smart thing to do would have been to turn around and, tail between my legs, retreat to the bikepacking route as mapped. But this branch of the creek didn't look too bad either, and I didn't want to carry the trailer back over what I had just worked so hard to get across.

Same drill. Sweating now from the effort. But I got across, hooked up, and rolled uphill toward where the cows had migrated, only to find that there was a third branch. Cussing ensued. It got worse when I saw this was not so much a creek crossing as a cow wallow. The creek pooled here, making it deeper and wider than the last two crossings. Plus, the little herd of cows had just crossed to get away from me, leaving who knew what in the murky water. The mud was squishy a good distance back from the bank, so I couldn't start from the water's edge on the bike like the last two crossings; I would only get mired before I got to the water. The pool was too deep to ride cross anyway. I would soak my shoes and the trailer, with all my gear, food, and bedding.

I walked back and forth across that twenty-yard space for ten minutes trying to find another way across. The fences on either side were strung with barbed wire and what looked like electric fence. I'd heard that once cattle touch an electric fence, you can turn it off because they'll respect it. I tested the top wire. *ZZZTTT!* That one was live, and a lot more of a shock than I'd expected. I walked the length of the wallow again and came back to the same place. Seems I'd read that only one wire was live, so I wonder if this bottom—*ZZZTTT!* Nope, it was live, too.

I finally concluded that the only way to cross was to take my shoes off and carry everything through the wallow. At this point I was less than a mile from the Pony Express Backpacking Trail. I'd have had to carry my gear and recross two branches of Willow Creek, but I could be back and on my way in twenty minutes or so. Or I could get across this wallow and keep going where so few are lucky enough to ride. The thought of going back was worse than the thought of going forward, so I took off my shoes and socks (noting the amount of poop on the soles of my shoes), and carried my gear in two trips across this disgusting little cow wallow, sinking calf-deep in the mud, knee-deep in murky water, and then through yet another poopy maze of cow tracks on the other side.

It could have been worse. Overland emigrants who ran out of water crossing dry stretches on the prairie actually *drank* out of buffalo wallows.

But this was as close as I wanted to get to reliving that particular feature of the overland emigrant experience.

By the time I dried my feet, reshod, and had the trailer hooked up and ready to go, the cattle were all huddled around the gate at the top of the hill. The gate I needed to get through. The rancher had told me to make sure to close all gates I opened, and with the cows there, I pictured them charging through the gate as soon as I opened it. I rode my bike directly at the cattle, yelling at them like a madman the entire time to get out of my way. To my great relief, they did.

All told it took me forty minutes to make that first mile after crossing onto the ranch, a huge waste of time so early in a long day's ride. The ride from there to Burnt Ranch was straightforward, if strenuous. Hills and valleys, soft sand, sharp rocks, prickly pear, and all the time wind, sometimes steady, sometimes gusting, always against me. But this was the Pony Express Trail, or so the concrete posts along the way told me. The Oregon, California, and Mormon Pioneer Trails. This was the trail I had set out to ride. In moments when I was thinking how difficult it was on a bike, I imagined how much more difficult it would have been for the overland emigrants walking in the heat while whacking oxen, or for handcart emigrants starving and huddled against the bitter cold with the remainder of their worldly possessions. I also thought about being the unfortunate Pony Express rider on this stretch, and what a dreary route this would be to have as your back-and-forth run. Especially in winter.

Many people who write about the Pony Express themselves express a sadness, a poignancy at its passing. They talk, for instance, about the "thankless dismissal of a faithful friend." All I have to say to that is good riddance. What an utter waste of so many lives and so many resources. The messages the Pony carried were essentially telegrams, notes on tissue paper to save weight, and sent mostly between businesses because the average person could not afford its rates. Two-thirds of the mail delivered by the Pony Express was sent by newspapers, and even then, only a few California papers could afford the service. With the invention of the telegraph, messages could be sent in minutes instead of ten days or more, without the need for scores of riders and station keepers, hundreds of horses, mountains of feed, or water that sometimes had to be carted to remote stations in the desert. The Pony Express was an enterprise that bled money from day one and did not accomplish any of the goals posthumously attributed to it. I have to wonder if the people who mark the Pony's passing with regret are, like me, the same people who get angry when their Amazon Prime purchases don't arrive in the specified two days. The progress of mail has always been toward faster, more reliable delivery. The telegraph beat the Pony Express as readily as the US Priority Mail beats standard mail, and who doesn't prefer faster service? The Pony Express of popular culture is a romantic fantasy, a fiction, and like all such fictions only looks beautiful from a safe distance. I challenge anyone who bemoans its passing to put their butt in a bike seat and ride the fifty-plus miles from Rock Creek Hollow over South Pass to Farson, Wyoming, to endure the mosquitoes and the wind and the utter isolation, and then tell me they still think the Pony is romantic, or that its demise was such a loss.

Having to carry your bike and gear through a cow wallow will engender rants like that.

Eventually, I descended off the plain toward the Ninth Crossing of the Sweetwater River at Burnt Ranch. The river was a welcome sight, its verdant strip of abundant life running like a green scar through the khaki hills. The current owners have a few buildings next to the river and a corral a little distance away. The map I was following marked the Emigrant Trail. It told me to go northwest to cross the Sweetwater. I rode in that direction and found a canal (unmarked on the map) between me and the crossing, but no bridge. Not being in the mood for more water crossings that day, I rode around the area looking for a trace of a trail, anything that might lead to the bridge I thought the map said existed. No luck. I reviewed the email the rancher had sent. His note mentioned a bridge to the south, so I went in that direction. I found the bridge easily and crossed it.

From there I had to work to the north to rejoin the trail, which meant another water crossing over Oregon Slough, which joins the Sweetwater just south of Burnt Ranch. But at the place the map showed a crossing over the slough, again, there was no bridge. Instead, the slough pooled into a catch basin far too wide and deep to carry a bike and trailer across. I rode back to the main ranch area, unhooked the trailer for greater mobility, and searched for the missing bridge. I crossed boggy land and small rivulets, my tires sinking into water-saturated earth that seemed to want to swallow my bike. The only good result of all this effort was that I stumbled across a couple of markers I'd missed earlier. One was a stainless-steel post marking the Sweetwater Pony Express Station. The other was a stone monument marking Burnt Ranch, with the "N" engraved backward.

Burnt Ranch and Sweetwater Station were just a couple of the historical names of this area. Others included Upper Sweetwater, Ninth Crossing, Gilbert's Station, South Pass Station, Camp Highland, and South Pass City, as well as Markham's Fort. Settlements in the area were deliberately set on fire in the area at least three times, in 1857, 1866, and 1868. The name Burnt Ranch dates from the third.

The site is less than ten miles from the Continental Divide at South Pass and was an important crossroads throughout the emigrant era. This is where the Seminoe Cutoff (which started back near the Sixth Crossing) rejoined the Emigrant Trail. It was also the eastern trailhead for the Lander Cutoff of the Oregon Trail, the first federally funded overland trail, which opened in 1858. Gold was discovered in the area in 1867, giving rise to the nearby town of South Pass City in 1868. Burnt Ranch also lay at the crossing for the north-south traffic to and from the mines.

In 1856, when the survivors of the Willie and Martin Handcart Companies crossed here, there were no buildings. The following year Mormons built the first permanent structures in the area, a stage stop and post office called Markham's Fort. This was one of the stations built for Brigham Young's fledgling mail and transportation company, Brigham Young Express. As with all the BYX stations, Markham's Fort was set up as much to support the Mormon emigration to Salt Lake as to service the mail operation. The suffering of the handcart emigrants the previous winter may have influenced the decision to build a station here. Within months, however, the Utah Expedition was on its way to chastise the Mormons. As with the BYX station at Deer Creek and Mormon settlements as far west as San Bernardino, California, Brigham Young called on Mormons to abandon the settlements and return home to help defend Salt Lake. Markham reportedly burned the buildings before leaving.

In 1858, John Hockaday had a station built across the river from the remains of Markham's Fort for his fledgling mail and stagecoach service, the Hockaday Salt Lake Mail. The station became known as Gilbert's Station, after its proprietor. Gilbert's Station was the most isolated of the thirty-six stations Hockaday established between the Missouri River and Salt Lake City. The next station to the east was eighty-five miles away at Devil's Gate, and the next one to the west was seventy-five miles away at Big Sandy Station on Green River.

In December 1858, just months after opening, Gilbert's Station probably saved the lives of two mail crews. A threatening snowstorm had prompted a westbound mail crew to hole up in a willow grove on Rocky Ridge, eight miles east. The storm kept them in camp for three days, during which nine of their ten mules froze to death. After the storm broke, they abandoned the mail and plowed their way to Gilbert's Station. It took them five hours to make the eight-mile trip.

During this same three-day storm, an eastbound mail crew left Big Sandy Station, only to return after making twenty-eight miles and deciding they would die if they continued. When they ventured out again, they made it over South Pass to the head of the Sweetwater River, where they abandoned the mail, their baggage, and their mules, and finally stumbled into Gilbert's Station just ahead of the westbound carriers. Gilbert's Station was converted into a makeshift hospital to care for the frozen men, though even with medical intervention some lost fingers and toes to frostbite. But Gilbert's was, first and foremost, a mail station. Despite the conditions, crews went out immediately in both directions to retrieve the abandoned mail.

After twenty minutes of riding around in circles, I tried calling the rancher. No cell service. In a pig-headed sort of way I decided I'd reattach the trailer and just stick to the mapped route and cross whatever obstacles I encountered. I didn't have to wait long. The first obstacle was that canal crossing. I rode around it, picked up what might have been a trail, and soon came to a creek that fed into the canal. The map said a bridge lay on the other side, so I went about crossing the creek. It was maybe too deep to ride through, but at least the water was clean and clear. Just to be on the safe side, I took off my shoes and socks and carried everything across. No problem. I dried my feet and put shoes and socks back on, reattached the trailer, and headed off according to the map. Water everywhere. Saturated ground. I plowed my way through anyway until I came to a dead end: a fence with no gate. I stopped my bike and put my foot down and felt it sink. If this were evening, my body would probably have been found weeks later, a shriveled husk of exsanguinated flesh sucked dry by Wyoming mosquitoes. Thankfully, the wind was strong enough to keep those blood suckers at bay.

I found a reasonably dry place to rest and surveyed the area for five minutes, thinking the entire time of how much time I had already lost that morning, of how much further I had yet to go. Finally, I came to the conclusion that this was dumb, there was no way forward, and the only bridge must be that one to the south. If I could not rejoin my planned route, the bridge road had to lead somewhere. Worst case was I would end up miles off course, but eventually I would find my way back to the Pony Express Route somewhere in Wyoming. I couldn't just sit at the ranch all day, and I sure wasn't riding all the way back and recrossing three streams just to get to the Pony Express Bikepacking Route and start the day over.

My first move was to recross the little creek. I stopped at the water's edge to reassess its depth. I had another forty-five miles to go, daylight was burning, and the wind was building. Rather than de-shoe, unhitch, and carry everything, I decided to save a few minutes and ride across the stream, and proceeded to soak my shoes and socks and everything in the trailer that wasn't protected inside my gear bag.

But no time to worry about that now. I recrossed the bridge to the south and stopped at the supposed crossing over the slough to double-check it wasn't bridged before shaking my head and moving on, resigned to finding an alternate route—only to discover an unmarked crossing a quarter mile further west. A low passage over a culvert, dry as toast. Now I really felt dumb. I crossed the slough, mounted a steep hill, and rejoined the route on the bluffs directly west of where I'd spent so much time searching for a phantom bridge.

By the time I was back on track I had lost an hour wandering around Burnt Ranch. My post-ride GPS track through this area looked like spaghetti. I'd ridden three miles looking for a bridge that wasn't there, and only progressed one mile toward my destination. So far that morning it had taken me two and a half hours to cover eight miles and I still had nearly fifty to go. Researching the ranch area more thoroughly weeks later, I realized the trail I had been following across Burnt Ranch led to the emigrant-era ford, not to a bridge site. Looking more closely at the Pony Express Bikepacking Route, I also discovered that the culvert across Oregon Slough was where the route ended its detour around Burnt Ranch. In short, I had no one but myself to blame for all my wasted time and effort that morning.

CHAPTER TWENTY-NINE

Uncle Sam's Backbone

BACK ON THE PLAIN FROM THE RIVER BOTTOM, I WAS ONCE AGAIN riding into the full force of the wind. Nothing to do but put my head down and do it. On and on I rode. I noticed more scat along this barren stretch than anywhere else on the trail. Maybe noticing it was just an indicator that I truly was face down trying to plow through the thick Wyoming wind. I did not stop to inspect it, and wouldn't know prong-horn scat from any other animal's, but it littered the scruffy growth between the tracks I was riding for miles.

As I neared South Pass, I passed interpretive signs placed by the Bureau of Land Management marking the Oregon Buttes and Twin Mounds. These, along with Pacific Butte, helped guide the emigrants over the pass. I hadn't seen another person since Keith left me at Rock Creek Hollow nearly twenty-four hours earlier, which made me wonder how many people actually approached South Pass on this trail, from this direction, and stopped to appreciate these signs.

Finally, I reached South Pass. It had taken me a month to ride this far. It took prairie schooner emigrants twice that long. For them South Pass marked the halfway point of the overland journey, and they often took a break here to celebrate this milestone. In spite of all the delays of the morning, I decided to follow suit and stopped to reflect on the accomplishment of making it to the crossing of Uncle Sam's Backbone, the Continental Divide.

South Pass has been called the Panama Canal of the Central Route, and the Gateway to the West. It is the primary topographic feature that defined the Oregon, California, Mormon Pioneer, and Pony Express trails. They all led to and away from this point because it was the only pass through the Rocky Mountain Cordillera between Marias Pass (near the Canadian border) and Guadalupe Pass (just above Mexico), wagons could traverse. Americans praised it as confirmation of the country's "Manifest Destiny."

The deeper significance of this "God-given pass" in the Rocky Mountains is that it enabled the transformation of the American West in little more than one generation. Up until 1846, crossing through South Pass meant leaving the United States. The United States and England shared possession of Oregon, which started at the crest of the Rocky Mountains, and Mexico owned the rest. By 1854, just eight years later, the United States owned it all. California was a state and the rest of the West had been divided and subdivided into territories: Oregon (1848), Utah (1850), Washington (1853), Kansas (1854), and Nebraska (1854). Others would soon follow: North Dakota and South Dakota (1861), Nevada (1861), and Colorado (1861). Idaho (1863), Montana (1864), and Wyoming (1868) followed soon after.

But in facilitating the rapid transformation of the West, this relatively easy passage "excavated by the finger of God" also encouraged American citizens and the US government to crush any and all indigenous people who might slow the juggernaut of the American empire. South Pass is not to blame—it is a topographical feature, not a sentient being—but the ease of westward movement it facilitated fit hand-in-glove with the American ideology of having a divinely given right to wipe anyone in its way off the face of the earth. Brigham Young, often cited as holding the belief that it was cheaper to feed and clothe Native Americans than fight them, epitomized the prevailing ethos: "If [the Utah Indians] continue hostile pursue them until you use them up. Let it be peace with them or extermination." The US government cleared the way for settlement by circumscribing ever-contracting boundaries for the Native American nations and restricting their movements, first through purchase (starting with the Fort Laramie Treaty Council of 1851), then increasingly through war and massacre.

As important as South Pass was to the overland emigration, from 1849 through 1860 only about one-third of the people bound for the Pacific Coast traveled this route. The rest went overland across the lower US or northern Mexico, took boats and crossed the isthmi of Tehuantepec or Panama and then steamed up the Pacific Coast, or took the sea voyage around Cape Horn, the most popular choice after the South Pass route.

The pass itself is anticlimactic. It is a twenty-mile-wide saddle, not a narrow gap. In his 1842 report, John Frémont estimated that the final approach was about equal "to the ascent of the Capitol hill from the avenue, at Washington." Emigrant descriptions often remarked how unremarkable South Pass appears. Some didn't even know they'd crossed it until they reached Pacific Springs a few miles further and noticed the river flowing west instead of east, or because they were now catching trout, which only live west of the Rockies.

The trail I was following was marked on maps as "Emigrant Trail," but there is no single historic place where the trail crosses the continent here. Emigrants spread out anywhere they could find a decent trail and forage, and in busy years, escape the dust of other wagon trains. I came across a few monuments and interpretive signs at the top of the pass on the trail. Ezra Meeker, who first crossed the continent to Oregon in 1852, placed a stone marker here in 1906 that reads, "Old Oregon Trail, 1843–57." Meeker's dates seem somewhat arbitrary, and the marker is a bit off the actual summit of the pass, but close enough. Next to it is another stone monument, placed in 1916 by Herman G. Nickerson, the same person who placed the Burnt Ranch monument back at the Ninth Crossing. This monument is to Narcissa Whitman and Eliza Spalding and reads,

NARCISSA
PRENTISS
WHITMAN.
ELIZA HART
SPALDING.

FIRST WHITE
WOMEN TO
CROSS THIS
PASS,
JULY 4, 1836

Unlike Meeker's monument, Nickerson's choices and inaccuracies are less innocuous.

These two women did cross the pass on that date, but about twenty-three miles north along what would eventually become part of the Lander Cutoff. More to the point, as historian Will Bagley suggests, is that while Nickerson's monument (and a mountain of annals of the West) celebrate the two women's accomplishment in sexist and racist terms, "History is too complicated to abide such narrow prejudices." Ms. Whitman and Ms. Spalding weren't the first women to cross South Pass and weren't even the first documented women to do so. Their accomplishment was not so much in crossing South Pass as traveling there from the Missouri River, a feat only noteworthy if you think, as their male contemporaries did, women weren't strong enough to make the journey. They rated a monument because unlike their predecessors they made the headlines. Once news got back to the States that two missionary women made the overland trip to Oregon, no one could argue credibly that women were incapable of making the trip. Six years later, entire families were emigrating along the Emigrant Trail.

As it happened, I was reading these monuments on July 2, 2021, just two days shy of 185 years after Narcissa Whitman and Eliza Spalding. During the overland emigrant period, making South Pass by July 4th meant emigrants were on track to get to the West Coast before early winter storms. For mail carriers, however, the fourth was just another day. They crossed South Pass throughout the year. Winters here were especially brutal. In the 1860s, Second Lieutenant Caspar Collins (namesake of Casper, Wyoming) called this area the "natural penitentiary of the United States." Another military officer stationed nearby called his deployment "an exercise in Siberian exile."

Reading about overland emigration in the 1850s, it seems every winter of that decade was the worst on record. The storm that nearly killed Hockaday's mail carriers near Gilbert's Station in 1858, for example, was said to be the "severest known in these parts for the last ten years," and "the worst storm in the memory of old-timers." Similarly, in 1856, the year of the Willie and Martin Handcart Companies disasters, it was reported that "Men who had been many times over the road had never seen so much snow along the Sweetwater."

Even in unexceptional years, winter on the Continental Divide was the crucible of the trans-Mississippi mail service. It was the largest impediment to steady mail service from the Missouri River to Utah and California four months of the year, and by this measure, every mail service failed. No early mail service was able to deliver over South Pass on schedule during winter, including the Pony Express. And yet being able to deliver mail on schedule throughout winter was exactly what the Pony Express had been established to prove.

By early 1860, when Russell launched the Pony Express via telegram to his son, there were a handful of overland mail services between the Missouri River and the West Coast. One service, the Butterfield Overland, dwarfed the others. It received the largest mail subsidy and the longest term: $600,000 per year for six years. At this time, Russell's Central Overland California and Pike's Peak Express (COC&PP) only ran between St. Joseph, Missouri, and Salt Lake City, Utah. Between Salt Lake City and Sacramento, California, mail and passengers carried by the COC&PP transferred to another service owned by George Chorpenning, whose operations had held that route since 1851. Russell's and Chorpenning's combined compensation for mail service was $205,000, around one-third of the Butterfield Overland's.

Recall that Russell, Majors & Waddell started in 1854 primarily to haul military freight across the plains. By November 1859, Russell had reshaped it (over his partners' objections) from a staid freighting firm to a transportation conglomerate that had the potential to move goods, mail, express, and passengers between the Missouri River and the West Coast. But that wasn't enough for Russell. He incorporated the COC&PP in November 1859 with an eye toward monopolizing transportation in the west. He had his sights on usurping Butterfield's contract when it came up for renewal in 1862. He also aimed to convince the US government to increase the subsidy from $600,000 to $1 million per year or more.

To achieve these goals, Russell had to demonstrate he could provide better mail and passenger service than the Butterfield Overland. At first blush, this didn't seem like an easy task. In contrast to other overland mail services, the Butterfield Overland's dependability was unimpeachable. From the first run of the Butterfield Overland's coaches, it consistently ran on schedule, year-round: twenty-five days or faster between its eastern termini and San Francisco, California. But the feature that enabled the Butterfield Overland to provide year-round service was also its Achilles' heel. The Butterfield Overland traced what came to be known as the Southern Route (because it ran along the southern border of the United States) and derided as the "ox-bow" route (for its semicircular shape). The Southern Route was 40 percent longer than the Emigrant Trail over South Pass—the Central Route—that the COC&PP and Chorpenning took between the Missouri River and the West Coast via Salt Lake City.

The Butterfield Overland did not propose using the Southern Route when it bid for the contract. Rather, Postmaster General Aaron Brown mapped the route and required Butterfield to use it. Knowing his move would be controversial, Brown submitted a letter to Congress in support of his actions. In that letter, Brown asserted that the record of mail service over the Central Route from 1851 through 1856 proved the impracticability of the route primarily due to winter conditions in the Rockies. Fans of the Pony Express often argue that Postmaster Brown's decision was political; that Brown, as a Southerner, was advancing Southern interests at the expense of faster mail service to California. That may be true. But even if Brown was being disingenuous, he wasn't wrong. Mail to Utah for November, December, and January 1850–1851 did not arrive until March. In 1852, storms were so severe the mail carrier had to turn back. The mails of February, March, and December of 1853 were impeded by deep snow. Those of January and February 1854 didn't arrive until April. In 1856, "the snow caused almost an entire failure for four months of the year." In 1857, after Brown had awarded the contract to the Butterfield Overland, the most experienced mail carriers in the West, Feramorz

Little and Ephraim Hanks, took seventy-eight days to deliver mail from Salt Lake to Independence, Missouri, on account of the winter weather.

There was an assumption at the time, which has become accepted truth in many Pony Express histories, that despite the well-documented winter disruptions the often impassible Central Route was superior to the longer, year-round Southern Route merely by virtue of being shorter. Russell, who was forced to use the Central Route under his mail contract, used this reductive logic to his advantage. He would take the contract from the Butterfield Overland by running a faster mail service over the Central Route. But simply providing a faster service wouldn't suffice. In order to prove convincingly he could transport mail and passengers on time throughout winter along the Central Route, and further, to win congressional approbation and its accompanying rewards, Russell felt he needed to do something "sensational, something that would be talked about the world over." The Pony Express was Russell's sensation, his magic bullet. In the end, he only managed to shoot himself in the foot.

William Russell is often lionized in the Pony Express literature as visionary. I think delusional is closer to the mark. He was undoubtedly ambitious. But if he were half the forward-thinking entrepreneur he is touted to have been, he would have known his gambit was doomed from the start.

Things started out well. In May 1860, just over a month after the Pony Express started running, the Post Office Department canceled Chorpenning's route between Salt Lake City and Sacramento and immediately awarded it to the COC&PP. It seems likely some chicanery was involved, but the COC&PP now operated an unbroken line the entire length of the Central Route. Finally, Russell was poised to go head to head against the Butterfield Overland. His next move was to provide faster service. The challenge, of course, was winter. Contrary to Pony Express dogma, winter won.

Every popular account of the Pony Express states that it delivered mail between St. Joseph and Sacramento in ten days. It often did. On the eve of its first and only winter, however, the Pony Express informed the public that after December 1st and throughout the winter, delivery time between St. Joseph and San Francisco would be extended to fifteen days. By mid-January, heavy snows delayed passage of the Pony Express by two days. By the end of January, the delay was four days. According to historian LeRoy Hafen, winter weather "often doubled the time to move the mochila across the country." The Pony Express, like every other mail service over the Central Route before it, could not maintain a regular schedule throughout winter. The raison d'être of the Pony Express was to disprove Postmaster General Brown's assertion that it was impracticable to maintain regular and certain service on the Central Route. Instead, the Pony Express confirmed Brown's assertion.

Ironically, the iconic feature of the Pony Express—the lone rider racing across a wilderness—was the primary reason the service could not keep a schedule. A single pony, no matter how stout-hearted, could not plow through the deep Rocky Mountain snow. It needed a daily run of a team of animals to break the trail.

These delays did nothing to disenchant the press, especially in California. But the flash of the Pony Express would never be enough to impress Congress, and Russell should have known it wouldn't. His predecessors, John Hockaday and George Chorpenning, whose mail routes he'd absorbed, had tried the identical strategy two years earlier. In December 1858 they had set out to prove mail could be delivered more quickly over the Central Route even in winter by proposing a contest. Three mail services—their combined overland route, the Butterfield Overland, and the Louisiana-Tehuantepec steamer service—would race to California to deliver a copy of President Buchanan's annual message. Hockaday and Chorpenning set up a one-time pony express to speed the message across the west. The Buchanan administration fixed the race by not providing the Hockaday-Chorpenning agent with an advance copy as it did for both other services. Consequently, the Hockaday-Chorpenning rider had to wait until the president's message was printed in a newspaper, which gave the other services an eight-day head start. Despite being last to arrive in California, however, the Hockaday-Chorpenning pony express was the fastest of the three: it beat the Butterfield Overland by two days and the Louisiana-Tehuantepec by four.

The newspapers were impressed with Hockaday and Chorpenning's achievement, but Congress wasn't. Even worse for mail contractors, there was a new postmaster general in town. The expansionist-minded Aaron Brown had died suddenly. Joseph Holt, Brown's successor, immediately set about slashing mail contracts in a vain effort to make the US Postal Service self-supporting. Holt slashed both Hockaday's and Chorpenning's subsidies by a third. Just months after providing the fastest overland delivery to California, John Hockaday was searching frantically for a sucker to take his debt-ridden mail route off his hands. One year later, George Chorpenning finally lost the futile battle he'd been waging to keep his mail contract despite chronic losses. Hockaday and Chorpenning's pony express had done nothing to save their businesses.

William Russell ended up with both mail contracts but gleaned nothing from his predecessors' experiences. His Pony Express didn't impress Congress any more than Hockaday and Chorpenning's did. The fact that Russell went ahead with his crack-brained scheme in spite of the facts before him does not strike me as the workings of an entrepreneurial genius. In fact, I might go so far as to say that the only two contemporary transportation magnates less qualified to run an enterprise on the scale of Russell, Majors & Waddell were Russell's partners, Majors and Waddell. After all, this feckless pair allowed and even enabled Russell to chase after rainbows to their collective, corporate, and personal financial ruin. Waddell in particular engaged in heated exchanges with Russell only to step back in line, seemingly cowered by Russell's raging tantrums.

Russell reportedly took on the Pony Express at the behest of Senator Gwin of California who wanted credit for providing faster mail service to California. Gwin promised in return to lobby for Russell's Central Route. As with the demonstrated inefficacy of Hockaday and Chorpenning's pony express as a marketing tool, Russell should have known better. To his detriment, he had relied on a similar oral agreement just two years earlier when the US Army came to Russell, hat in hand, to ask him to arrange a late-season freighting operation to support the Utah Expedition. At that time, the assistant quartermaster in Leavenworth promised Russell his firm would be fully compensated. Yet Russell, Majors & Waddell was still fighting with Congress to get reimbursed for their losses in the Utah Expedition when Russell was spending money freely to start up his Pony Express on the equally ephemeral basis of Senator Gwin's promise.

Unsurprisingly (to everyone but Russell, it seems), Senator Gwin's promise never resulted in a million-dollar contract. In March 1860, the House of Representatives passed a bill to provide improved mail service over the Central Route with a $900,000 subsidy. Had Gwin supported the bill when it came before the Senate, Russell would likely have received his lucrative contract, and the Pony Express would probably have been an arcane footnote to US mail service history. But the bill had been introduced by a Republican and Senator Gwin, a Democrat, could not afford to hand the Republicans a victory. Instead, he made a deal with the administration to stall the bill in the Senate in exchange for an order for improved service over the Central Route from the postmaster general. After Gwin killed the bill, however, Postmaster General Holt refused to order any such improvement. Senator Gwin then went to President Buchanan, who also refused to act. Russell's reliance on Gwin's promise, as his reliance on the assistant quartermaster's promise two years earlier, was misplaced.

Neither Majors nor Waddell wanted to take on the Pony Express; both knew it would lose money. Years later, Alexander Majors wrote that he and Waddell felt they had no choice but to go along. Even though Russell had not consulted them before promising to start the Pony Express, they felt bound to honor Russell's word. Given Majors's and Waddell's record of being led by Russell from one financial disaster to the next, Majors's explanation sounds more like ex post facto justification.

I suspect ego was the motivating factor behind Russell's disastrous mismanagement of Russell, Majors & Waddell. He had nothing to do with the day-to-day operations of the firm. Despite being known as Napoleon of the West, he spent most of this time on the East Coast looking after the firm's interests by entertaining government officials and living large on other people's money. I have to imagine that owning a freighting firm was the nineteenth-century equivalent of owning a garbage-truck service. It paid the bills, but a stagecoach company featuring prancing ponies and top-of-the-line Concord coaches would have been more prestigious. In that sense, the Pony Express was probably the nineteenth-century equivalent of a commercial spaceline. Russell couldn't resist the prestige of owning the flashiest transportation service of his time. But his partners could, and they should have done more to rein him in.

Russell's Pony Express drove the already debt-laden Russell, Majors & Waddell into irredeemable financial ruin. In December 1860, Russell embezzled government bonds in a last-ditch effort to stave off ruin. His accomplice confessed, and the Napoleon of the West spent Christmas Eve 1860 in jail. Ironically, just a few months later Congress did award a million-dollar overland mail contract to conduct mail and passengers along the Central Route. But it went to the Butterfield Overland, not to the COC&PP. And it was not because the Central Route was superior. Congress directed the Butterfield Overland to move its line to the Central Route because the Civil War had started and raiders had destroyed Butterfield's stations in Texas. In light of the Southern states' secession, the Central Route became the only viable route between the Union and the West. The COC&PP was still operating, but given its moribund financial status and Russell's recent shenanigans, the best it could do was operate the eastern part of the line under a subcontract from the Butterfield Overland.

Breaktime over, I found myself once again crossing the barren Wyoming steppe in the face of the howling wind. The west side of the pass, the weather side, was even less hospitable than the east. Barren, exposed rock and washed-out road. It trended downhill, but the trail was in such bad condition I still had to ride slowly.

The first camp west of South Pass for emigrants was Pacific Springs. Like the Sweetwater on the other side, it cut a lush, green swath through the desolation, but the road stayed up higher and was more exposed. With another four or so hours to ride, I didn't feel I had time or energy enough to take a side trip to get a better look.

After some more miles of riding, I reached Highway 28. It was busy, but the smooth pavement was a welcome break from the trails I'd ridden up to that point. Five miles west I came to a pullout with a monument marking the Parting of the Ways. In the early days of the overland emigration, only one trail led west from South Pass. Overlanders to both California and Oregon continued southwest from South Pass to Fort Bridger in the southwest corner of Wyoming before turning northwest toward Fort Hall near present-day Pocatello, Idaho. Forty miles further, at the Raft River, the trails to California and Oregon diverged. It was an indirect route, but one that followed water and forage as much as possible.

In 1844, Caleb Greenwood led a party of emigrants over what came to be known as the Sublette Cutoff. Rather than continue southwest toward Fort Bridger, it went west. The cutoff led over the waterless Little Colorado Desert, but it saved about fifty miles and seven days' travel. As with the Central Route for mail service, emigrants came to assume the Sublette Cutoff must be superior to the old trail merely by virtue of being shorter. Sublette Cutoff grew in popularity and the area where it left the main trail came to be known as the Parting of the Ways.

During the overland emigration period, a sign purportedly stood near the parting. On it was written "Oregon," with an arrow pointing right, and "California" with an arrow pointing left. It was said that those who could read turned right and that the rest turned left—an anecdote written by an Oregonian, no doubt.

As it turned out, the modern monument I saw stood at a point known as "False Parting of the Ways." The real spot was some miles west off a gravel road. The Pony Express Route left the highway at the False Parting to take that road, so in a sense, I found myself at a personal parting of the ways: I could veer off the highway and continue over gravel roads or I could continue on pavement. Both roads led to Farson, the gravel road less directly so. On the bikepacking route map, the notes after the turnoff stated that the trail had areas of deep sand and to expect slow going. I had to wonder, *Wasn't that deep sand I had just ridden through? Hadn't I spent most of the day struggling over miles of slow-going trail? If so, and if there were no notations on that section, how much worse would the next section be?* The choice came down to what kind of ride I wanted to have. It wasn't a hard decision to make. The sky was filling with clouds, threatening rain. The wind whipped around me. There was no way I was up to adding another two or three hours to my ride just to stick to the Pony Express Trail. Honestly, I didn't think I had it in me. I kept to the highway.

From the False Parting of the Ways to Farson, Wyoming (a little over twenty miles), I engaged in a three-hour grudge match with the wind. It blew at me from left, right, and center, but never swung abaft the beam. It was a shoving, bullying wind. I imagined it as a devil, teasing me, trying alternately to push me into traffic or knock me off the shoulder into the sand. When a gust blew head on, it sometimes stopped me dead, at which point I was so fed up I'd yell, "Thank you for that!" Though occasionally I'd substitute a more emphatic word for "thank."

To say it was an exhausting three hours is an understatement. In taking the paved road I'd traded difficulty for tedium. I kept wishing someone would pull over and offer me a ride, kept considering stopping and sticking out my thumb. There were certainly enough pickup trucks in Wyoming. Anyone could easily have hauled me and my gear. The frustrations of the morning—fording the creeks, getting lost at Burnt Ranch, wasting so much time—had burned up so much of the morning energy that usually propelled me far into the day's ride I had little reserve left.

The road itself didn't help. Though smooth, there weren't a hundred continuous feet of level surface at a time. The only grace was whereas east Kansas roads might have two or three hills per mile, Highway 28 had hills that rolled for two or three miles. Some were steeper than I would have wished. Then again, any hill at this stage was steeper than I would have wished.

As in most of Wyoming, there was no shade. The surrounding land was even more featureless than east of the pass. I had entered the Green River Basin, which I'd be riding through the next two days, until Fort Bridger. It is a wind-blown sagebrush and greasewood desert that, as one writer notes, "redefines monotony."

At length, I made it to the Eden Valley, where Farson sits. The road dropped down a gentle decline, and almost as if brought to heel, the wind blew steadily out of the northwest. It was still strong, still in front of rather than behind me. But it was a tame wind, a polite wind that kept to its lane. I could work with that for the last few miles.

By the time I hit Farson, Wyoming, I'd been on the bike eight hours. Not an incredibly long day by some standards, but they were not an easy-going eight hours. I was beat. Farson is a tiny high-desert town, a crossroads of two highways on the Big Sandy River. Back at the Sixth Crossing: Mormon Trail Site Visitors' Center, Keith had told me that the Farson Mercantile ("Home of the Big Cone") sold ice cream, and that he was pretty sure they had a camping area near the store. I didn't know if either piece of information was true, or if so, which would make me happier.

I sat a while on the Mercantile's outside deck and drank electrolytes and had a snack and generally stabilized myself to the point where I could walk a straight line and speak coherently, two things I had not needed to do for the previous thirty or so hours. I went inside and was happy to see they offered five sizes of ice cream, from "baby scoop" to "four scoops." I ordered the four-scooper and I swear it was at least a quart of ice cream. Everyone in the shop who saw me carrying it away pointed or laughed.

As I was paying, I asked about camping. The clerk told me there was free, primitive camping behind the store. I felt a huge wave of relief. No matter how primitive the camping was, it meant no more riding that day. And I had a boatload of ice cream to eat in the meantime. Life had turned from bleak to plush in the space of an hour. Farson didn't become my new favorite town, but it was a lifesaver that afternoon.

CHAPTER THIRTY

Simpson's Hollow

I GOT AN EARLY START THE NEXT MORNING. I WANTED TO MAKE Granger, Wyoming, about fifty-five miles away. I knew the second half of the ride would be on dirt, but I didn't know what kind of dirt. After the ride I'd had the day before, I didn't want to get a late start and find out it would be all bad.

For the same reason, I deviated from the Pony Express Bikepacking Route out of Farson. The route stuck to the off-road Emigrant Trail, which ran parallel to a perfectly good highway. It did not pass any Pony Express stations or other historical sites before it rejoined the highway and I wanted some early miles under my belt, so I stuck to the pavement.

Farson grew up near the confluence of the Big Sandy and Little Sandy Rivers and now sits at the intersection of US 191 and Wyoming Highway 28. It was a natural crossroad and has a surprising number of historical monuments. Two monuments marking the Big Sandy Pony Express Station sat between US 191 and the Big Sandy River. Another monument nearby celebrated the "Brave men who rode the Pony Express," and yet another commemorated the meeting of the first east and westbound Pony Express riders. There is no record of the riders passing each other, one westbound, the other east, but it is believed they passed one another about fifteen miles west of Farson, between there and the Green River.

There are very few records concerning the Pony Express at all. The absence of documented facts leaves plenty of room for speculation, one of the hallmarks of Pony Express literature. Some have blamed the loss of company records, assuming they existed at one time, on the rapid demise of Russell, Majors & Waddell. It has also been argued that the Civil War and Reconstruction so preoccupied historians that none thought about studying and preserving the history of the Pony Express for posterity. I suspect that because it was superseded by the telegraph, people were as interested in preserving the memory of the outdated Pony Express as people who grew up in the era of email might be about guaranteeing the legacy of the fax machine. But that may be because I'd had to pull a tick trying to embed its way into my stomach that morning, so I was starting to sour on Farson, Wyoming.

There were more markers around the corner on Highway 28 where it crossed the Big Sandy River. One was a large interpretive sign noting the history and importance of the crossing. Another marked the 1847 meeting between the legendary mountain man Jim Bridger and Brigham Young, who was leading the first contingent of Latter-Day Saints to Salt Lake Valley. Bridger had trapped and scouted throughout the West for twenty years. Seeing the end of the free-trapper era, he and fellow mountain man Luis Vasquez had set up an emigrant trading post, Fort Bridger, about one hundred miles southwest near the present-day town of Lyman, Wyoming. Bridger had an encyclopedic knowledge of the land and spent the evening telling Young what he knew about the Great Salt Lake Valley. The meeting of these two legends of Western history is even more interesting given that just a few years later Bridger abandoned his fort in the middle of the night, fearing Brigham Young had sent men to kill him.

There were other markers some miles north and east of town I would have passed had I ridden into Farson from the bikepacking route the day before. But Granger was calling. More accurately, the day was quickly warming. I was southbound, the opposite direction from the markers, and I needed to get going if I was going to beat the worst of the weather.

Highway 28 follows the Big Sandy River until its confluence with the Green River in the Seedskadee National Wildlife Refuge. Well before then I had to pull over and remove my right pedal to oil it. Slogging through so much water the two previous days had caused an irritating squeak. Pedal reattached, I made good time down the little highway. By and by I came to another place I had been anticipating: Simpson's Hollow.

There is a pullout with monuments and interpretive signs. The hollow itself wasn't visually striking—an otherwise indistinguishable depression between a pair of bracketing bluffs—but it was here that the Mormons won a war against the United States without firing a shot.

When Brigham Young led the Mormons to Great Salt Lake Valley in 1847, he planned to establish a kingdom: "Hierarchic, theocratic, patriarchal." Young intended his realm to cover most of the Great Basin, a square area roughly one thousand by eight hundred miles, or equal to one-sixth of the area of the United States. Given the history of Mormon persecution, he sent missionaries to establish settlements near all of the approaches through which enemies could invade: Fort Limhi on the Salmon River in Idaho; Genoa, at the base of Carson Pass in Nevada; San Bernardino, California, which secured Cajon Pass and gave the Mormons access to ports on the Pacific Ocean; and Las Vegas on the Spanish Trail, a route between California and Utah that was passable year-round.

Fort Bridger, on the Emigrant Trail, guarded the northeast approach to Echo Canyon, which led directly to Salt Lake through the Wasatch Mountains. That's why, depending on whose story you believe, the Mormons either bought out or forcibly evicted Jim Bridger in 1853. Mormons wanted the fort and also claimed Bridger was selling guns to the Utes, with whom the Mormons were at war in 1853. Bridger got word a posse was coming to arrest him and escaped. The Mormons moved in and made some improvements until abandoning the fort at the onset of the Utah War in 1857.

Great Salt Lake Valley, where the Mormons settled, had transferred to the United States at the end of the Mexican-American War. As US property, there were three options for its governance: it could exist as an unsupervised provisional state, as a US territory, or as a state of the Union. Initially, the Mormons created the provisional state of Deseret and filled its offices with Mormons. Brigham Young intended to use that infrastructure as a basis to lobby Congress for statehood, which would give the Mormons the most extensive rights. As Mormon elections tended to list only one slate, Young would control who would be elected to state offices and hold temporal power over his people. Congress, however, voted to make Utah a territory. This was the worst of the three options for Young. US territories did not have the sovereign status states enjoyed. Moreover, Young wouldn't be able to dictate leadership in Utah because territorial officials were not elected, but rather appointed by the US government.

Over the next seven years the Mormons pushed and Uncle Sam pulled in a contest of autonomy and control exacerbated by ignorance and misinformation on the part of both parties. For example, the US government sent out teams to settle Native American rights to land occupied by Mormons and to survey it, legitimate steps toward establishing title; Mormons hindered the survey work because they saw this as a first step in confiscating their hard-won land and giving that title to non-Mormons. Brigham Young, in his role as superintendent of Indian affairs for Utah Territory, purported to pursue a policy of coexistence with the local Native Americans; US Indian agents accused Young of currying favor with Native Americans to incline them to side against the United States. In 1851, three appointed officials had managed to offend the Mormons so thoroughly that they left Utah fearing for their lives just months after arriving. Between 1850 and 1856, of eight district judges appointed to Utah, five fled, two died, and one was not reappointed.

Reports from territorial officials from 1851 to 1857 on the situation in Utah stoked the embers of distrust back in the States ignited by repulsion at the Mormon doctrine of "spiritual wives" (aka "the Practice" or polygamy); fear of Danites (Mormon execution squads); anger over the ever-growing jurisdiction of Mormon probate courts staffed by Mormon judges with Mormon juries told by the church how to decide; as well as a belief that Utah was working toward declaring itself an independent state. Many more factors and incidents increased tensions during this contentious period, but a fuller discussion of the history leading up the Utah War (also called the Mormon War, the Mormon Rebellion, and the Utah Conflict) is beyond the scope of this book. The upshot is by May 1857, President Buchanan decided that Mormon actions evidenced a rebelliousness that threatened to weaken the fabric of the Union. Brigham Young's tenure as governor of the territory had ended back in 1854 and he had continued under a clause that allowed him to retain office until a replacement took his position. Buchanan's response to Mormon intransigence was announcing the Utah Expedition, the *posse comitatus* sent out to install Brigham Young's replacement as governor of Utah Territory and to ensure his safety.

Buchanan announced the Utah Expedition in late May, but the troops didn't set off until July 18, 1857. As noted in the previous chapter, overland emigrants were well past South Pass by that date every year. All of Russell, Majors & Waddell's freight supply caravans for the army were already spread across the plains to supply the army's posts. Army General Winfield Scott counseled against setting off so late in the season, but the president ordered troops sent anyway. Despite increased cost and the difficulty of finding adequate equipment, animals, and men with sufficient skill, Russell, Majors & Waddell put together the resources to transport three million pounds of supplies to support the expedition.

The march to Utah was poorly organized. Troops and supplies traveled at different speeds and as a result, Russell, Majors & Waddell supply caravans found themselves without military escort. On October 4, 1857, mounted Mormons surrounded two caravans, and after allowing the bullwhackers to save their personal belongings, burned the wagons and took the animals. The following day, they did the same to a third caravan led by Lewis Simpson, after which the area I was overlooking became known as Simpson's Hollow. Altogether the army and Russell, Majors & Waddell lost seventy-two wagons, nine hundred oxen, and three hundred thousand pounds of food supplies in these raids, enough to provision the Utah Expedition for three months.

Note the date, October 4, 1857. On October 20 the previous year an early winter storm broke across Wyoming. Over the following weeks severe winter storms coupled with inadequate clothing and food had killed more than two hundred Mormon handcart emigrants between Last Crossing (Casper, Wyoming) and Fort Bridger, Wyoming. Now the weather that had terrorized the Mormons the previous year had become their best defense. Mormon troops did not have to kill anyone to defend their home; once they deprived the Utah Expedition of adequate food and clothing, winter would do it for them. Mormons had ten years of winter traveling experience throughout the region and had mounted a massive rescue effort across the mountains for the handcart emigrants the previous year. They roamed the high country between Salt Lake and Fort Laramie at will. In contrast, the Utah Expedition wandered aimlessly for a time before abandoning any hope of making it to Salt Lake City before spring. General Albert Sidney, who'd taken over command of the expedition from General Harney, settled the troops in for the winter near the ruins of Fort Bridger, which the Mormons had burned down to deny the army shelter.

By the time the troops converted Fort Bridger into the makeshift Camp Scott, winter had set in. Draft animals died along the trail and freight wagons were abandoned for lack of animals to pull them. Temperatures were dropping below zero at night, and for the remaining animals what little forage was left after being burned by retreating Mormons was buried under snow. That troops did not die in droves as the Mormon emigrants had the year before was largely thanks to Captain R. B. Marcy, who led a heroic midwinter expedition across the Rockies to Fort Union in New Mexico to arrange for resupply.

By the following spring, Buchanan had sent a secret envoy to negotiate peace with the Mormons. When General Sidney finally led his army through Salt Lake City on June 26, 1858, the troops marched through an empty, silent city. They kept going to the future site of Camp Floyd, located about forty miles south: close enough to keep an eye on the Mormons, but far enough to minimize conflicts between troops and civilians. Notably, the camp was named in honor of US Secretary of War John Floyd, "the War Department's foremost Mormon-hater."

Between November 1857, when the expedition hunkered down at Camp Scott, and June 1858, when General Sidney led his troops through Salt Lake City, public opinion back in the States had turned against the Utah Expedition. Congress was asking the Buchanan administration for explanations, and some found one in labeling the Utah Expedition a "Contractor's War." In their view, Buchanan had sent troops to Utah in order to enrich Russell, Majors & Waddell.

On the contrary, supplying the Utah Expedition constituted a big step toward the firm's inexorable death. Between Mormons and winter, Russell, Majors & Waddell suffered losses of hundreds of wagons, nearly two thousand oxen frozen to death or run off, wages for employees who had to winter at Camp Scott, and the cost of additional supplies over the initial amount requested by the army. Russell estimated the damage at around $500,000. Foolishly, he had committed his firm to supplying the expedition on the strength of an assistant quartermaster's word that the firm would be reimbursed for all of its costs, including losses. When Russell submitted bills of lading to the War Department, he was told the department had already overdrawn its annual appropriation and had no money to pay him. Russell then prepared and submitted a claim to Congress. But the quartermaster's word was not binding. The predominant attitude in Congress cast Buchanan's war as a blunder and military freighters as profiteers. There was no compelling reason to reimburse Russell, Majors & Waddell, and Congress never did.

The firm had gone heavily into debt to supply the Utah Expedition and never recovered from the loss. It might have, but only if Russell had focused on retiring old debt instead of chasing after the next shiny thing that caught his eye: a stagecoach line to the gold findings at Pike's Peak.

About halfway into my ride, I came to Seedskadee National Wildlife Refuge, which borders the Green River. The name comes from Crow Indians who lived in the area and called the river Seedskadee Agie, Prairie-Chicken River. The riverbanks were nearly as barren as the surrounding desert. There were a few far-off trees, more sagebrush and greasewood, lots of sand. The river itself was wide and beautiful. Its placid surface gave no hint of the havoc it wreaked during emigrant years. It was a particularly treacherous stretch of water, wide and cold, and during its flood stage early in the emigration season could be from ten to twenty feet deep. Mountain men, including Jim Bridger, had established a ferry near this spot in 1843. By 1847 there were several ferries across the river from this area up to the Sublette Cutoff near Farson. By the early 1850s mountain men and Mormons were feuding over the right to ferry emigrants across.

Interpretive signs and a replica of the ferry, which came to be known as Lombard's Ferry, stood nearby. Rather than wander over to see it, I took a break in the only oasis I could find, a tiny triangle of shade created by a three-panel interpretive sign on the far side of the parking area.

From here I left the highway and the Big Sandy and Green Rivers to keep southwest toward Granger, Wyoming. Except for short sections of pavement at the beginning and end, I followed a two-track trail over sand and gravel the rest of the ride. The Green River Valley between Farson and Granger, Wyoming, is known as the Little Colorado Desert. Descriptions of it from the emigrant era to the present all rely heavily on synonyms for "barren" and "desolate." Burton reported it was known as the "First Desert," and in the dry season was "a terrible *jornada* [a long, waterless stretch of desert] for laden wagons with tired cattle." The land was "scabby," "bone-dry," with short buttes "like flat-topped warts on a sagebrush skin." The passage was over "broken, barren prairie, covered with sand and gravel," its "hard-faced soil as hard as cast iron and barren of anything but sage." The descriptions are apt. For miles a khaki-mustard landscape of sagebrush and greasewood were all I could see in every direction, except from hilltops, where I could follow the winding dun-colored tracks cut into the dusty brown-green earth.

After a short flat, the road climbed out of the river bottom up a steepish hill strewn with loose rock. I rode to the top thinking if the trail looked to be this bad for the entire length, I might have to retrace to the paved road and stay the night in Green River instead of Granger. Luckily, that first climb was the worst, and though the trail wasn't the best I'd ridden, it wasn't too bad. The sand was loose, but not deep, and kept favorably solid by small rocks throughout.

The air warmed to the low nineties and the wind rose to about ten knots, but after the day before, the weather felt moderate. In fact, the ride turned out to be pleasant. I found the emptiness peaceful. So long as my bike rolled along and the wind didn't stand in my way, I was happy to be riding through the desert.

After Seven Mile Gulch, the road became rougher. The land was more broken here and the trail was severed in several places by dry washes, places where water rushing down from nearby bluffs during cloudbursts or storms had scoured riverbeds two to three feet deep with vertical walls. They may have been from earlier that season or maybe were ten years old. There was no way to tell. If there were no alternatives, I would have had to detach my trailer and carry it and my bike across each one. Luckily, I could circumvent the gullies by following tracks that wound uphill to where the walls weren't so steep.

Closer to Granger, the landscape changed again. The road became littered with shale, flat shards of sharp-edged rock. I passed through without issue, but woe to any rider with lighter-weight tires.

At length I hit US 30 and followed it a mile before turning onto Wyoming Highway 375 and followed Blacks Fork (of the Green River) into Granger, Wyoming. It was early afternoon. The wind was building and clouds were gathering. I was glad to be nearly done for the day. Nearly, because I still didn't know where I was going to sleep. There were no campgrounds or motels in the area. For supplies, there was only one lightly stocked convenience store and a closed restaurant. The town allowed camping in its park, but the Fourth of July fireworks were going to be held in the park that evening, a day early, so I couldn't stay there. Logistically, it would have made more sense to camp back by the Green River in the Seedskadee National Wildlife Refuge, but that was too short of a ride. Alternately, I could have stayed on the highway back at Seedskadee and ended up at Little America, Wyoming, about eight miles away off I-80. But Antelope Crossing Pub, the closed restaurant in Granger, still operated as a caterer. I'd been in touch with Jessica, who owns the pub with her husband, Ed, and she was willing to prepare vegetarian meals for me. She had also told me she had some recommendations for places nearby to camp on BLM land.

Granger sits at the confluence of Hams Fork and Blacks Fork. Like Farson, it is a natural crossroads. The 1834 fur trappers' rendezvous took place in this area along Hams Fork. During the Utah War in 1857, the US Army set up Camp Winfield near here as a temporary headquarters. Lewis Simpson and the other teamsters from the freight caravans burned by the Mormons walked from Simpson's Hollow to Camp Winfield to report their losses. And though I couldn't locate the spot, I'm pretty sure Jack Slade (in his capacity as captain of a wagon caravan) shot Andrew

Ferrin (a mutinous teamster in his crew) somewhere nearby, the only documented killing in the notorious Slade's life.

The Overland Stage Trail (opened to stagecoach use in 1862) rejoined the original Emigrant Trail at Hams Fork Crossing, which lay nearby. The Overland Stage Line maintained a station here known as the Granger Stage Station (according to one sign on the lot), also known as the South Bend Stage Station (according to a stone monument nearby). The old depot and the ruin of another stone building stand in an undeveloped lot, though there is some doubt whether the building on the site ever was a stage station. The Hams Fork Pony Express Station stood about a half-mile away, south of Blacks Fork. The Transcontinental Railroad was built through here in the 1860s, Lincoln Highway in the late 1910s, and just a few miles south, I-80 in the 1950s. A lot of transportation history for a town of fewer than two hundred.

Incongruously for such a historically important transportation hub, Granger's streets were gravel, giving it a rough appearance. I learned later that they used to be paved, but when the city contracted to have the water lines redone a few years earlier, the bid failed to include repaving and they'd been gravel ever since.

Antelope Crossing Pub is a small wooden building at a gravel intersection across from the Transcontinental Railroad tracks. I'd last crossed these tracks two weeks earlier in Sidney, Nebraska, before starting along the 550-mile northwest arch that led though South Pass. When I rode up, Jessica was in the shade of the front deck grilling vegetables for the lasagna she'd planned to bake for me. After she was done, she went into the pub and told me I was welcome to hang out while she cooked. Outside was heat, wind, and possibly rain. Where else would I go? I followed her inside.

I sat in one of two recliners in the bar area, and in the dim light of the cool room, I became sleepy. Minutes later, I was out. When I woke Jessica told me that she'd spoken to Ed and they'd agreed I could stay in the pub that night if I wanted. By that point nothing about sleeping in a tent under a bridge next to the river appealed to me. Sleeping arrangements made, I settled in and spent the rest of the afternoon talking with Jessica while she cooked—a pleasant, wandering conversation about nothing in particular.

Ed came in while we were eating—that is, while Jessica nibbled and I shoveled down two entire dinners. He was just as friendly, but he had his prickly side, too. Where Jessica might drop a hint as to her politics, Ed seemed to want to provoke a debate ("Are you going to vote for your governor again?"). I'm pretty sure my votes have negated Ed's in every federal election since 1976, so I sidestepped any discussion of politics. But our different opinions didn't stand in the way of getting along. In addition to putting me up for the night, Ed offered, practically insisted, that he put me and my gear in his truck the next morning so he could get me safely to Salt Lake City. It was as if now that I was in his place, I was his responsibility, and he'd do whatever he needed to keep me safe. Even if I did vote for President Obama.

PART FIVE

THE WASATCH—
GRANGER, WYOMING, TO
SALT LAKE CITY, UTAH

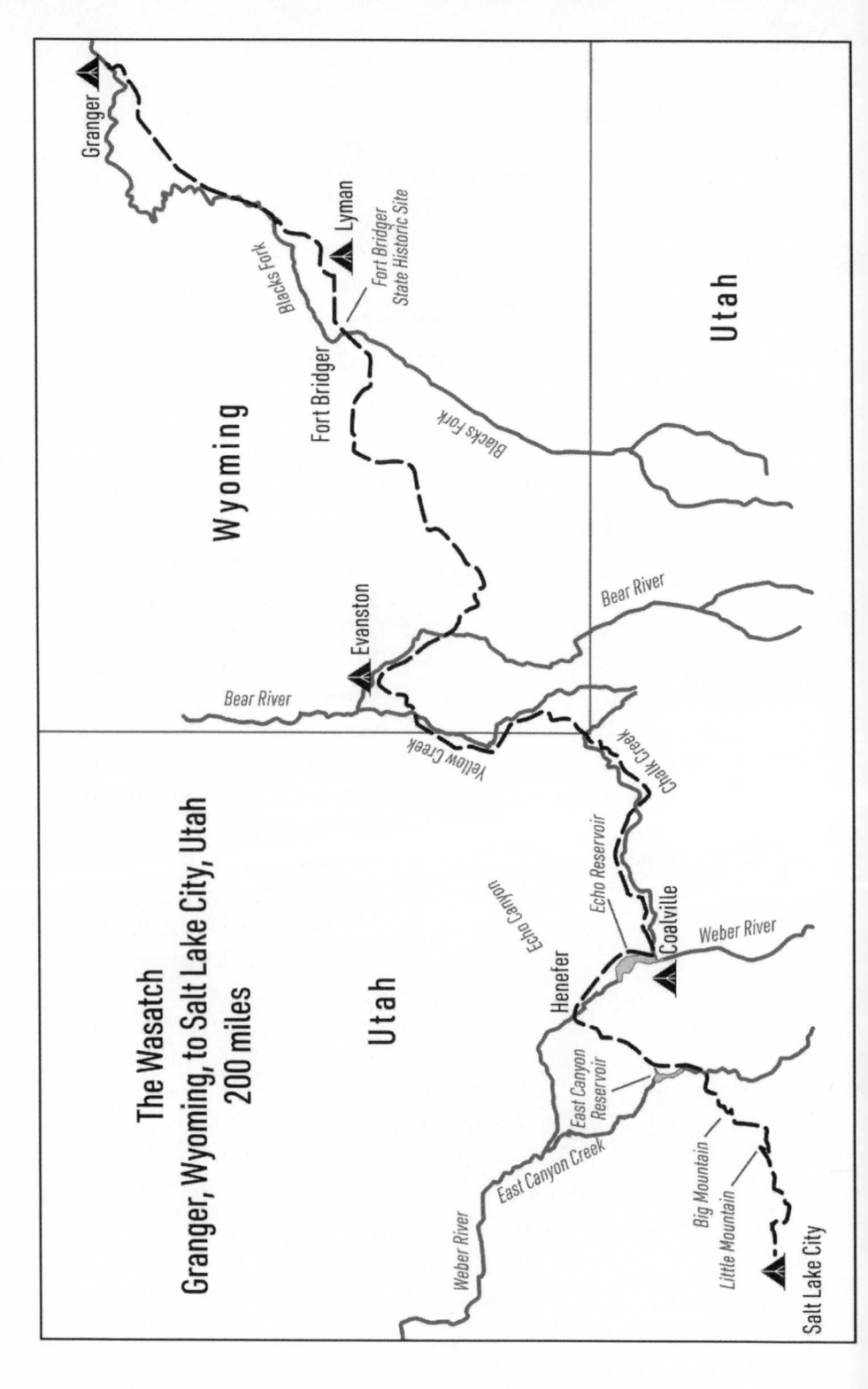

The Wasatch
Granger, Wyoming, to Salt Lake City, Utah
200 miles

Wyoming

Utah

Granger

Blacks Fork

Lyman

Fort Bridger

Fort Bridger
State Historic Site

Blacks Fork

Evanston

Bear River

Bear River

Yellow Creek

Chalk Creek

Echo Reservoir

Echo Canyon

Coalville

Weber River

Henefer

Utah

East Canyon
Reservoir

East Canyon Creek

Weber River

Big Mountain

Little Mountain

Salt Lake City

CHAPTER THIRTY-ONE

Fort Bridger

TRAINS RUMBLED THROUGH GRANGER ALL NIGHT. I WOKE EARLY BUT took my time leaving. Jessica came back and made breakfast and packed a lunch for me. It was the best I'd eaten since Marilyn and Dale had fed me way back at Rock Creek Station State Recreation Area, Nebraska. As I was leaving, Jessica became very serious and said, "You have my number. Call if you need anything." This wasn't an empty offer. She said as a mother she'd hate to know her son was out on the road without any support, so she was offering hers. She made a point of making eye contact and getting me to promise I would call if I needed help.

As it turned out, that day was one of the easiest of the entire ride. It was about forty miles, not much climbing, with mild temperatures and fair winds. I was back on the Lincoln Highway, which I would follow all day. The road was dirt and gravel, but it had seen a lot of vehicle traffic, so the bed was mostly compact and easy to ride.

A dozen miles along I passed Church Butte, and with it, the unmarked site of Church Butte Pony Express Station. Church Butte stands out from the road, its multicolored strata of weather-beaten rock rising to a point nearer to the road and taller than any other formation for miles, making it a well-known landmark in emigrant days. A little further along, the road nestled up next to Blacks Fork and followed it over a couple of Lincoln Highway–era bridges and under an I-80 overpass into my destination for the day, Lyman, Wyoming ("A Great Place to Grow").

It was Sunday, July 4, Independence Day, and in this largely Mormon town, the Sabbath. As a result, most businesses were closed. I wanted to spend some time at Fort Bridger, which was five miles past Lyman, so I kept going. On the way through Lyman, I saw a laundromat and a self-serve car wash, both open. I knew how I was going to spend my afternoon.

From Lyman I dropped down a long hill into Bridger Valley and the town of Fort Bridger. The word "fort" along the Emigrant Trail did not necessarily designate a military installation. Most trading posts were called forts. Some, such as Fort Laramie, were purchased by the US government and converted into fortified army posts.

Fort Bridger was the first trading post along the Emigrant Trail built specifically to service the emigrant trade. Earlier developments, such as Fort Laramie, were built for trade with Native Americans and later adapted to accommodate overlanders. As such, the emergence of Fort Bridger in 1842 signaled the end of the fur trade. Its initial summer of business saw the first surge in overland emigration, the Great Migration of 1843. The fort was a joint business run by Jim Bridger and Louis Vasquez, both veteran mountain men who'd come west in the 1820s as trappers. Bridger and Vasquez were separately credited with "discovering" the Great Salt Lake in 1824. Bridger was the first to provide a firsthand account, so he usually receives the credit.

Jim Bridger, aka Old Gabe, seems to have some personal connection to nearly every event of note in this era of the West. He was one of the first party of fur trappers to come out from the Missouri in 1822; at the trapper's rendezvous in 1835, missionary and doctor Marcus Whitman extracted an arrowhead Bridger had been carrying in his back for three years. Bridger was at his fort when the Donner Party decided to follow a new road being touted by Lansford Hastings, and he selfishly encouraged them in making that poor decision. He rode with the Shoshone Indians into the Horse Creek Treaty negotiations in 1851 and worked as a guide for Colonel Albert Sidney Johnston during the Utah Expedition in 1857. He also guided Lieutenant Colonel William Collins when his troops came west in 1862, and along the way taught Collins how to distinguish between tribes, as well as bands within tribes, a level of understanding most army commanders didn't bother to learn. Though Bridger was illiterate, his knowledge of the American West was so thorough he could sketch out any section in detail on buffalo skin with a piece of charcoal delineating mountains, streams, and holes (circular valleys) accurately. In 1850 he laid out a shorter trail from the South Platte to Fort Bridger for Captain Stansbury of the US Corp of Topographical Engineers using a burnt stick on parchment. This is the route that the Overland Stage, Transcontinental Railroad, and Lincoln Highway followed across the Rocky Mountains; I-80 still follows it today.

The site Bridger and Vasquez selected for their trading post was perfectly suited to the emigrant trade. They received a grant from the Mexican Government for a nine square mile parcel about halfway between Fort Laramie and Fort Hall. Though the fort lies in the Green River Basin, Blacks Fork separates into smaller streams at the head of a valley, creating the "best piece of pastureland between Salt Lake City and Horseshoe Station." The Emigrant Trail led here before crossing the Bear River Divide and turning northwest toward Fort Hall. It was a good place for overlanders to purchase supplies, make repairs, and recruit their cattle on the rich grass. They could also sell their worn-out oxen and replace them with new animals, albeit at a considerable markup.

In 1844, a year after Fort Bridger opened for business, Caleb Greenwood led the first party of emigrants over the Sublette Cutoff, which bypassed the fort. Many emigrants still came to Fort Bridger, but traffic slowed. Starting in 1846, emigrants who made it to the fort had another choice of routes. That was the year Lansford Hastings rode east from California to advertise his new route to California via Salt Lake. From then on, overlanders at Fort Bridger could stay on the old road to Fort Hall, or they could try to save some time by keeping southwest to Salt Lake City instead via Hastings Cutoff, which was reported to cut hundreds of miles off the Fort Hall route. Three parties swallowed Hastings's Kool-Aid that first year and followed his cutoff. But more about that later.

There may or may not have been a Pony Express station at Fort Bridger. If there was, nothing much of note happened there. During the Utah Expedition, the US Army leased Fort Bridger. Before the army would pay, however, it wanted proof of title, which Bridger couldn't produce.

It is largely the remaining army structures that occupy Fort Bridger State Historic Site today, along with a reconstruction of the original trading post. I walked around a little to look at some of the old buildings and the reconstructed ones and read the interpretive signs. But the importance of Fort Bridger was its strategic location as both a waypoint on the Emigrant Trail and gateway to Salt Lake City. With Bridger Valley subdivided, plowed, irrigated, built on, and occupied, I couldn't get a good sense of what it must have been like by walking the grounds.

I stopped in at the visitor center to find a bathroom. The center is in a building that housed the sutler's store when the army took over. The woman working there showed me where the restrooms were and we got to talking. She told me the residents in the area had pretty much ignored COVID until there was a local outbreak, at which point the Fort Bridgerians started wearing masks. That is, until a local store put up a sign requiring masks inside, at which point the masks came off.

Side trip over, I rode the five miles back uphill to Lyman through intermittent drizzle, went straight to the laundromat, and washed every piece of clothing I could. After, I checked into my motel and emptied my bike trailer so I could take it and my bike to the car wash. It was only then, two days after the fact, that I remembered I had run water over the gunwales, as it were, crossing the stream back at Burnt Ranch. Everything at that level was sealed, and so remained dry, but the trailer bed and a few things I had stored under my gear bag were damp and a little funky. No disaster. But it bothered me that I had not taken better care of my gear.

With every restaurant and fast-food place in town closed, I ended up boiling water in the room's coffee maker and reconstituting a couple of dehydrated dinners. I watched an old Robert Redford movie, waited for the fireworks to die off, then went to bed—only to be woken up by partying Fourth of Julyers returning to the room right above me around midnight. I turned the air conditioner on for the white noise, and when that wasn't enough, inserted earplugs and eventually was able to get some sleep. But I had to wonder—why couldn't I have been downstairs from men who do laundry when they get away from home instead of going all *Guys Gone Wild*?

The ground was wet the next morning, and the sky overcast. But the chance of more rain was slight. I started off by retracing the five miles to Fort Bridger, Wyoming. The wind was calm, just a very light breeze (in the wrong direction, of course). The sky to the west was full of clouds, dropping rain in the Uinta Mountains further south. As the clouds neared where I was riding, they lifted and dissipated. I didn't see any rain at all that day. What I did see, which was unexpected, was a lot of climbing. The west side of Bridger Valley is buttressed by Bigelow Bench, a series of buttes. The huge turbines of a wind generator farm stood on top. I'd been seeing those generators since the day before, and they seemed high. I never would have guessed I'd be climbing up to that point. The climb was not huge, but I wasn't ready for it so early in the ride.

The payoff was a screaming downhill on the far side, which led to another climb up Muddy Creek. The road turned southwest to follow the creek. Just past the turnoff, I passed a couple of markers. One was a steel rail historical marker placed by the Oregon-California Trails Association to mark the Hastings Cutoff. Another nearby interpretive sign marked Muddy Creek Crossing, where apparently everyone and everything westbound in the mid-1800s crossed (including the transcontinental telegraph and railroad), and Muddy Creek Camp, where everyone camped. I also came across a different type of sign: a diamond-shaped warning sign that said "Handcart Crossing." There were signs for handcart camps all along Muddy Creek indicating side roads that led to empty lots. During a normal season, this area probably swarmed with sweaty, teenaged Mormons in period dress pushing handcarts around. There likely would also have been support vehicles plying the roads and kicking up dust. In this second summer of COVID, however, the road and the camps were empty.

Over the next couple of hours I enjoyed a gradual, uncommonly steady climb. The creek canyon and surrounding hills were beautiful, the empty road peaceful. At one point it finally dawned on me that this was the first real improved gravel road I had been on for days. That is, instead of just flattening the sagebrush under oversized vehicle tires, or scraping a narrow swath through the sand and maybe pouring gravel on top, the depressions were filled in to keep the road at an even grade for a steady climb instead of dipping into and climbing up out of every cross-ravine.

I suddenly felt rejuvenated, grateful to the Wyoming Department of Transportation and maybe even the Mormons who probably had a hand in making the road to their camps easier to travel. The surface was bad at times, but I didn't mind. The drop-offs where the road crossed ravines were steep and unguarded, but so what? I wasn't riding in the actual tracks of the emigrants, but who cares? It could have been me down there, struggling up those steep, sandy banks. Instead, I was up here, spinning easily up a steady grade. A little slowly, perhaps, but that was okay. I felt as if I had dodged a bullet I didn't even know had been fired. There is nothing like a decent road to improve a cyclist's mood.

I tried to picture how much worse it would have been for the eighty-plus members of the Donner Party humping their wagons over this ground. As tedious as it might have been for me, it would have been tortuous for them to ascend Muddy Creek without road improvements. And this would have been one of the easiest parts of the trail for them between Fort Bridger and California.

I passed by the Piedmont Kilns, built to supply charcoal to the settlement at Salt Lake, and the reflective waters of Piedmont Reservoir (also known as Guild and Dean's Reservoir). I topped the climb, then descended to Sulfur Creek Reservoir. I stopped by the boat launch area to use the pit toilet. There were some bass boats on the water, and a couple of adults trying to herd kids toward the beach while dealing with complaints about sunblock and toys and lunch and a diaper that needed changing. It was such a familiar scene, the chaos of excited young children and harried young parents, but seemed out of place given the terrain I had just crossed. I was only about fifteen miles from I-80 at this point, but because we came from two different worlds that morning—mine from 175 years ago and theirs from breakfast that day—it felt incongruous.

What seemed even more incongruous was that here, on the edge of a reservoir, there was no drinking water available.

I left the Pony Express Route at this point to ride Highway 150, which follows Bear River—the longest river in North America not to reach an ocean—to Evanston, Wyoming. When planning my route, I could not find a place to stay or camp along the route between Lyman, Wyoming, and the Echo Lake area in Utah, a distance of eighty-five miles. That was further than I wanted to ride in one day. This was also my eighth straight day of riding since leaving Casper, so I planned to stay in town two nights and rest up from riding across the western Wyoming high desert before making the final push over the Wasatch Mountains to Salt Lake City.

Just past the turnoff were two more monuments. One was dedicated to the Mormon pioneers who'd passed that spot on July 12, 1847. The second was granite marker for the Bear River Pony Express Station, the last station in Wyoming. It was Monday, July 5, a national holiday, and the highway was packed. All those patriotic revelers (including the people above me the night before, no doubt) were headed home in caravans of trucks and RVs towing trailers full of recreational gear, all of them whooshing by me at seventy miles per hour, sometimes moving over, more often not, everyone in an awful hurry to get back to God knows where. A headwind was coming up the river valley, but it wasn't nearly as bad as it could have been, especially with all the square-faced vehicles pushing the wind my way.

Evanston sits at the junction of Wyoming Highway 150 and I-80. With all the mammoth recreational vehicles lumbering around in search of gas, snacks, bathrooms, etc., traffic near the interchange was a little hairy. Things were much quieter in the old downtown further up from the freeway. Downtown Evanston was a lot like many of the old downtowns I'd seen on this trip: stone and brick buildings, old advertisements painted on the walls, wide streets, a cool 1940s-vintage theater, not to mention music piped through speakers mounted on light posts. I will never understand that (who chooses the playlist?), but here it was again.

Sadly, Evanston doesn't tout a town motto. But it does house the head-quarters of the Jamaican Bobsled Team. Park City, Utah (sixty miles away) has one of the few bobsled tracks in the United States, so some years ago a local attorney coaxed the team to make its homebase in Evanston with the promise of a few perqs. In early July you'd never guess there would be world-class snow so close. I'd forgotten that I'd been riding at a mile or higher elevation since just past Casper, Wyoming. Evanston sits at 6,700 feet above sea level and averages sixty inches of snow every year.

Evanston started as a railroad town, not a trail town, so I didn't spend a lot of time looking for landmarks. Rather, a little lunch and pie seemed to be in order and from the looks of downtown, the prospects seemed promising. As it turned out, my choices were few. There weren't many restaurants to begin with, and most of those decided to take the holiday off. I found a coffee house and sat out on the sidewalk in the shade to keep an eye on my bike. I relaxed for quite a while out there, talked with a couple traveling home from Boise to Cheyenne, and when the time came, I mounted up and rode the half mile, uphill, to the hotel. I'd ridden fifty-five miles and climbed two thousand feet, but all in all it had been a pretty quiet day on the trail.

Mounting Up

When I say "mounting up," I'm not being facetious. It was a process. My backpack (with a water bladder and a drinking tube so I could stay hydrated while riding) went on first, and I had to remember to secure the chest and belly straps so it wouldn't slide all over. Next I pulled gloves onto my hands, put a sweat cap on my head, then the helmet over that. Fully dressed, I turned on the taillight at the back of the trailer, the radar/taillight under my saddle, and the running light on my handlebars. Then I reactivated the iPhone on my handlebars and made sure my nav app was still active and checked that I hadn't left anything on the table or resting on the trailer (which I have done in the past). Everything accounted for, attached, turned on, and secure, I'd swing my leg over the bike, check traffic in both directions (pedestrian and vehicular) to make sure I wouldn't hit anything or anyone, or vice versa, and only then would I roll forward to raise the trailer kickstand and get going.

CHAPTER THIRTY-TWO

Up One Creek and Down Another

I woke the next morning in Evanston knowing I didn't have to ride, which was its own special feeling of relaxation. I didn't mind riding every day—in fact I wanted to ride—but it was mentally liberating not having to deal with the logistics of where I would stay and when I would get there, what I would eat and what the wind would do, wondering if it would rain, etc. On layover days the elements could do what they wanted and it wouldn't affect me. I could eat whenever I wanted and not have to worry about eating too much or too little or too late to save myself from bonking; I could drink whatever and however much I wanted without making sure to leave enough to last the entire ride or worrying it wasn't as much as my body needed. Not having to think and plan may have been the real rest I got on these off days.

The following day I slept in a little and started my fifty-mile ride to Coalville, Utah, a little after 8:00 a.m. My route was essentially up one river valley, over a small divide, then down another river valley. The ride profile looked promising. It resembled a caret (^), or chevron, only with a shallower incline and a longer descent. It seemed too good to be true.

The first half of my ride was up Yellow Creek on Yellow Creek Road, a quiet, smoothly paved, two-lane road with a gentle grade. About ten miles in I came to a sign marking the Historical View Site of the Needles. Richard Burton described the Needles as "a huge Stonehenge, a crown of broken and somewhat lanceolate perpendicular conglomerates or cemented pudding-stones." I don't know that I would describe it as that exactly. For one thing, I've never had the chance to use "lanceolate" in a sentence. But also, like Church Butte back near Granger, Wyoming, and other land-marks along the trail, the feature itself wasn't impressive so much as it was distinct from its surroundings. In this case, outcroppings of rock against the otherwise smoother surface of the hills. Then again, I was viewing the Needles from the south, whereas Sir Richard approached the rocks from the northeast. Maybe they were more impressive from his angle.

Sir Richard and I saw the Needles from different vantage points because I wasn't following the historic trails, but rather had intersected them near the site of Needle Rock Pony Express Station. I'd left the Oregon Trail for good three days earlier when I turned south out of Fort Bridger, Wyoming, and the Oregon Trail turned northwest toward Fort Hall (near Pocatello, Idaho). My route had still been following the Mormon Pioneer, California, and Pony Express National Historic Trails toward Salt Lake City, but only as far as the Bear River Pony Express Station monument by Sulfur Creek Reservoir. Where I had turned north onto Highway 150 to go to Evanston, Wyoming, the historic trails continued southwest toward the Needles. The land between these points, Bear Creek Station and Needle Rock Station, was privately owned and inaccessible. My detour to Evanston, which took me around the private land, followed two sides of a triangle; the original trails formed the base of that triangle by following Coyote Creek across the privately held land. The place where I was standing was the bottom corner of that triangle. From here, the historic trails continued on their southwest line through Echo Canyon. I couldn't follow them because I-80 now fills most of Echo Canyon, leaving no through-road for bikes. As a result, I had to keep riding up Yellow Creek Road to get to Chalk Creek Canyon, a bike-accessible route that ran parallel to Echo Canyon. I wouldn't be trac-ing the historic trails again until I rejoined them near the town of Echo, Utah, at the mouth of Echo Canyon on Weber River.

Somewhere in here I passed out of Wyoming and into Utah, though I didn't see a sign. Further ahead I'd cross back into Wyoming before leaving it for good. The breeze was still light and what little there was followed me up the canyon. I wondered whether Wyoming was apologizing for the last two weeks, or maybe just giving me a good send-off to fool me into thinking wind there wasn't so bad after all. I'd corresponded with a local cyclist who'd told me the second half of the ride, down Chalk Creek, had strong headwinds in the afternoon. I hoped to reach Coalville before the wind worked itself up to full speed.

A few miles further up, the road climbed out of the valley and into foothills and the pavement gave way to a hard-packed gravel road. Then I came to a junction. The county highway I was on turned left and deteriorated; the hardpack turned right, up a steep hill. My route told me to go right, but it looked like private land for a mining operation. I could see on my nav app that the county highway went through but was longer. I opted for the better, shorter, steeper road—the cutoff, if you will—hoping it wasn't blocked to public use further along. It turned out to be open the entire way, but true to the tradition of the old cutoffs, there were some tough climbs. Soon enough I picked up Chalk Creek Road, which took me all the way down to my destination, Coalville, Utah, on the eastern end of Echo Reservoir.

By this point I had rejoined the Pony Express Bikepacking Route. Even so, there were no historical markers after Needle Rock Station because this was not on the emigrant route. Chalk Creek Road does, however, have a history loosely related to Pony Express.

At the time of the Utah War, the most direct approach to Salt Lake City for the US Army was through Echo Canyon, a narrow defile with steep walls. The Mormons erected defensive fortifications in the crenelated canyon walls, blocking the army's advance. After the war, when the army established Camp Floyd about forty miles south of Salt Lake City, General Albert Johnston wanted an alternate route separate from Echo Canyon to ensure there would always be an open route from the east to Camp Floyd in case of future hostilities. To that end, Captain James H. Simpson of the US Army's Corps of Topographical Engineers surveyed a new route that followed White Clay Creek from the Weber River to the Bear River. When the road work was done, Russell, Majors & Waddell rerouted their supply caravans over the new route because it was faster and had more grass and water than the older trail through Echo Canyon. The Pony Express stayed to the old route, which was more direct between Salt Lake City and Fort Bridger.

What Chalk Creek Valley lacked in historical markers, it made up for in increasing grandeur. I was getting further into the east side of the

Wasatch Mountains. Rocky outcroppings and larger formations seemed to increase as I went along. The valley was beautiful, and even better, trended downhill. As I suspected, the wind rushed up to greet me and there were some uphill sections where the road tended away from the creek and had to mount a rise, so my ride was not quite as fast and effortless as I might have hoped. Nevertheless, it was very pleasant overall. I saw my first recreational road cyclists here since Scottsbluff, Nebraska. Two separate couples out for a day's exercise, clad in Lycra, not carrying anything beyond what they needed for a few hours on the road. I envied their lighter loads.

I rode into Coalville much earlier than I had planned, around 12:30 p.m. Coalville got its start in 1858 as Chalk Creek. Its name changed after Brigham Young sent men out to investigate a reported discovery of coal in the area. It had a nice little downtown of older brick buildings. I would like to have found a café to hang out in, but there weren't any. I am not sure if that was because it was a predominantly non-coffee-drinking Mormon town, but regardless I had to find some other place that would allow a sweaty, dirty, stinky cyclist to escape the midnineties heat for a couple of hours until I could check in. Fortunately, I found a place for lunch. Unfortunately, as per usual the only nonmeat item was a grilled cheese sandwich.

By and by two o'clock rolled around and I decided to go by the hotel to see if I could check in early. Once in my room, I started my usual routine: charging devices, showering, changing, taking a short nap, then finding a table off the hotel lobby to write. A few hours later I wandered over to a nearby gas station c-store and bought some chocolate for the evening and electrolytes to pack for the next day. Back at the room I prepacked and double-checked everything so I would have the fewest items and tasks to forget in the morning. As evening fell I found I wasn't very hungry, so I skipped dinner.

I reviewed my route for the next day—three mountain passes—and thought I should get to bed early. Just then I realized the route I had mapped would only take me into downtown Salt Lake City. I was planning to stay with relatives who lived south of town, but had no idea how to get to their house. I went to the hotel business center and used their computer to update the route to my actual destination and downloaded the maps on all my devices. Part of me congratulated myself on catching that oversight, because figuring the route on the fly after fifty miles of hill climbs would have been tough. Another part, however, wondered how I ever missed that omission in the first place. Nevertheless, everything ready, route set, I watched a movie until it was time to go to bed.

In retrospect, my afternoon and evening sounded so civilized— showering, writing, watching a movie, using a business center to update electronic maps. This was not real bikepacking, let alone anything like the emigrant crossing or riding for the Pony Express. I admit I was not a dyed-in-the-wool bikepacker, nor was I a historical reenactor. Then again, I hadn't set out to experience the trail the way others did. I welcomed these conveniences at the end of the day, and even more so as I neared the end of the ride.

Besides, cycling has its own demands. On a bike, everything is about my immediate present, the right now: Paying attention to the pavement to make sure I don't run over anything that will cause a flat or a crash; staying attuned to the wind, especially in canyons where the breeze suddenly shears to go around obstacles, pushing me toward the road or the outer edge of a narrow shoulder; listening for the sound of cars approaching from behind; watching the cars ahead to make sure they see me and are staying in their lane; scanning the clouds as they gather for signs of rain or light- ning and anticipating the direction and strength of the wind they might push ahead of themselves; gauging my hunger, my thirst, my need to urinate; monitoring any pain in my arms, neck, butt, perineum, and legs; and all the while trying to take in scenery that is ever changing, trying to record it mentally, deciding whether it's worth stopping to take a picture. My mind runs through this constant cycle of gauging, checking, and evaluating while I cycle along.

It can be mentally taxing. But that immersiveness, the absolute presence cycling requires, is one of the things that makes long-distance cycling so addictive. It can be a complete escape from your day-to-day preoccupations.

The Most Efficient Means of Travel

Perhaps surprisingly, the physical aspect of riding a bike is one of the least demanding. Cycling is the most efficient form of human-powered propulsion. Over 98 percent of the cyclist's pedal effort is used to spin the wheels. Those who walk/jog are only 65 percent efficient. Running is even less efficient. Cycling is five times more efficient than running on flat surfaces with a still wind.

In the same sense, in order to relax it was just as important for me to clear my head at the end of the day, to get as far away as I could from the immediacy of cycling, the neediness of it, like a crying child you can't ignore. I found that writing was the answer. To recall all I had experienced during the day's ride, the ideas and the memories I wanted to preserve as well as the data points of my constantly running checklist of sensory bombardment, and to dump it out in the form of writing was the perfect antidote, the ideal counterweight. I had not planned to write as much or so often as I did. I never would have thought I'd have the energy or motivation at the end of each day's ride. But I'd come to realize that the days after I wrote I was more relaxed, more present, than the days I'd had to skip. It was the same whether I wrote from a camp chair in my tent or at a nice workspace in a motel. Though I'd be lying if I didn't admit that a hot shower and a clean bed, running water and air conditioning did make writing that much easier.

CHAPTER THIRTY-THREE

The City of the Saints

THE LAST DAY OF MY RIDE STARTED WARM AND CLEAR. I CROSSED OVER I-80, rode back through Coalville, then northwest toward the little town of Henefer, Utah ("Located on the historic Mormon Pioneer Trail") on a rail-to-trail path along the north edge of Echo Reservoir. As a former railroad track, the trail had a steady grade, in this case slightly downhill. It was nice not to have to ride the undulations of the road and not to be riding next to cars.

Between Coalville and Henefer is Echo, Utah, a town at the mouth of Echo Canyon. A monument for the Weber Pony Express Station sits just east of town, at the intersection of Echo Canyon and the Weber River. From this point, the Pony Express Bikepacking Trail rejoins the Mormon Pioneer, California, and Pony Express National Historic Trails and follows them the rest of the way into Salt Lake City.

There was not much in the town of Echo, but the red rock towering behind it and up the canyon were impressive. I took a couple of photos and moved on. Five miles further I came to Henefer, Utah, a tidy little town with few historical monuments. This was the point at which the Donner Party left the Weber River to find its way through the mountains to the Great Salt Lake. The Mormon Pioneer, California, Pony Express National Historic Trails, and the Pony Express Bikepacking Route all follow Highway 65 between Henefer and Salt Lake City along the path that the Donner Party blazed in 1846 and the Mormon Pioneers turned into a road in 1847.

The Donner Party—the first wagons over the Wasatch Mountains—camped in this area for five days waiting for Lansford Hastings to guide them. Hastings had published a guidebook in 1845 that stated emigrants would find the most direct route to California by leaving the established trail about two hundred miles east of Fort Hall and "bearing west southwest, to the Salt Lake." His cutoff would then reach the established California Trail along the Humboldt River by passing south of the lake. The book didn't detail the exact route, but historians estimate his cutoff would save anywhere from 150 to 400 miles off the Fort Hall route. If you compare the Fort Hall route to Hastings Cutoff on a map, it's easy to see why someone would want to risk it. Like my detour through Evanston, the two routes create a triangle, with Hastings Cutoff forming the much shorter and more direct straight-line base.

But cutoffs from the original trail were a double-edged sword. While they promised shorter distances between two points, they were more difficult, with longer distances between water, less forage, and worse terrain. And those were the best cutoffs, the ones blazed by knowledgeable guides. At the time Hastings published his guidebook, he had never seen the cutoff he had described, and no wagons had ever attempted it. Hastings's first attempt to follow the trail he had recommended was when he rode east from California in 1846 with veteran mountain men Jim Clyman and James Hudspeth to convince emigrants to follow him back west. The three men had an extremely hard time navigating the Wasatch Mountains above Salt Lake. According to Clyman, they barely got through, and they were on horses, which, unlike wagons, didn't need a road.

But that didn't stop Hastings. He wanted to be the Brigham Young of California. Or the Sam Houston. He thought California could easily be taken from Mexico, that he was the man to lead the revolution, and that afterward, he would be the one to lead the new republic. All he needed was the weight of an influx of American emigrants to back his play. In that sense, he wanted to be Moses, too.

Hastings led a wagon train of emigrants he'd recruited from Fort Bridger, the Harlan-Young Party of sixty-six wagons, to the Great Salt Lake. "Leading" in this case means not guiding so much as simply riding in front. Rather than follow his eastbound route, Hastings took the Harlan-Young Party down Weber River. Hastings had never traveled this route either, but knowing the route he'd taken east was not passable by wagons, he blindly hoped the river route would be better. It wasn't. The going was so bad they were sometimes cutting a road, other times climbing their wagons over boulders through the bed of the river and hauling wagons up mountainsides by ropes. Over the course of a week, they made only a mile and a half each day. They finally emerged from the mountains near the middle of the west shore of the Great Salt Lake, just south of Ogden, Utah.

Hastings had promised to return to guide the Donner Party after leading the Harlan-Young Party to the Great Salt Lake. But when the Donner Party arrived at the future site of Henefer, all they found was a note from Hastings pinned to a cleft stick. Remember Hastings was taking the Harlan-Young Party down the Weber River because he thought his eastbound route over the Wasatch Mountains too difficult for wagons. Unfortunately for everyone, he found going down the Weber River worse. At some point, Hastings returned to the crossing of the Weber near Henefer and left the note the Donner Party found. The note told anyone who'd made it this far along his cutoff that the Weber River was too hard to travel, and to ride ahead and fetch him and he'd return to guide them through the mountains. The Donner Party went into camp while James Reed and two others rode ahead. Reed came back alone five days later; the other two riders' horses had broken down. He'd found Hastings, but rather than return to guide the group, Hastings only took Reed a short way up a mountain and pointed the way across the Wasatch: that is, his eastbound route, the one he'd decided earlier was impassable by wagons.

Highway 65 was narrow and had no shoulder, but was well paved, lightly traveled this time of the morning, and had a gentle rise. Until it didn't. Once it started to lift toward the first pass, the going got slow. The sun was hidden probably half the time behind morning clouds, but when it came out it felt every bit as strong as you might expect for a midninety-degree forecast. Winds were very light. It wasn't long before my shirt was soaked.

Let me clarify: The back of my shirt, under my hydration pack, was perpetually wet, pretty much all day, every day of the ride. This morning, with this climb and under these conditions, my entire shirt was soaked.

After a five-mile climb I reached the top of the first rise, called Hogsback Summit. It was also nicknamed Heartbreak Ridge because the

Mormon emigrants reached this point after a long, hard pull (to which I can attest), only to get a good view of the much taller mountains they still needed to climb. From there the road descended into Dixie Hollow along East Canyon Creek. The creek has been dammed so most of the Hollow is now East Canyon Reservoir. The East Canyon Pony Express Station languishes somnolent somewhere under that water. When I rode past there were kayakers and paddle boarders playing on the lake. The air was so still I could hear their voices from quite a distance across the water.

For me, this was a nice, flat stretch, a good place to rest up before the biggest climb of the day. For the Donner Party it was hell. After Reed returned from his meeting with Hastings, the Donner Party started south, possibly on the route Hastings indicated, but with no way of knowing for certain. From Hogsback Summit, the Donner Party found the descent so steep and the vegetation so thick they had to cut a road skirting along the hillside through Broad Hollow, which risked tipping the high-wheeled, top-heavy wagons. Back in the river bottom they had to cut through willows "thick as a porcupine's quills and hardly less troublesome to get through." Even after the passage of the Donners and improvement by the Mormons, the trail forded East Canyon Creek "ten or more times," and the cut willow stubs tore at oxen hoofs and gashed their legs.

The climb up Big Mountain on Highway 65 started just a little past the south end of East Canyon Reservoir, up Dutch Hollow. In 1846 the vegetation was so thick here that the Donner Party camped for three days while the men went forward to hack a trail, hewing their way yard by yard by felling "willow, alder, and aspen twenty feet tall intertwined with service-berries and wild rose." A year later, Mormon scouts followed the Donner Party's faint track. Mormon diarists deemed this thirty-six-mile stretch from Henefer to Salt Lake City the worst part of the Mormon Trail. It had taken the Donner Party eleven days to hack their way through. It took the Mormon road crew, Orson Pratt and forty-two men who traveled ahead to make the road passable by the main body of the pioneering party, six days to rework the path the Donner Party had cut the year before. According to Wallace Stegner, the Mormons "fell into camp every night with a respect approaching awe" for the work the Donner Party had faced. One hundred years later there was still no paved road over Big Mountain. Crews were constructing it when Irene Paden traveled this area in 1946.

It took the Donner Party more than two weeks in August 1846 to hack a road through the Wasatch Mountains. They still had to cross the Great Salt Desert and all of Nevada. By the time they reached the base of what came to be known as Donner Pass in the Sierra Nevada Mountains it was October 31, and the pass was blocked with snow from an early winter storm. They shacked up on the east side of Donner Lake, and as has been well documented, survived the winter by resorting to cannibalism. By the time the last of the survivors had been brought down from the Sierra Nevadas in April 1847, forty of the party members had died out of eighty-seven who had crossed the Wasatch Mountains, thirty-five of those over the winter. That number doesn't include two Native American rescuers, Luis and Salvador, whom a few of the more desperate surviving emigrants killed and ate on the western slope of the Sierra Nevadas.

The Donners had unwisely laid over at various points during their overland trek. But the combination of delay and fatigue they incurred blazing a trail through the Wasatch Mountains, followed by their *jornada* across the salt flats, brought them to the Sierra Nevadas long after and in far worse shape than if they'd followed the advice of two experienced mountain men, Jim Clyman and Joseph Walker, who personally told them to stick to the Fort Hall route instead.

At the base of the climb up Big Mountain, the Pony Express Bikepacking Route leaves the highway at a fork in the road to take a gravel route along East Canyon Creek, then up Little Emigration Canyon to Big Mountain. The route note for this section started with the phrases, "Hike-a-Bike" and "Mormon Trail Overgrown," which translate to "You'll have to get off your bike and push it through bushes." And that was the easier section of the trail. The trail leaves East Creek to climb Little Emigration Canyon to the top of Big Mountain on a singletrack mountain bike trail referred to as "Mormon Puke Hill" for the brutal climbs near the top. There was no way I was going to try to push my trailer up that mountain bike route. I stuck on Highway 65, which was hard enough.

I have never been a good climber. Even in my best shape I get dusted by other cyclists. My ungrateful son, Kazu, will practice one-handed wheelies on the mountain bike I bought for him while I trail behind in first gear, gasping for air, tongue hanging out like a dehydrated dog. It's embarrassing how slow I can be. I settled in for a long, slow climb up the appropriately named Big Mountain. My mantra at times like these is a haiku by Issa Kobayashi:

O snail
Climb Mount Fuji
But slowly, slowly

But there you have it. I crawled up the north side of Big Mountain slowly, slowly, until at last I made the pass. The elevation at Big Mountain Pass is 7,420 feet, slightly higher than South Pass at the Continental Divide. In January 1853, Feramorz Little and the Mormon mail carriers had hauled two seventy-pound bags up and over this pass in the snow. They cached it at the base and made a seventeen-mile dash from there to Salt Lake City. Even today maps note that this highway is closed in winter from Henefer south. I was glad to be sitting at the top, but compared to the Donner Party, Feramorz Little and his cohorts, and countless others of the time, mine was not such an impressive achievement. In fact, the closer I got to Salt Lake City, the more cyclists there were. Not travelers, like me, but folks riding up Big Mountain for exercise. You know, fun.

There was a parking area at the pass with pit toilets and some monuments, interpretive signs, and historical markers. I took a break and read them all. Big Mountain Pass also affords a view down through the canyons to the south and into the Salt Lake Valley. The Wasatch Mountains are steep-sided and precipitous, and the view over the lower peaks and down the canyons is spectacular. Do you need to ride a bike up Big Mountain to appreciate the view? No. My suggestion is to drive.

The descent down the north slope of Big Mountain was a white-knuckle ride. Some years ago, while descending a hill like this in the Sierra Nevadas during an ultradistance ride, another rider passed me. When we got to the bottom, he slowed to share his joy. "I need a cigarette," he said. Big Mountain was that kind of rush. I had outfitted my bike for this ride with oversized disc brake rotors and beefed-up, four-piston calipers to handle the extra weight I'd planned to carry. Even controlling my speed on the descent, the bike got up to nearly forty miles per hour, dangerously fast considering my trailer's manual advised a top speed of fifteen miles per hour.

Taking the Lane

On narrow roads, such as the stretch of Highway 65 south of Big Mountain, the best defensive move for a cyclist is to ride in the middle of the road. This is known as "taking the lane." To stay to the right is to invite a vehicle to pass, and on a narrow road like this with no shoulder and not enough room, riding to the right increases the chances the cyclist will be forced off the road. I held to the middle of the lane until I heard my radar beep. Without it, I would never have known cars were behind me for the whistle of the wind in my ears. Once I heard the alarm, I waved over my shoulder to let the driver know I knew they were behind me, signaled that I was moving to the right, then slowly moved over.

Eventually the road flattened out into an area known as Mountain Dell. From there I had one more climb, over Little Mountain Summit. This summit is possibly where Hastings pointed out the route over the Wasatch to James Reed. The climb was not particularly long, not particularly steep. But it had to be done, and after the climb up Big Mountain I rode up the hill more slowly than I might have otherwise. Eventually, though, there I was, looking down at the reservoirs at the upper end of Parley's Canyon and looking forward to a final, long descent down Emigration Canyon.

Another screaming ride down the upper part of the winding canyon. There weren't too many cars or bikes, so the ride never felt sketchy that way. The slope transitioned into a long, pleasant descent, less steep than the upper canyon. Soon I was on the outskirts of the city, riding down a tree-lined street past houses and parked cars, and with them the potential to be doored. I made it through without incident, stopping to take pictures of monuments at Donner Hill—a place where the emigrants were so tired of hacking through brush and climbing over boulders they went straight up a hill instead—and the last camp of the Mormon Pioneers. In a way it was kind of a big finish, this slalom ride down historic Emigration Canyon into the City of the Saints.

I sped past This Is The Place shrine, not feeling up to a dose of Mormon mythology just then. The shrine marks the spot where Brigham

Young, on nearing the Salt Lake Valley in 1847, is supposed to have called for the carriage carrying him to stop and, after remaining a moment as if lost in a vision, said "It is enough. This is the right place, drive on." That's not exactly how it happened—the words seem to have been put in Young's mouth some thirty-three years later—but like so many tales about the West, it makes a good story.

Soon enough I was in the thick of it, and saints or no, it was just like riding in any other big city. Four lanes of traffic all rushing from one red light to the next. Watching out for cars turning left in front of me or speeding up to pass and cut me off by turning right. I had mapped out a purportedly bicycle-friendly route through the city, but sometimes that meant no more than a nominal bike lane alongside that rush. My destination was in the suburbs south of downtown, so eventually I turned left. Happily, south was downhill and downwind, so I had an easy time of it, except for the bus driver who kept passing me only to stop at his stop, then pull out again to cut me off rather than pass me again. I was relieved when he finally turned off after a couple of miles of this cat-and-mouse.

I made it to a café I had marked on the map just a short distance from where my cousins, Connie and Mike, lived, which was where I was going to stay for a couple of days. I thought I'd rest and recuperate and evaporate off a little more sweat before invading their home. But the place turned out to be a drive-through with no seating area. Quick search. Another promising place a mile or so away, up a hill, naturally. But once I arrived, worth the ride. Feeling recruited, I remounted the bike and rolled downhill. Connie was home and I stopped her from hugging me then explained about all the sweating I had done earlier and all of the grit I had no doubt picked up since. One shower later we were sitting and talking and waiting for Mike to get home from work.

It was lovely in a way I don't know how well I can convey. To Mike and Connie it was simple. This was how you treated family. But for me, to ride so far, to be on my own for such long stretches of time, to ride through such remote places, and then to be in the hands of family, relatives by marriage who welcomed me and treated me as blood, was a comfort and a blessing beyond my ability to describe.

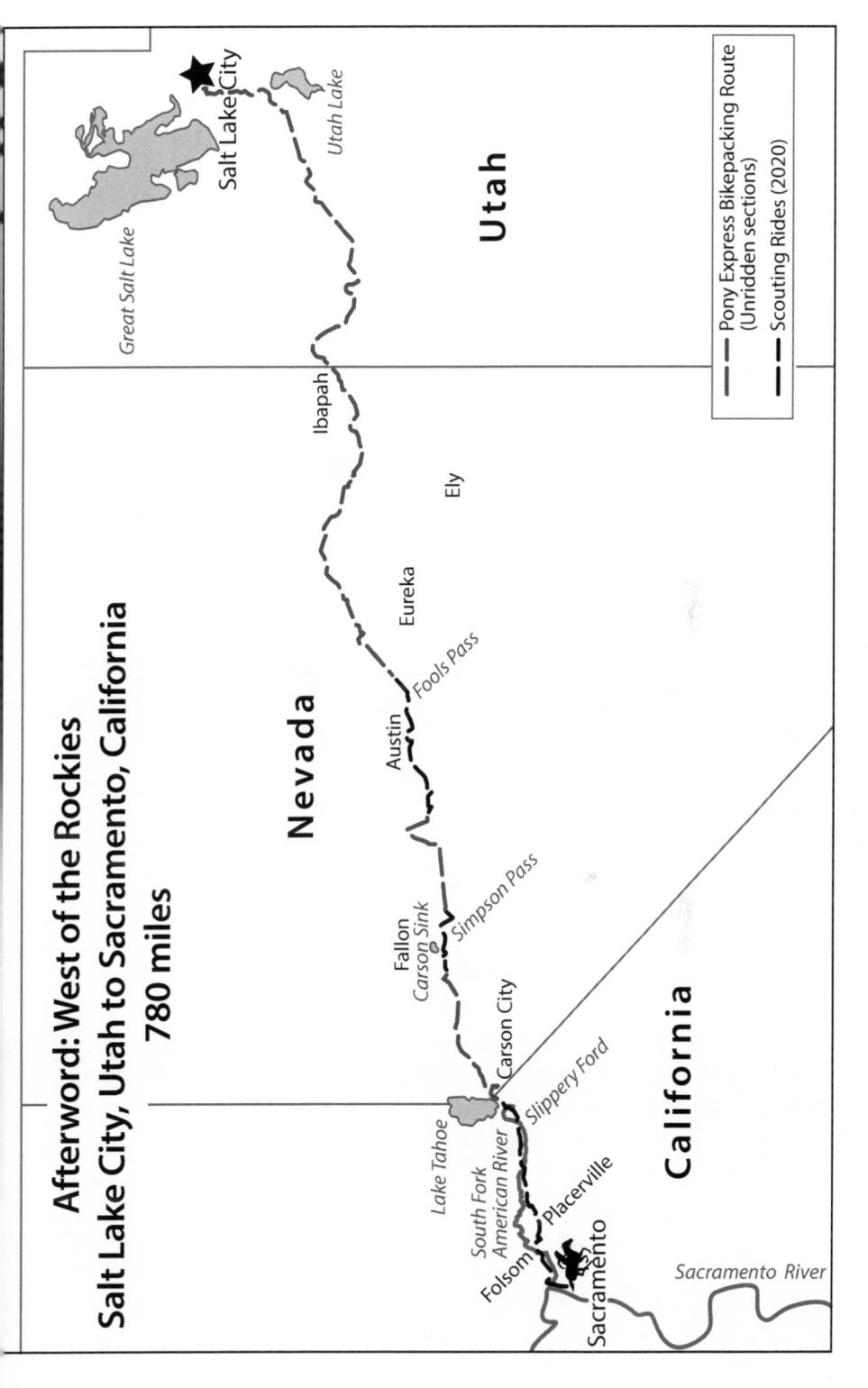

Afterword: West of the Rockies
Salt Lake City, Utah to Sacramento, California
780 miles

Great Salt Lake

Salt Lake City

Utah Lake

Utah

Ibapah

Ely

Eureka

Fools Pass

Austin

Nevada

Fallon

Carson Sink

Simpson Pass

Carson City

Lake Tahoe

Slippery Ford

South Fork
American River

Placerville

Folsom

Sacramento

California

Sacramento River

- - - Pony Express Bikepacking Route
(Unridden sections)

— — Scouting Rides (2020)

Afterword

The Mormon Pioneer Trail ended in Salt Lake City. The California and Pony Express Trails continued, but parted ways from there: The California Trail went north and west, while the Pony Express Trail went south. I took Amtrak's California Zephyr back home to California from Salt Lake City. The tracks followed roughly along the same course as Hastings Cutoff and the California Trail along the Humboldt River. And so, for the first time in six weeks, I found myself nowhere near the Pony Express Trail.

I had planned from the start to end my ride at Salt Lake City. By the time I arrived, I was glad I did. Though I had only ridden two-thirds of the Pony Express Route on this trip, it was now the second week of July. It was high summer in the Great Basin, more than five hundred miles of desert riding between Salt Lake City and Carson City, Nevada. Unlike the overland emigrants trying to beat the Sierra Nevada snow, or Pony Express riders who didn't have a choice, there was no rational reason for me to suffer the worst of the desert heat. Other factors also came into play. The western United States was in the worst drought since 2000. Water, scarce across the Great Basin in summer, might not be available at all from otherwise dependable sources. Air quality from California to Utah was poor. There were so many fires raging across the Northwest and of such magnitude that their smoke filled Salt Lake Valley. By the time I boarded the train, the front range of the Wasatch, so clear and close when I had arrived, was obscured behind a gauzy veil of smoke.

Though I didn't ride the section between Salt Lake City, Utah, and Sacramento, California, on this trip, I had scouted substantial portions the year before. I'd explored alternate trails in California and helped fill in some gaps in the draft Pony Express Bikepacking Route through central Nevada.

These scouting rides were out-and-back day trips, which meant minimal gear and no trailer, and they were still tough—by far the most technical trails I encountered on the route. I'd hike-a-biked over the river-rock section of Slippery Ford and pushed my bike up steep, loose, winding singletrack on my way to Echo Summit near Lake Tahoe. I'd scrambled up and down sketchy, shale-strewn trails over passes, such as Fool's Cutoff near Dry Creek Pony Express Station west of Austin, Nevada. I got mired in the playa of Four Mile Flat and filled my shoes with sand walking my bike up and over Simpson's Pass near Farson, Nevada.

In short, I knew what I was missing and I didn't miss it at all.

Nevertheless, though I didn't ride through this portion on my trip, the story of the Pony Express west of the Rockies is an integral part of the saga. Events in the Great Basin nearly ended the Pony Express as soon as it began. And if it weren't for California, there might not have been a Pony Express at all.

THE PAIUTE WAR

From Salt Lake City, the Pony Express Trail first headed south to Camp Floyd before turning west to cut more or less straight across the Great Basin to the foot of the Sierra Nevada Mountains at Genoa, Nevada (near Carson City). It followed a route surveyed in 1859 by Captain James Simpson, the same topographical engineer who'd surveyed the Chalk Creek route to Camp Floyd the year before. Simpson's job was to survey and lay out a wagon road that could resupply the army station at Camp Floyd from the west. He sought the most direct route possible, taking into account having to go around mountain ranges (Nevada has nearly one hundred, all running north–south) and having to deviate off course to find water.

After returning from his expedition in August 1859, Captain Simpson published notices in Salt Lake City newspapers extolling the virtues of his route. One person who took notice was George Chorpenning, who had the contract to deliver mail between Sacramento and Salt Lake City. Chorpenning had shifted his route across Nevada a few times during the previous eight years and welcomed the opportunity to shorten it. By early 1860, Chorpenning was busy setting up stations along Simpson's new route. In May 1860, however, the US postmaster general annulled Chorpenning's contract and gave it to Russell, Majors & Waddell. Along with Chorpenning's route, the firm acquired the mail stations he had built, apparently without compensating him.

Finally, Russell had his long-sought-after route from the Missouri River to California. But at what cost? While the US postmaster general was canceling Chorpenning's contract and handing it to Russell, a motley collection of miners in western Nevada were singing their way to their likely deaths at the First Battle of Pyramid Lake. This was the opening of the Paiute War.

Causes of the Paiute War reached back at least thirty years to 1832 when mountain man Joe Meek shot and killed a Shoshone man on the Humboldt River because he "looked as if" he were going to steal something. The following year, members of another expedition killed scores of Native Americans in the same area, possibly as many as seventy-five. For the next thirty years, overland emigrants and Native Americans fought along the Nevada portion of the California Trail. In 1859, the discovery of the Comstock Lode near Virginia City, Nevada, led to a headlong rush of people to the area. As in other rushes, a great number of miners chasing after instant riches invaded Native American land and destroyed their sources of food—in this case, driving the tribes to the point of near starvation.

The immediate cause of the Paiute War was that some number of Paiute women, sometimes reported to be teenagers, were kidnapped, held captive, and presumably raped at Williams Station in Nevada. The husband of one of the women tried to rescue her and failed, after which he returned with others, rescued the women, then killed the three men they found at the station and burned it. The killings occurred on May 7, 1860, and were discovered the next day by stationmaster James Williams, who had reportedly been out rounding up lost stock. Williams rode to the nearest Pony Express station and sent the rider with the news to Virginia City. By the time the rider dismounted, the story had somehow grown. He reported seven men killed by a combined force of five hundred Paiutes, Shoshones, and Pitt River Indians who had chased Williams for miles before giving up.

Some went out to Williams Station to investigate. Others got drunk and vowed revenge. Within days a ragtag force of 105 volunteers had assembled to punish the purported offenders. They trundled off toward Pyramid Lake, thinking it would be fun. Their motto was "An Indian for breakfast and a pony to ride." The Paiutes knew a force would come, so they set a trap. They sent out a few horsemen to lure the attacking force into a narrow space then closed off the escape and had a turkey shoot of their own. During this First Battle of Pyramid Lake, the Paiutes killed more than seventy of the volunteers and injured others.

Later in May, Shoshones attacked two Pony Express stations further east, killing employees at Dry Creek Station and Simpson Park Station. A second, better organized force of volunteers went out in June and engaged the Paiutes in a Second Battle at Pyramid Lake. After a few more skirmishes, the parties negotiated a truce.

Meanwhile, some who went out on the initial investigation concluded it was unlikely any Native Americans were involved in the initial murders. Nothing about the scene or the assailants' actions was consistent with such attacks: None of the stock had been driven off; a storehouse filled with provisions and powder was untouched; no other stations had been attacked; and the only thing taken from Williams Station was money. They concluded it more likely that someone who had recently lost at cards killed the men to retrieve his money and burned the scene to hide his act.

The Paiute War shut down eastbound Pony Express deliveries for over a month and caused interruptions in both directions for a number of months more as conflicts continued throughout eastern Nevada and western Utah. In the aftermath of the war, Russell, Majors & Waddell found itself saddled with the dual burdens of lost income and having to spend even more money it didn't have to rebuild destroyed stations across the Great Basin with more substantial, defendable structures.

In retrospect, one can see how the losses incurred as a result of this war became one more in a series of financial mishaps and missteps to Russell, Majors & Waddell's early grave. The firm started by incurring debt to fund its initial startup in 1855; took on more debt and absorbed huge losses supplying the Utah Expedition in 1857–1858; expended more money it didn't have to bail out Russell and Jones's Leavenworth and Pikes Peak Express in 1859; and borrowed heavily again to fund the start-up costs of the Pony Express in early 1860. The costs incurred throughout the summer of 1860 to rebuild its line through the Great Basin after the Paiute War rendered the firm's crushing debt insurmountable and hammered the penultimate nail in Russell, Majors & Waddell's coffin. Russell's desperate, ham-handed embezzlement of Indian Trust Funds later that year sealed it for good.

At the same time, the Paiute War arguably gave later champions of the Pony Express its greatest feat: the legendary ride of Pony Bob Haslam, who purportedly rode 380 miles in thirty-six hours during the worst of the raids on the Nevada stations. Pony Bob started his normal route from Friday Station (by South Lake Tahoe) to Buckland's Station (near Farson, Nevada) just as Paiutes and Shoshones were attacking stations and stealing horses throughout western Nevada. He kept riding when there was no one to relieve him or when the relief rider was too afraid, rode on the same tired horse when there was none to replace it, and through it all kept within hours of the Pony Express's scheduled time.

That's the nearly incontrovertible legend, anyway. Pony Bob's heroic effort went unreported at the time and wasn't written about until thirty years later when it appeared in Alexander Majors's autobiography. Despite numerous factual flaws and inconsistencies in Haslam's account, his unsubstantiated story was lifted wholesale from Majors's autobiography and reprinted in the first book on the Pony Express and has been dutifully repeated for more than a hundred years. Despite being undocumented, Pony Bob's ride stands proudly in Pony Express lore as the epitome of the speed, dedication, endurance, and bravery of our red-flannelled riders of the purple sage.

GOING TO CALIFORNIA

California was the beginning and the end of the Pony Express. The clamoring of Californians for better mail service led to the creation of an overland mail route between the Missouri River and the Golden Gate. The purpose of the Pony Express was to demonstrate the viability of the

Central Route for delivering mail quickly and consistently to and from California. It failed for the same reasons all previous efforts had failed: the severity of winter weather in the Rocky Mountains.

Which begs the question: What did the Pony Express accomplish? The answer to some is nothing less than to save the United States by holding California and its vast wealth to the Union at the brink of the Civil War. To them, this was the higher purpose the Pony Express served.

When Abraham Lincoln was elected president in November 1860, the United States was a financial wreck. President Lincoln viewed California's mineral wealth as vital to the Union. Yet in the months leading up to the Civil War it was unclear where Californians stood. There was a strong proslavery Democrat contingent in the state government, including the governor, the legislature, and four of its congressional representatives. The US Army's Department of the Pacific, headquartered in San Francisco, was led by Southerner and slaveholder General Albert Sidney Johnston (late of the Mormon War), who later resigned his commission to fight for the Confederacy. The population of the southern half of California, like the legislature, was overwhelmingly proslavery. In 1859 the California legislature voted to set off six southern counties and form a separate territorial government that would legalize slavery. The people of these counties voted three to one in favor of dismemberment.

Jefferson Davis, president of the Confederate States, had felt certain California and other western states would join the Confederacy, or at least be disloyal to the United States. California Democrats in favor of disloyalty advocated secession from the United States to create an independent Pacific Republic. Backers of this movement, known as "Copperheads," hoped keeping California independent would weaken the Union by denying it California's money and at the same time drain Union resources by requiring a force to keep the state neutral.

The Pony Express's purported role in this drama was that the news it delivered to California buttressed the state's silently complacent pro-Union majority. For example, reports of Pennsylvania's vote in favor of Abraham Lincoln in October 1860 encouraged California Republicans to "put forth their greatest effort to carry the state for Lincoln." The army also used the Pony to communicate with the Department of the Pacific. Arguably, the Pony's communications helped the army maintain control over potentially anti-Union forces in California. Ultimately, California's pro-Union forces rose up and the state contributed substantially to the success of the United States during the Civil War.

While it is indisputable that the Pony Express brought the most recent news to California, and further, that the news helped keep California in the Union, there is nothing to suggest that *but for* the Pony Express, California would not have helped elect Lincoln or support the United States. There is nothing to indicate that California's allegiance depended on the Pony Express, or to put it another way, that California only stayed loyal because it received mail in ten days rather than eighteen or twenty, that had the news been slower in coming, things might have gone differently.

Moreover, if the Pony Express did play a vital role in keeping California loyal, then it is the greatest irony of the entire Pony Express saga. The Pony Express was a proslavery institution from the top down. All three principals, William Russell, Alexander Majors, and William Waddell, were slaveholders. It has even been alleged that the partners' success was "deeply entwined with their slaveholding status," and that the firm "likely relied heavily on slave labor in their businesses."

Bear in mind the time and place that fostered Russell, Majors & Waddell. Just months before the firm incorporated and established its base in Leavenworth, Kansas, Congress made Kansas a territory by passing the Kansas-Nebraska Act of 1854. This act overruled the Missouri Compromise of 1820 by enabling each territory to determine the legality of slavery in its jurisdiction. The measure passed largely because Congress members assumed Nebraska would vote to be a free territory and that Kansas would allow slavery, keeping the balance of power in Washington. But Eastern abolitionists, seeking to make Kansas Territory free, sponsored antislavery emigrants to settle in Kansas. In response, proslavery emigrants, primarily from Missouri, staked out claims in Kansas and regularly went across the border to vote illegally to allow slavery. Clashes became violent, resulting in the epithet "Bleeding Kansas." Between

November 1, 1855, and December 1, 1856, an estimated two hundred people were killed in a war of retribution and retaliation between the two factions. Violence was so fierce that in 1857 General Harney was pulled away from the task of leading the Utah Expedition against the Mormons in order to quell riots in Kansas even though it meant the Utah Expedition had to start west without a commanding officer or any supporting cavalry.

In this milieu, John Russell, Alexander Majors, and William Bradford Waddell personally and corporately "threw their weight as the most influential capitalists in the territory on the side of slavery." Proslavery groups, known as "Border Ruffians," boarded incoming steamboats on the Missouri River, took any equipment "Free-Staters" had with them, then turned the Free-Staters away from Kansas. Russell, Majors & Waddell allowed the Border Ruffians to use its warehouse as a depot for selling these confiscated goods. The firm accepted funds on behalf of proslavery immigrants. The town where the firm set its headquarters, Leavenworth, Kansas, was headquarters for the proslavery faction dedicated to making Kansas a slave state.

While all three were involved, Russell was a particularly active supporter. He joined the proslavery Law and Order Party when it was organized in 1856 and became its treasurer. He was also one of the signatories of a flyer it sent out asking for donations and recruiting proslavery immigrants to move to Kansas to vote in favor of slavery.

Nor does the Pony Express's proslavery contingent end there. Senator Gwin of California, credited with suggesting to Russell that he start a Pony Express, was strongly pro-South. While sitting as a senator he still held a large plantation in Mississippi that relied on enslaved labor, and he brought enslaved people with him when he moved to California. In a speech before the Senate, he argued that the Southern states could secede, "violently if necessary." Benjamin Ficklin, supervisor over the entire Pony Express line, was a major in the Confederacy in charge of the Virginia quartermaster's ordinance department. The indomitable Pony Express Division Superintendent Jack Slade once told one of his bullwhackers that if he intended to get back to the States with his scalp, "never let me hear you again say you are an abolitionist." M. Jeff Thompson, the mayor of St. Joseph, Missouri, who gave a speech at the launch of the Pony Express on April 3, 1860, became a brigadier general in the Missouri state militia during the Civil War. He led a raid on a US arsenal, cut down a US flag from the St. Joseph Post Office, and according to a display at the Patee House Museum, was a "rebel adulterer."

Moreover, hostility toward the United States didn't come only from Confederate ranks. In Utah and east Nevada, Pony Express station keepers and riders were Mormons, who as a group were antagonistic toward both the North and the South. Joseph Smith had foretold the Civil War in 1832. To Brigham Young, the coming of the war in 1861 fulfilled Smith's prophecy and the carnage was payback for persecution the Mormons had suffered back in the States. His policy was to stay neutral and "pray both parties prevailed." Maybe then the Mormons would be left to govern themselves in peace.

Given the proslavery stance of the partners and leadership of the Pony Express, as well as the distain of the Mormons for the United States, it is difficult to see what satisfaction any of these men would have gained from learning their efforts helped save the Union.

Enough with the myths.

The Pony Express did not save the United States. Neither were Russell, Majors, or Waddell patriots. William Russell wasn't a genius. Alexander Majors wasn't a saint. As a group, Pony Express riders were not God-fearing Christians. Their horses weren't semimythic beasts.

It has been the onus of the Pony Express to be the skeleton on which each successive wave of writers and enactors heaps layers of meaning according to their predilections. Buffalo Bill created the action-figure version of the Pony Express to pad his résumé and add excitement to his Wild West Show. The Daughters of the American Revolution and others since have burnished that image by giving it a patriotic sheen. Ever since, the Pony Express has been glorified as exemplary, symbolic, or patriotic, described as heroic, sentimental, or romantic, each characterization further obscuring rather than elucidating the singular accomplishment of the Pony Express.

Which is this: For a brief period, an army of people moved a small amount of mail across the American West as quickly as humanly possible under exceptionally difficult conditions. Riders braved long, lonely rides, at times across barren stretches of land in extremely harsh weather. Station keepers withstood loneliness, isolation, boredom, and sometimes grave personal danger to support them. The rank and file who operated the Pony Express, the people whose pay was so intermittent they nicknamed the COC&PP "Clean Out of Cash and Poor Pay," were mail carriers in the best sense of a tradition at least as old as Persia's Angarium from the fifth century BCE: "Neither snow nor rain nor heat nor gloom of night stays these couriers from the swift completion of their appointed rounds." The Pony Express was a trans-Mississippi mail service in the mid-1800s. Nothing more, and nothing less.

BIBLIOGRAPHY

ARTICLES

Ackley, Richard Thomas. "Across the Plains in 1858." *Utah Historical Quarterly* 9, no. 1–4 (October 1941): 190–228.

Allin, Lawrence C. "'A Mile Wide and an Inch Deep': Attempts to Navigate the Platte River." *Nebraska History* 63 (1982): 1–15.

Anderson, Harry. "The Controversial Sioux Amendment to the Fort Laramie Treaty of 1851." *Nebraska History* 37 (1956): 201–20.

Applegate, Jesse. "A Day with the Cow Column in 1843." *Quarterly of the Oregon Historical Society* 1, no. 4 (1900).

Bailey, W. F. "The Pony Express." *Century Magazine* 41 (October 1898): 882–92.

Beehrer, George W., and Julie Beehrer Colyer. "Freighting across the Plains." *Montana: The Magazine of Western History* 12, no. 4 (1962): 2–17.

Beeton, Barbara. "James Hervey Simpson in the Great Basin." *Montana: The Magazine of Western History* 28, no. 1 (1978): 28–43.

Bennett, Colin. "Compacts and Compromises: Thomas S. Twiss and West Point Influence in the Antebellum South Carolina College." *South Carolina Historical Magazine* 109, no. 1 (2008): 7–37.

Bernholz, Charles D. "Citation Abuse and Legal Writing: A Note on the Treaty of Fort Laramie with Sioux, Etc., 1851 and 11 Stat. 749." *Legal Reference Services Quarterly* 29 (2010): 133–48.

Bigler, David L. "'A Lion in the Path': Genesis of the Utah War, 1857–1858." *Utah Historical Quarterly* 76, no. 1 (2008): 4–21.

Brown, Randy. "The Grave of Susan C. Haile." *Overland Journal* 25, no. 1 (Spring 2007): 24–36.

Carley, Maurine, comp. "Second Segment of the Oregon Trail in Wyoming: Cold Spring to Fort Fetterman." *Annals of Wyoming* (October 1970): 252–70.

Carter, John Denton. "Before the Telegraph: The News Service of the San Francisco Bulletin, 1855–1861." *Pacific Historical Review* 11, no. 3 (September 1942): 301–17.

Chamber of Commerce, Austin, Nevada. "Austin-Toiyabe Mountain Bike Trail Guide." n.d.

Chapman, Arthur. "Slade of the Overland." *Union Pacific Magazine*, January 1931.

Clark, William. "A Trip across the Plains in 1857." *Iowa Journal of History and Politics* 22, no. 2 (April 1922): 163–223.

Clow, Richmond L. "General William S. Harney on the Northern Plains." *South Dakota Historical Society Quarterly* 16, no. 3 (1986): 229–48.

Considine, John L. "Eleven Days to St. Joe!" *Sunset Magazine* 51, no. 4 (October 1923): 36, 80–81.

Darley, Reverend G. M. "The End Gate of the Mess Wagon." *The Trail: A Magazine for Colorado* 1, no. 1 (n.d.): 18–19.

Davies, J. Kenneth. "Mormons and California Gold." *Journal of Mormon History* 7 (1980): 83–99.

Drum, General Richard C. "Reminiscences of the Indian Fight at Ash Hollow, 1855." *Collections of the Nebraska State Historical Society* XVI (1911): 143–51.

Eisele, Kimi. "Thoughts by the Way: Women's Written Perceptions of the American Frontier Landscape." *Middle States Division of the Association of American Geographers*, 1993.

Eldridge, John. "The Utah War: A Photographic Essay of Some of Its Important Historic Sites." *Utah Historical Quarterly* 76, no. 1 (2008): 38–64.

"Emigration from Iowa to Oregon in 1843." *Oregon Historical Quarterly* 15, no. 4 (December 1914): 285–99.

Ericson, Robert, and D. Rebecca Snow. "The Indian Battle for Self-Determination." *California Law Review* 58, no. 2 (March 1970): 445–90.

Fixico, Donald L. "Ethics and Responsibilities in Writing American Indian History." *American Indian Quarterly*, Special Issue: *Writing about American Indians* 20, no. 1 (Winter 1996).

Ford, Dixon, and Lee Kreutzer. "Oxen: Engines of the Overland Emigration." *Overland Journal* 33, no. 1 (Spring 2015): 4–29.

Franklin, William E. "The Archy Case: The California Supreme Court Refuses to Free a Slave." *Pacific Historical Review* 32, no. 2 (May 1963): 137–54.

Goodwin, Victor O. "Development of Emigrant Routes of Northern Nevada." *Nevada Historical Society Quarterly* VIII, no. 3–4 (Fall–Winter 1965): 25–40.

Gray, John S. "Fact Versus Fiction in the Kansas Boyhood of Buffalo Bill." *Kansas History* 8, no. 1 (Spring 1985): 2–20.

———. "The Salt Lake Hockaday Mail, Part 1 (of 2)." *Annals of Wyoming* 56, no. 2 (Fall 1984): 12–19.

———. "The Salt Lake Hockaday Mail, Part 2 (of 2)." *Annals of Wyoming* 57, no. 1 (Spring 1985): 2–12.

Gudger, E. W. "Marco Polo and Some Modern Things Old in the Asia of His Day." *Scientific Monthly* 37, no. 6 (December 1933): 496–510.

Guenther, Todd. "The Burnt Ranch Saga: A History of the Last Crossing of the Sweetwater." *Overland Journal* 17, no. 4 (Winter 1999–2000): 2–32.

———. "'Could These Bones Be from a Negro?'" *Overland Journal* 19, no. 2 (Summer 2001): 42–55.

Guinn, J. M. "Early Postal Service of California." *Historical Society of Southern California* 4, no. 1 (1897): 18–26.

Hafen, LeRoy R. "A Winter Rescue March across the Rockies." *Colorado Magazine* IV, no. 1 (January 1927): 7–13.

Hagerty, Leroy W. "Indian Raids along the Platte and Little Blue Rivers, 1864–1865 (I)." *Nebraska History* 28, no. 3 (1947): 176–86.

———. "Indian Raids along the Platte and Little Blue Rivers, 1864–1865 (III)." *Nebraska History* 28, no. 4 (1947): 239–60.

Hammond, Andy. "The Look of the Elephant: Scott's Bluff." *Overland Journal* 25, no. 2 (Summer 2007): 59–62.

Hauck, Louise Platt. "The Pony Express Celebration." *Missouri Historical Review* XVI, no. 4 (July 1923): 435–39.

Hill, Burton S. "The Great Indian Treaty Council of 1851." *Nebraska History* 47 (1966): 85–110.

Hoopes, Alban W. "Thomas S. Twiss, Indian Agent on the Upper Platte, 1855–1861." *Mississippi Valley Historical Review* 20, no. 3 (1933): 353–64.

Jackson, W. Turrentine. "The Army Engineers as Road Surveyors and Builders in Kansas and Nebraska, 1854–1858." *Kansas History: A Journal of the Central Plains* 17, no. 1 (February 1949): 37–59.

Jenkins, Perry W. "Kiskadden-Slade." *Annals of Wyoming* 21, no. 1 (January 1949): 89–92.

Johansen, Dorothy O. "A Working Hypothesis for the Study of Migrations." *Pacific Historical Review* 36, no. 1 (February 1967): 1–12.

Kelly, Pete. "Plans for the Pony Express Re-Run, July 19, 1960." *Nevada Historical Society Quarterly* III, no. 2 (Spring 1960): 41–44.

Kemble, John Haskell. "The Gold Rush by Panama, 1848–1851." *Pacific Historical Review* 18, no. 1, *Rushing for Gold* (February 1949): 45–56.

Landstrom, Karl S. "How We Acquired Our Landed Estate, Part 2." *Our Public Lands* 8, no. 4 (April 1959): 6–7.

Lapp, Rudolph M. "Negro Rights Activities in Gold Rush California." *California Historical Society Quarterly* 45, no. 1 (March 1966): 3–20.

Lisa, Gregory C. "Bicyclists and Bureaucrats: The League of American Wheelmen and Public Choice Theory Applied." *Georgetown Law Journal* 84 (1995): 373–98.

Luce, W. Ray. "The Mormon Battalion: A Historical Accident?" *Utah Historical Quarterly* 42, no. 1 (1974): 27–38.

MacKinnon, William P. "And the War Came: James Buchanan, The Utah Expedition, and the Decision to Intervene." *Utah Historical Quarterly* 76, no. 1 (2008): 22–37.

———. "The Buchanan Spoils System and the Utah Expedition: Careers of W. M. F. Magraw and John M. Hockaday." *Utah Historical Quarterly* 31, no. 2 (1963): 127–50.

MacMurphy, Harriet S. "The Heroine of the Jules-Slade Tragedy." *Collection of Nebraska Pioneer Reminiscences*, 1916, 322–25.

Martin, George P. "Bull-Whacking Days." *Publications—Nebraska State Historical Society*, Proceedings and Collections of the Nebraska State Historical Society, V (1902).

Martin, Jill E. "'The Greatest Evil' Interpretations of Indian Prohibition Laws, 1832–1953." *Great Plains Quarterly* 23 (Winter 2003): 35–53.

Mason, Patrick Q. "God and the People: Theodemocracy in Nineteenth-Century Mormonism." *Journal of Church and State* 53, no. 3 (Summer 2011): 349–75.

Mattes, Merrill J. "The Sutler's Store at Fort Laramie." *Annals of Wyoming* 18, no. 2 (1946): 93–138.

———. "A Tribute to the Emigrant Graves at Robidoux Pass." *Overland Journal* 25, no. 2 (Summer 2007): 54–57.

Mattes, Merrill, and Paul Henderson. "The Pony Express: Across Nebraska from St. Joseph to Fort Laramie." *Nebraska History* 41 (1960): 83–122.

McArthur, Lewis A. "Earliest Oregon Postoffices as Recorded at Washington." *Oregon Historical Quarterly* 41, no. 1 (March 1940): 53–71.

McCann, Lloyd E. "The Grattan Massacre." *Nebraska History* 37 (1956): 1–25.

McMechen, Edgar. "Slade's Virginia Dale Days." *Union Pacific Magazine*, March 1931.

Mead & Hunt. "Nebraska Historic Buildings Survey: Historic Highways in Nebraska." Nebraska State Historical Society and Nebraska Department of Roads, August 2002.

Meschter, Daniel Y. "The First Transmountain Mail Route Contracts, 1850–1862, Part IV: Route No. 5043 The Dalles, Oregon to Salt Lake City, Utah July 1, 1851 to June 30, 1854." *La Posta: A Journal of American Postal History*, The First Transmountain Mail Route Contracts, 1850–1862, 27, no. 1 (Whole No. 157) (March 1996): 19–26.

Miller, Robert J. "The Doctrine of Discovery: The International Law of Colonialism." *Indigenous Peoples' Journal of Law, Culture & Resistance* 5, no. 1 (2019): 35–42.

Miller, William, ed. "The Pyramid Lake Indian War of 1860, Part 1." *Nevada Historical Society Quarterly* I, no. 1 (Summer 1957): 37–53.

———. "The Pyramid Lake Indian War of 1860, Part 2." *Nevada Historical Society Quarterly* I, no. 2 (Fall 1957): 98–113.

Morris, M. Patricia. "Joe Nardone's Long Ride on the Trail of the Pony Express." *California State Library Foundation Bulletin* 78 (2007): 2–9.

———. "Pony Express Historian Joe Nardone's Gifts from the Trail." *California State Library Foundation Bulletin* 121 (2018): 2–9.

Muir, Florabel. "The Man Who Was Hanged for a Song." *Liberty Magazine*, June 30, 1928.

Nettles, Curtis. "The Overland Mail Issue During the 1850s." *Missouri Historical Review* XVIII, no. 4 (July 1924): 521–34.

Neville, Alan L., and Kaye Anderson. "The Diminishment of the Great Sioux Reservation: Treaties, Tricks, and Time." *Great Plains Quarterly* 33, no. 4 (Fall 2013): 237–51.

Olch, Peter D. "Treading the Elephant's Tail: Medical Problems on the Overland Trail." *Bulletin of the History of Medicine* 59, no. 2 (Summer 1985): 196–212.

Pack, Mary. "The Romance of the Pony Express." *Union Pacific Magazine* II (August 1923): 6–9, 28–30.

Paden, Irene D., and Carl P. Russell. "The Ira J. Willis Guide to the Gold Mines." *California Historical Society Quarterly* 32, no. 3 (September 1, 1953): 193–207.

Parker, Mrs. C. F. "Old Julesburg and Fort Sedgwick." *Colorado Magazine* VII, no. 4 (July 1930): 139–46.

Paul, R. Eli, ed. "Battle of Ash Hollow: The 1909–1910 Recollections of General N. A. M. Dudley." *Nebraska History* 62 (1981): 373–99.

"The Pony Express Rides Again." *Kansas Historical Quarterly* 25, no. 4 (Winter 1959): 367–85.

Rea, J. "Seeing the Elephant." *Western Folklore* 28, no. 1 (January 1969): 21–26.

Redd, Emmett, and Nicole Etcheson. "'Sound on the Goose': A Search for the Answer to an Age Old 'Question.'" *Kansas History: A Journal of the Central Plains* 32 (Autumn 2009): 204–17.

Root, George A., and Russell K. Hickman. "Pike's Peak Express Companies, Part I—The Solomon and Republican Route." *Kansas Historical Quarterly*, Pike's Peak Express Companies, 1 of 4, 13, no. 3 (August 1944): 163–95.

———. "Pike's Peak Express Companies, Part II—Solomon and Republican Route—Concluded." *Kansas Historical Quarterly*, Pike's Peak Express Companies, 2 of 4, 13, no. 4 (November 1944): 211–42.

———. "Pike's Peak Express Companies, Part III—The Platte Route." *Kansas Historical Quarterly*, Pike's Peak Express Companies, 3 of 4, 13, no. 8 (November 1945): 485–526.

———. "Pike's Peak Express Companies, Part IV—The Platte Route—Concluded." *Kansas Historical Quarterly*, Pike's Peak Express Companies, 4 of 4, 14, no. 1 (February 1946): 36–92.

Roth, David D. "Lakota Sioux Terms for White and Negro." *Plains Anthropologist* 20, no. 68 (1975): 117–20.

Rydell, Raymond A. "The Cape Horn Route to California, 1849." *Pacific Historical Review* 17, no. 2 (May 1948): 149–63.

Schindler, Harold. "Utah's First Post Office and Postmaster." *Utah Historical Quarterly* XXX (1962): 347–51.

Schlissel, Lillian. "Women's Diaries on the Western Frontier." *American Studies* 18, no. 1 (1977): 87–100.

Settle, Raymond W. "The Pony Express, Heroic Effort—Tragic End." *Utah Historical Quarterly* 27, no. 2 (April 1959): 103–26.

Settle, Raymond W., and Mary Lund Settle. "The Early Careers of William Bradford Waddell and William Hepburn Russell: Frontier Capitalists." *Kansas Historical Quarterly* 26, no. 4 (Winter 1960): 355–82.

———. "Napoleon of the West." *Annals of Wyoming* 32, no. 1 (April 1960): 5–47.

———. "Origin of the Pony Express." *The Bulletin, Missouri Historical Society* 26, no. 3 (April 1960): 199–212.

Sharp, Pauline Settle. "Flying Ponies Blazed Hot Trail Over Old West." *The Pioneer, News of the Sons of Utah Pioneers* 18, no. 3 (June 1971): 7–8.

Smith, Stacey L. "Remaking Slavery in a Free State: Masters and Slaves in Gold Rush California." *Pacific Historical Review* 80, no. 1 (February 2011): 28–63.

Spaulding, Imogene. "The Attitude of California to the Civil War." *Annual Publication of the Historical Society of Southern California* 9, no. 1/2 (1912): 104–31.

Stanley, Gerald. "Senator William Gwin: Moderate or Racist?" *California Historical Quarterly* 50, no. 3 (September 1971): 243–55.

Steele, Mrs. C. F., and George W. Hansen. "How the Sons of George Winslow Found Their Father's Grave." *Collection of Nebraska Pioneer Reminiscences Cedar Rapids: The Torch Press*, 1916, 169–74.

Sydenham, Moses H. "Freighting across the Plains in 1856—A Personal Experience." *Proceedings and Collections of the Nebraska State Historical Society*, Second Series, I, no. 1 (January 1895): 164–84.

Taylor, Allan R. "Note Concerning Lakota Sioux Terms for White and Negro." *Plains Anthropologist* 21, no. 71 (1976): 63–65.

Townley, John M. "Stalking Horse for the Pony Express: The Chorpenning Mail Contracts between California and Utah, 1851–1860." *Arizona and the West* 24, no. 3 (1982): 229–52.

Trennert, Robert A. Jr. "The Mormons and the Office of Indian Affairs: The Conflict Over Winter Quarters, 1846–1848." *Nebraska History* 53 (1972): 381–400.

Villard, Henry. "To the Pike's Peak Country in 1859 and Cannibalism on the Smoky Hill Route." *Colorado Magazine* VIII, no. 6 (November 1931): 225–36.

Walker, Margaret F. "A Woman's Work Is Never Done: Or the Dirt on Men and Their Laundry." *Overland Journal* 16, no. 2 (Summer 1998): 4–13.

Walker, Ronald W., and Matthew J. Grow. "The People Are 'Hogaffed or Humbugged': The 1851–52 National Reaction to Utah's 'Runaway' Officers: Part 2." *Journal of Mormon History* 40, no. 1 (Winter 2014): 1–52.

Webb, Walter Prescott. "The Story of Some Prairie Inventions." *Nebraska History* 34, no. 4 (1953): 229–43.

Westover, Mary C. "Monument to Pony Express." *Daughters of the American Revolution Magazine* XLIII, no. 4 (October 1913): 619–21.

Whitcomb, E. W. "Alfred Slade at Close Range." *The Trail: A Magazine "for Colorado"* XIV, no. 6 (November 1921): 11–15.

Wishart, David J. "The Dispossession of the Pawnee." *Annals of the Association of American Geographers* 69, no. 3 (1979): 382–401.

Wyman, Walker D. "The Military Phase of Santa Fe Freighting, 1846–1865." *Kansas Historical Quarterly* 1, no. 5 (1932): 415–28.

BOOKS

Alter, James Cecil. *James Bridger: A Historical Narrative*. Salt Lake City: Shepard Book Company, 1925.

Angel, Myron. *History of Nevada*. Oakland: Thompson and West, 1881.

Avey, Loren. *The Pole Creek Crossing*. Bloomington: Author House, 2010.

Bagley, Will. *Across the Plains, Mountains, and Deserts: A Bibliography of the Oregon-California Trail, 1812–1912*. Salt Lake City: National Park Service, 2014.

———. *South Pass: Gateway to a Continent*. Norman: University of Oklahoma Press, 2014.

Bancroft, Hubert Howe. *History of California*. Vol. VI, 1860–1890. San Francisco: The History Company, 1888.

Beck, Paul Norman. *The First Sioux War: The Grattan Fight and Blue Water Creek, 1854–1856*. Lanham, MD: University Press of America, 2004.

Berwanger, Eugene H. *The Frontier Against Slavery: Western Anti-Negro Prejudice and the Slavery Extension Controversy*. Chicago: University of Illinois Press, 1967.

Beveridge, Thomas R. Revised by Jerry D. Vineyard. *Geologic Wonders and Curiosities of Missouri*. Educational Series No. 4. Missouri Department of Natural Resources Division of Geology and Land Survey, 1990.

Biggs, Donald C. *The Pony Express: Creation of the Legend*. San Francisco: printed privately, 1956.

Bigler, David L. *Forgotten Kingdom: The Mormon Theocracy in the American West, 1847–1896*. Norman, OK: Arthur Clark Company, 1998.

Bloss, Roy S. *Pony Express—The Great Gamble*. Berkeley: Howell-North, 1959.

Bradley, Glenn D. *The Story of the Pony Express, An Account of the Most Remarkable Mail Service Ever in Existence and Its Place in History*. Chicago: A. C. McClurg & Company, 1913.

Bratt, John. *Trails of Yesterday*. Lincoln: University Publishing Company, 1921.

Brown, Randy, and Reg Duffin. *Graves and Sites on the Oregon and California Trails*. 2nd ed. Independence: Oregon-California Trails Association, 1998.

Bryant, Edwin. *What I Saw in California: Being the Journal of a Tour by the Emigrant Route and South Pass of the Rocky Mountains, Across the Continent of North America, the Great Desert Basin, and Through California in the Years 1846, 1847*. New York: D. Appleton, 1849.

Buck, Rinker. *The Oregon Trail*. New York: Simon & Schuster, 2015.

Buel, J. W. *Heroes of the Plains, or, Lives and Wonderful Adventures of Wild Bill, Buffalo Bill, Kit Carson, Capt. Payne, Capt. Jack, Texas Jack, California Joe, and Other Celebrated Indian Fighters, Scouts, Hunters and Guides: Including a True and Thrilling History of Gen. Custer's Famous "Last Fight" on the Little Big Horn, with Sitting Bull*. New York: N. D. Thompson, 1882.

Burton, Richard Francis. *The City of the Saints and Across the Rocky Mountains to California*. New York: Harper & Brothers, 1862.

Carter, Kate B. *Riders of the Pony Express*. Third printing, 1952. Daughters of Utah Pioneers, 1947.

Chandless, William. *A Visit to Salt Lake City: Being a Journey Across the Plains and a Residence in the Mormon Settlements at Utah*. London: Smith, Elder, and Co., 1857.

Chapman, Arthur. *The Pony Express: The Record of a Romantic Adventure in Business*. Reprint, New York: Cooper Square Publishers, Inc., 1971. New York: G. P. Putnam's Sons, 1932.

Clayton, William. *The Latter-Day Saints' Emigrants' Guide: Being a Table of Distances from Council Bluffs to the Valley of the Great Salt Lake*. Reprint, 1983. Gerald: Patrice Press, 1848.

Clifford, Henry H. (comp.). *A Brief History of the Mail Service, Settlement of the Country, and the Indian Depredations Committed upon the Mail Trains of George Chorpenning on the Several Routes between Salt Lake and California from May 1 St, 1850 to July, 1860*. San Francisco: Grant Dahlstrom, 1972.

Cole, Cornelius. *Memoirs of Cornelius Cole, Ex-Senator of the United States from California*. New York: McLoughlin Brothers, 1908.

Collins, Dabney Otis. *The Hanging of Bad Jack Slade*. 1st ed. Denver: Golden Bell Press, 1966.

Corbett, Christopher. *Orphans Preferred: The Twisted Truth and Lasting Legend of the Pony Express*. New York: Broadway Books, 2004.

Coutant, Charles G. *The History of Wyoming from the Earliest Known Discoveries*. Vol. I. 3 vols. Laramie: Chaplin, Spafford & Mathison, 1899.

Davenport, Frances Gardiner, ed. *European Treaties Bearing on the History of the United States and Its Dependencies to 1648*. Washington, DC: Carnegie Institution of Washington, 17.

Dawson, Charles. *Pioneer Tales of the Oregon Trail and of Jefferson County*. Topeka: Crane & Company, 1912.

De Quille, Dan. *History of the Big Bonanza: An Authentic Account of the Discovery, History, and Working of the World Renowned Comstock Silver Lode of Nevada, Including the Present Condition of the Various Mines Situated Thereon*. Hartford: American Publishing Company, 1877.

De Voto, Bernard. *Across the Wide Missouri*. Boston: Bonanza Books, 1947.

———. *The Course of Empire*. Boston: Houghton Mifflin Harcourt, 1952.

———. *The Year of Decision, 1846*. Boston: Houghton Mifflin, 1942.

DeFelice, Jim. *West Like Lightning: The Brief, Legendary Ride of the Pony Express*. Illustrated edition. New York: William Morrow, 2018.

DiCerto, Joseph J. *The Saga of the Pony Express*. Sixth printing, 2017. Missoula: Mountain Press Publishing Company, 2002.

Dimsdale, Thos. J. *The Vigilantes of Montana, or, Popular Justice In the Rocky Mountains: Being a Correct and Impartial Narrative of the Chase, Capture, Trial and Execution of Henry Plummer's Road Agent Band*. Virginia City: D. W. Tilton, 1882.

Dodge, Richard Irving. *Hunting Grounds of the Great West*. London: Chatto & Windus, 1877.

Egan, John. "Home on the Range No More: Boom and Bust in Jeffery City." In *Readings in Wyoming History*, edited by Phil Roberts. 2nd rev. ed., 17–26. Laramie: Skyline West Press/Wyoming Almanac, 1995.

Ellis, Jerry. *Bareback!* New York: Delacorte Press, 1993.

Ely, Glen Sample. *The Texas Frontier and the Butterfield Overland Mail, 1858–1861*. Norman: University of Oklahoma Press, 2016.

Faragher, John Mack. *Women and Men on the Overland Trail*. New Haven: Yale University Press, 1979.

Fike, Richard E., and John W. Headley, with US Bureau of Land Management, Utah State Office. *The Pony Express Stations of Utah in Historical Perspective*. Salt Lake City: Bureau of Land Management, Utah, 1979.

Franzwa, Gregory. *Maps of the Oregon Trail*. Gerald: Patrice Press, 1982.

Frederick, J. V. *Ben Holladay, the Stagecoach King: A Chapter in the Development of Transcontinental Transportation*. Reprint, Lincoln: University of Nebraska Press, 1989. Glendale: Arthur H. Clark Company, 1940.

Furniss, Norman F. *The Mormon Conflict: 1850–1859*. New Haven: Yale University Press, 1960.

Gallagher, Winifred. *How the Post Office Created America*. New York: Penguin, 2016.

Garrard, Lewis Hector. *Wah-To-Yah, and the Taos Trail: Or, Prairie Travel and Scalp Dances, with a Look at Los Rancheros from Muleback and the Rocky Mountain Camp-Fire.* Reprint, Norman: University of Oklahoma Press, Fourth Printing, 1966. Cincinnati: H. W. Derby & Company, 1850.

Godfrey, Anthony. *Historic Resource Study: Pony Express National Historic Trail.* US Dept. of the Interior, National Park Service, 1994.

Gowans, Fred R. *Rocky Mountain Rendezvous.* Provo: Brigham Young University Press, 1975.

Gregg, Josiah. *Commerce of the Prairies.* Edited by Max L. Moorhead. 2nd ed., 1958. Norman: University of Oklahoma Press, 1954.

Guinn, James Miller. *History of the State of California and Biographical Record of Oakland and Environs: Also Containing Biographies of Well-Known Citizens of the Past and Present.* Vol. I. 2 vols. Los Angeles: Historic Record Company, 1907.

Guthrie, A. B. *The Way West.* New York: Sloane, 1949.

Gwynne, S. C. *Empire of the Summer Moon: Quanah Parker and the Rise and Fall of the Comanches, the Most Powerful Indian Tribe in American History.* New York: Scribner, 2010.

Hafen, LeRoy R. "Louis Vasquez." In *The Mountain Men and the Fur Trade of the Far West*, edited by LeRoy R. Hafen, 6:321–38. Glendale: Arthur Clark Company, 1968.

———. *The Overland Mail, 1849–1869: Promoter of Settlement, Precursor of Railroads.* Reprint 2004. Norman: University of Oklahoma Press, 1926.

———, ed. *The Mountain Men and the Fur Trade of the Far West.* 10 vols. Glendale: Arthur Clark Company, 1968.

Hafen, LeRoy, and Frances Marion Young. *Fort Laramie and the Pageant of the West, 1834–1890.* First Bison Book Printing, 1984. Lincoln: University of Nebraska Press, 1938.

Hämäläinen, Pekka. *The Comanche Empire.* New Haven: Yale University Press, 2008.

Hammond, Gerald, and Austin Busch, eds. *The English Bible: King James Version: The New Testament and the Apocrypha.* Vol. 2. New York: Norton, 2012.

Hardesty, Donald L., and US Bureau of Land Management, Nevada State Office. *The Pony Express in Central Nevada: Archaeological and Documentary Perspectives.* Reno: Bureau of Land Management, Nevada State Office, 1979.

Hearty, Patrick, and Joseph Hatch. *The Pony Express in Utah.* Charleston: Arcadia Publishing, 2015.

Hebard, Grace Raymond. *Marking the Oregon Trail, the Bozeman Road, and Historic Places in Wyoming, 1908–1920.* Laramie: Daughters of the American Revolution of Wyoming, 1922.

Henderson, Timothy J. *A Glorious Defeat: Mexico and Its War with the United States.* New York: Hill and Wang, 2007.

Herlihy, David V. *Bicycle: The History.* New Haven: Yale University Press, 2004.

Hill, William E. *The Pony Express Trail: Yesterday and Today.* Caldwell: Caxton Press, 2010.

Hollars, B. J. *Go West, Young Man: A Father and Son Rediscover America on the Oregon Trail.* Lincoln: University of Nebraska Press, 2021.

Hopkins, Sarah Winnemucca. *Life Among the Paiutes: Their Wrongs and Claims*. Edited by Mrs. Horace Mann. New York: G. P. Putnam's Sons, 1883.

Horner, William B. *The Gold Regions of Kansas and Nebraska: Being a Complete History of the First Year's Mining Operations. Also, Geographical, Climatological, and Statistical Description of the Great Northwest*. Chicago: W. H. Tobey & Company, 1859.

Howard, Major-General O. O. *Famous Indian Chiefs I Have Known*. New York: Century Company, 1908.

Hyde, George E. *The Pawnee Indians*. Denver: University of Denver Press, 1951.

———. *Red Cloud's Folk: A History of the Oglala Sioux Indians*. Fifth printing. Norman: University of Oklahoma Press, 1984.

———. *Spotted Tail's Folk: History of Brulé Sioux*. Norman: University of Oklahoma Press, 1961.

Irving, Washington. *The Adventures of Captain Bonneville*. Reprint: New York: John B. Alden, 1886.

Ismert, Cornelius M. "James Bridger." In *The Mountain Men and the Fur Trade of the Far West*, edited by LeRoy R. Hafen, 6:85–104. Glendale: Arthur Clark Company, 1968.

Jackson, W. Turrentine. *Wagon Roads West: A Study of Federal Road Surveys and Construction in the Trans-Mississippi West, 1846–1869*. Lincoln: University of Nebraska Press, 1979.

Johnsgard, Paul A. *A Guide to the Natural History of the Central Platte Valley of Nebraska*. Lincoln: University of Nebraska, 2007.

Jones, Robert Huhn. *Guarding the Overland Trails: The Eleventh Ohio Cavalry in the Civil War*. Frontier Military Series 24. Spokane: Arthur H. Clark, 2005.

Kappler, Charles J. *Indian Affairs: Laws and Treaties*. Vol. 2. Senate, 58th Congress, 2nd session, Senate Document No. 319, part 2. Government Printing Office, 1904.

Katz, William. *The Black West: A Documentary and Pictorial History of the African American Role in the Westward Expansion of the United States*. New York: Simon & Schuster, 1996.

Kenderdine, Thaddeus S. *A California Tramp and Later Footprints; or, Life on the Plains and in the Golden State Thirty Years Ago, with Miscellaneous Sketches in Prose and Verse . . . Illustrated with Thirty-Nine Wood and Photo-Engravings*. Newton: [Philadelphia, Press of Globe printing house], 1888.

Larimer, William H. H., and Herman S. Davis. *Reminiscences of General William Larimer and of His Son, William H. H. Larimer, Two of the Founders of Denver*. Lancaster: New Era Printing Company, 1918.

Lecompte, Janet. "John Poisal." In *The Mountain Men and the Fur Trade of the Far West*, edited by LeRoy R. Hafen, 6:353–58. Glendale: Arthur Clark Company, 1968.

Leslie, Edward E. *The Devil Knows How to Ride: The True Story of William Clarke Quantrill and His Confederate Raiders*. New York: Random House, 1996.

Lewis, Tom. *Divided Highways: Building the Interstate Highways, Transforming American Life*. New York: Viking, 1997.

Little, James A. *Biographical Sketch of Feramorz Little*. Salt Lake City: Juvenile Instructor Office, 1890.

Macaulay, G. C., trans. *Herodotus, The Histories*. Vol. II. 2 vols. London: Macmillan and Company, 1914.

Madsen, Susan Arrington. *The Second Rescue: The Story of the Spiritual Rescue of the Willie and Martin Handcart Pioneers*. Salt Lake City: Deseret Book Company, 1998.

Mahoney, Eugene T. *The Oregon Trail, Rock Creek Station, Nebraska to Fort Laramie, Wyoming*. Nebraska Game and Parks Commission, 1981.

Majors, Alexander. *Seventy Years on the Frontier: Alexander Majors' Memoirs of a Lifetime on the Border*. Edited by Colonel Prentiss Ingraham. Chicago and New York: Rand & Company, 1893.

Marcy, Randolph Barnes. *The Prairie Traveler. A Hand-Book for Overland Expeditions. with Maps, Illustrations, and Itineraries of the Principal Routes Between the Mississippi and the Pacific*. Reprint, Old Saybrook: Applewood Books, 1986. New York: Harper, 1859.

Marks, Herbert, ed. *The English Bible: King James Version: The Old Testament*. Vol. 1. New York: Norton, 2012.

Mason, Dorothy. *The Pony Express in Nevada*. Carson City: Nevada State Museum, 1996.

Mattes, Merrill J. *The Great Platte River Road: The Covered Wagon Mainline via Fort Kearny to Fort Laramie*. Vol. XXV. Nebraska State Historical Society Publications. Lincoln: Nebraska State Historical Society, 1969.

McClernan, John B. *Slade's Wells Fargo Colt: Historical Notes*. Hicksville: Exposition Press, 1977.

McLynn, Frank. *Wagons West: The Epic Story of America's Overland Trails*. New York: Grove Press, 2003.

Meldahl, Keith Heyer. *Hard Road West: History and Geology along the Gold Rush Trail*. Chicago: University of Chicago Press, 2012.

Moody, Ralph. *The Old Trails West*. New York: Promontory Press, 1963.

———. *Stagecoach West*. New York: Promontory Press, 1967.

Moody, Ralph, and Bob Riger. *Riders of the Pony Express*. First Nebraska paperback, Lincoln: University of Nebraska Press, 2004. New York: Dell, 1958.

Moore, Shirley Ann Wilson. *Sweet Freedom's Plains: African Americans on the Overland Trails, 1841–1869*. Norman: University of Oklahoma Press, 2016.

Ormsby, Waterman Lilly. *The Butterfield Overland Mail*. Edited by Lyle Henry Wright and Josephine M. Bynum. Third paperback and tenth printing, 1998. San Marino: Huntington Library, 1942.

Paden, Irene Dakin. *Prairie Schooner Detours*. New York: Macmillan Company, 1949.

———. *The Wake of the Prairie Schooner*. New York: Macmillan Company, 1943.

Parkman, Francis. *The Oregon Trail; Sketches of Prairie and Rocky Mountains Life*. Reprint, New York: Blue Ribbon Books, 1912. New York: George P. Putnam, 1849.

Petersen, Jesse G. *A Route for the Overland Stage: James H. Simpson's 1859 Trail across the Great Basin*. Logan: Utah State University Press, 2008.

Rea, Tom. *Devil's Gate: Owning the Land, Owning the Story*. Norman: University of Oklahoma Press, 2006.

Reinfeld, Fred. *Pony Express*. Bison Book. Lincoln: University of Nebraska Press, 1973.

Revised Feasibility and Suitability Study for Additional Routes of the Oregon, Mormon Pioneer, California, and Pony Express National Historic Trails: Appendix A: Study Route Descriptions and Historical Overviews. National Park Service, 2017.

Roberts, David. *Devil's Gate: Brigham Young and the Great Mormon Handcart Tragedy.* New York: Simon & Schuster, 2008.

Root, Frank A., and William Elsey Connelley. *The Overland Stage to California.* Topeka: Crane & Company, 1901.

Rosa, Joseph G. *They Called Him Wild Bill: The Life and Adventures of James Butler Hickok.* Norman: University of Oklahoma Press, 1964.

Rosenberg, Bruce A. *The Code of the West.* Bloomington: Indiana University Press, 1982.

Rottenberg, Dan. *Death of a Gunfighter: The Quest for Jack Slade, the West's Most Elusive Legend.* Yardley: Westholme, 2010.

Russell, Don. *The Lives and Legends of Buffalo Bill.* Omaha: University of Oklahoma Press, 1960.

"Sagebrush Shrublands." In *Wyoming State Wildlife Action Plan—2017,* 19. Wyoming Game and Fish Department, 2017.

Schlissel, Lillian. *Women's Diaries of the Westward Journey.* Studies in the Life of Women. New York: Schocken Books, 1992.

Scott, Robert. *Slade!: The True Story of the Notorious Badman.* Glendo: High Plains Press, 2004.

Seagraves, Anne. *Soiled Doves: Prostitution in the Early West.* Hayden: Wesanne Publications, 1994.

Settle, Raymond W., and Mary Lund Settle. *Empire on Wheels.* Palo Alto: Stanford University Press, 1949.

———. *Saddles and Spurs: The Pony Express Saga.* New York: Bonanza Books, 1955.

Simpson, J. H. *Report of Explorations across the Great Basin of the Territory of Utah: For a Direct Wagon-Route from Camp Floyd to Genoa in Carson Valley in 1859.* Washington, DC: Government Printing Office, 1876.

Snowshoe Thompson: His Life and Adventures. Carson Valley Historical Society, 1991.

Stegner, Wallace. *Beyond the Hundredth Meridian: John Wesley Powell and the Second Opening of the West.* Boston: Houghton Mifflin, 1954.

———. *The Gathering of Zion: The Story of the Mormon Trail.* First Bison Book Printing. Lincoln: University of Nebraska Press, 1992.

Stewart, George Rippey. *The California Trail: An Epic with Many Heroes.* Lincoln: University of Nebraska Press, 1983.

———. *Ordeal by Hunger: The Story of the Donner Party.* First Bison Book Printing, 1986. Lincoln: University of Nebraska Press, 1936.

Stuart, Granville. *Forty Years on the Frontier, as Seen in the Journals and Reminiscences of Granville Stuart.* Edited by Paul C. Phillips. Vol. I. 2 vols. Cleveland: Arthur H. Clark Company, 1925.

Tate, Michael L. *Indians and Emigrants: Encounters on the Overland Trails.* Norman: University of Oklahoma Press, 2014.

Thacker, Robert. *The Great Prairie Fact and Literary Imagination.* Albuquerque: University of New Mexico Press, 1989.

Thompson, David. *The Tennessee Letters: From Carson Valley, 1857–1860*. Danberg Historical Series. Reno: Grace Danberg Foundation, Inc., 1983.

Thornton, J. Quinn. *Oregon and California in 1848*. Vol. 1. 2 vols. New York: Harper & Brothers, 1855.

Tomkins, William. *Indian Sign Language*. New York: Dover Publications, 1969.

Towle, Virginia Rowe. *Vigilante Woman*. New York: Barnes & Yoseloff, 1967.

Twain, Mark. *Roughing It*. Hartford: American Publishing Company, 1891.

Unruh, John David. *The Plains Across: The Overland Emigrants and the Trans-Mississippi West, 1840–60*. 1st unabridged paperback. Urbana: University of Illinois Press, 1993.

Urbanek, Mae. *Wyoming Place Names*. Second printing, June 1990. Missoula: Mountain Press Publishing Company, 1988.

Utley, Robert M. *A Life Wild and Perilous: Mountain Men and the Paths to the Pacific*. New York: Henry Holt and Company, 1998.

Visscher, William Lightfoot. *A Thrilling and Truthful History of the Pony Express: Or, Blazing the Westward Way, and Other Sketches and Incidents of Those Stirring Times*. Chicago: Charles T. Powner Co., 1946.

Walker, Henry Pickering. *The Wagonmasters: High Plains Freighting from the Earliest Days of the Santa Fe Trail to 1880*. Norman: University of Oklahoma Press, 1966.

Walske, Steven. *Overland Mails of the Westward Expansion: 1832 to 1869*. Siegel Auction Galleries, n.d.

Walske, Steven C., and Richard C. Frajola. *Mails of the Westward Expansion: 1803 to 1861*. Western Cover Society, 2015.

Ware, Eugene F. *The Indian War of 1864: Being a Fragment of the Early History of Kansas, Nebraska, Colorado, and Wyoming*. Topeka: Crane & Co., 1911.

Warren, Louis S. *Buffalo Bill's America: William Cody and the Wild West Show*. New York: Alfred A. Knopf, 2005.

Watrous, Ansel. *History of Larimer County Colorado*. Fort Collins: Courier Printing & Publishing Company, 1911.

Webb, Walter Prescott. *The Great Plains*. Reprint, First Bison Book Printing, Lincoln: University of Nebraska Press, 1981. Lincoln: University of Nebraska Press, 1931.

Weinell, Don. *Bicycling the Oregon Trail*. Caldwell: Caxton Press, 2017.

West, Elliott. *The Contested Plains: Indians, Gold Seekers, & the Rush to Colorado*. Lawrence: University Press of Kansas, 1998.

Williams, R. H. *With the Border Ruffians; Memories of the Far West, 1852–1868*. London: J. Murray, 1908.

Wirth, Conrad Louis. *Great Explorers of the West*. The National Survey of Historic Sites and Buildings, XV, Westward Expansion and Extension of the National Boundaries 1830–1898. Washington, DC: National Park Service, 1960.

Young, Charles E. *Dangers of the Trail in 1865: A Narrative of Actual Events*. Geneva, NY: Press of W. F. Humphrey, 1912.

COURT DECISIONS
Anderson, Alexander. *In re Perkins*, 2 Cal. 424 (California Supreme Court, 1852).

Burnett, Peter H. *In re Archy*, 9 Cal. 147 (California Supreme Court, 1858).

Marshall, John. *Johnson v. M'Intosh*, 7 Wheat. 543 (US Supreme Court, 1823).

Taney, Roger Brooke. *Dred Scott v. Sandford*, 60 U.S. 393 (Supreme Court of the United States, 1856).

DOCUMENTS AND MANUSCRIPTS

Atchison, David Rice. "The Voice of Kansas, Let the South Respond." Law and Order Party, June 24, 1856.

Chamber of Commerce, Austin, Nevada. "Austin-Toiyabe Mountain Bike Trail Guide," n.d.

Gothenburg Visitor's Guide 2021. Gothenburg: Gothenburg Community Development Office, 2021.

Historical Department. "Journal History of the Church," June 13, 1847.

Little, Feramorz. "Mail Service Across the Plains." Salt Lake City, 1884. Unpublished manuscript, Bancroft Library, University of California–Berkeley.

Mead & Hunt. "Nebraska Historic Buildings Survey: Historic Highways in Nebraska." Nebraska State Historical Society and Nebraska Department of Roads, August 2002.

"The Paiute Indian War of 1860." Robert A. Siegel Auction Galleries, Incorporated, 2013.

Trepel, Scott R. "The Impact of Indian Attacks on the Pony Express in 1860." Robert A. Siegel Auction Galleries, Incorporated, 2014.

US Postal Service. "Overland Mail to California in the 1850s," n.d.

GOVERNMENT DOCUMENTS

An Act to Organize the Territories of Nebraska and Kansas, 277 § Thirty-Third Congress, Sess. 1, Ch. 59, 1854. 10 Stat. 277 (Chapter 59). (n.d.).

Haaland, Deb. Declaring "Squaw" a Derogatory Term and Implementing Procedures to Remove the Term from Federal Usage., Pub. L. No. 3404 (2021).

Legislative Resolution 3, § Nebraska Unicameral Legislature (1992).

Treaty of Fort Laramie with Sioux, Etc., 1851, Pub. L. No. 11 Stats. 749 (1851).

US Statutes at Large, Volume 2 (1799-1813), 6th through 12th Congress. Vol. II. Boston: Charles C. Little and James Brown, 1845.

MOVIES AND TV SHOWS

"The Doomsday Machine." *Star Trek*, October 20, 1967.

National Lampoon's Animal House. Universal Pictures, 1978.

The Right Stuff. Warner Bros., 1983.

NEWSPAPERS

Axtell Anchor. "Early History of the St. Joseph and Western Railroad." May 29, 1884.

Davis, Kenneth S. "Hoofbeats of History." *New York Times*, June 6, 1954.

Finney, William. "Advertisement." *Sacramento Daily Union*. March 19, 1860.

The Frontier Guardian. "The Mail Arrived from the Salt Lake." September 3, 1849.

Greeley, Horace. "The Republican Position." *New York Tribune*. December 17, 1860.

Hammel, Paul. "'Marker Geek' Shares Tales in Book on Nebraska Monuments." *Omaha World Herald*, November 26, 2020.
Koch, Hugo. "Early Days in Wyoming, Parts 1–12." *Wind River Mountaineer*, 1908.
———. "Hugo Koch Obituary." *Wind River Mountaineer.* January 16, 1914.
New York Times. "New Overland Telegraph." November 23, 1866.
———. "The President and Senator Gwin," July 12, 1860.
Our Special Correspondent. "Important from Kansas: Missouri River Piracy—And Other Outrages." *New York Tribune,* July 17, 1856.
Shearing, W. H. "Deseret News 1861-04-24 Difficulties and Grievances Epitomized—Deseret News 2—Digital Collections." Accessed December 16, 2020.
Theodore, Lauren. "Historian Has Reason for Saddle Soreness." *Tahoe Daily Tribune*, December 19, 2001.
Thompson, Don. "Historian Finds Pony Express Ad." *San Diego Union-Tribune*, March 20, 2005. https://web.archive.org/web/20120313183122/http://legacy.signonsan diego.com/uniontrib/20050320/news_1n20ponyexp.html.

THESES AND DISSERTATIONS
Bresee, Floyd. "Overland Freighting in the Platte Valley 1850–1870." Master's thesis, University of Nebraska, 1937.
Coffman, Natalie Brooke. "The Mormon Battalion's Manifest Destiny: Expansion and Identity during the Mexican-American War." Master's thesis, University of Vermont, 2015.
Embleton, Raelyn. "Racial Conflict in Early Utah: Mormon, Native American and Federal Relations." Master's thesis, Utah State University, 2019.
Mason, Philip P. "The League of American Wheelmen and the Good-Roads Movement, 1880–1905." PhD diss., University of Michigan, 1957.
McBride, Ralph L. "Utah Mail Service before the Coming of the Railroad, 1869." Master's thesis, Brigham Young University, 1957.
Peterson, Heather King. "Colorado Stagecoach Stations." Master's thesis, University of Colorado at Denver, 2001.
Poulson, Alton B. "The Mormon Outpost of San Bernardino, California." Master's thesis, University of Utah, 1947.

WEBSITES
Adams County Nebraska Historical Society. "The Oregon Trail in Adams County." Accessed October 15, 2021. https://www.adamshistory.org/index.php?option=com _content&view=article&id=119:oregon-trail-tour&catid=11&Itemid=48.
American Legion. "American Legion Post 77 in Cozad Purchases Willow Island Pony Express Station," January 1, 1936. https://centennial.legion.org/nebraska /post77/1936/01/01/american-legion-post-77-cozad-purchases-willow-island -pony-express.
"Auto Tour Route Interpretive Guides: Pony Express Trail (US National Park Service)." Accessed May 15, 2021. https://www.nps.gov/articles/000/auto-tour-route-inter pretive-guides-pony-express-trail.htm.

Beaver Water District. "May 2015—River or Creek?" May 28, 2015. https://www
.bwdh2o.org/blog/2015/05/may-2015-river-or-creek/.
Brown, Randy. "Ham's Fork Crossing." WyoHistory, May 21, 2018. https://www.wyohis
tory.org/encyclopedia/hams-fork-crossing.
Brown, Sheldon. "A Comfortable Bicycle Saddle." Sheldon Brown's Bicycle Technical
Info. Accessed October 28, 2021. https://www.sheldonbrown.com/saddles.html.
Cassinelli, Dennis. "Pony Bob Haslam and the Pony Express." DennisCassinelli.com,
May 13, 2014. https://denniscassinelli.com/2018/06/16/episode-007-pony-bob
-haslam-and-the-pony-express/.
City of Bridgeport. "About Us." Accessed January 29, 2022. https://www.cityofbport
.com/about-us-1.
City of Cozad, Nebraska. "Historical Sites in Cozad." Accessed January 4, 2022. https://
cozadne.net/history-of-cozad.
City of Douglas, Wyoming. "City of Douglas, Wyoming," n.d. Accessed April 21, 2022.
https://www.cityofdouglas.org/.
Cochran, Jason. "By Advertising That They Are 'American Owned,' A Number of U.S.
Motels Are Engaging in Utterly Improper Racism," May 11, 2013. https://www
.frommers.com/blogs/arthur-frommer-online/blog_posts/by-advertising-that
-they-are-american-owned-a-number-of-u-s-motels-are-engaging-in-utterly-im
proper-racism.
Facebook. "Seneca Pony Express Museum." Accessed December 14, 2021. https://www
.facebook.com/PonyExpressMuseum/.
Federal Highway Administration. "Ask the Rambler: Was the Lincoln Highway the
First Transcontinental Highway?" last modified 2017. https://www.fhwa.dot.gov
/highwayhistory/lincoln.cfm.
———. "Why President Dwight D. Eisenhower Understood We Needed the Interstate System." Accessed November 12, 2001. https://www.fhwa.dot.gov/interstate
/brainiacs/eisenhowerinterstate.cfm.
Gage County Historical Society and Museum. "Our Locations." Accessed December 12,
2021. https://www.gagecountyhistory.org/our-locations.
Ghost Bikes. "Ghost Bikes." Accessed November 11, 2021. http://ghostbikes.org.
Gothenburg Pony Express Station. "History of the Pony Express." Accessed January 2,
2022. https://www.ponyexpressstation.org/history.
Hadley, Craig. "A 19th Century Slang Dictionary." studylib.net. Accessed December 7,
2020. https://studylib.net/doc/7895287/a-19th-century-slang-dictionary.
Herlihy, David V. "Bicycle Saddle Vs. Seat, Part 2." Pedal Chile, August 12, 2020. https://
pedalchile.com/blog/seat-vs-saddle.
Historic Nebraska—People, Places and Landscapes. "Nebraska Historical Marker:
Dobytown," January 18, 2018. http://www.e-nebraskahistory.org/index.php?title
=Nebraska_Historical_Marker:_Dobytown.
Historical Marker Database. "The Great Smoke: The Horse Creek Treaty," June 16, 2016.
https://www.hmdb.org/m.asp?m=79439.
———. "Plum Creek Massacre Site, August 8, 1864," June 16, 2016. https://www.hmdb
.org/m.asp?m=62794.

History Nebraska. "1864 Indian Raids." Accessed December 24, 2021. ttps://mynehis
tory.com/items/show/378?tour=5&index=35.

Kampen, Todd von. "Marker Overland Ranch WEB.jpg." *The North Platte Telegraph*, May 5, 2020. https://nptelegraph.com/marker-overland-ranch-web-jpg
/image_90132698-9715-11ea-a100-678aaa2984fc.html.

Kansas Heritage Group. "The Palmetto & Roseport Railroad: Early History of the St.
Joseph and Western Railroad." Accessed October 22, 2021. http://kansasheritage
.org/research/rr/p&r.html.

Legends of America. "Cheyenne War of 1864, Nebraska." Accessed December 24, 2021.
https://www.legendsofamerica.com/cheyenne-war-1864-nebraska.

———. "Julesburg, Colorado—Wicked in the West." Accessed November 19, 2021.
https://www.legendsofamerica.com/julesburg-colorado/2/.

Marx, Rebecca Flint. "Cross-Country, by a Road Less Traveled." *New York Times*, July
23, 2013. www.nytimes.com/2013/07/07/travel/cross-country-by-a-road-less-trav
eled.html.

Measuring Worth. "Seven Ways to Compute the Relative Value of a U.S. Dollar Amount,
1774 to Present." Accessed January 15, 2022. http://www.measuringworth.com
/uscompare.

Museums of Marysville, Kansas. "Pony Express Barn & Museum." Accessed December
14, 2021. https://www.marysvillemuseumsks.org/about2-c17d6.

National Park Service. "Auto Tour Route Interpretive Guides: Pony Express Trail,"
October 22, 2021. https://www.nps.gov/articles/000/auto-tour-route-interpretive
-guides-pony-express-trail.htm.

———. "Sand Creek Massacre." Accessed December 24, 2021. https://www.nps.gov
/sand/learn/historyculture/index.htm.

———. "Series: National Historic Trails Auto Tour Route Interpretive Guides." Accessed
November 2, 2021. https://www.nps.gov/articles/series.htm?id=EAE02D51
-0A44-462F-B215B0D870200444.

National Pony Express Association. "Pony Express Re-Ride 2020 Canceled." Accessed
December 12, 2021. https://nationalponyexpress.org/item/pony-express-re-ride
-2020-canceled/.

Nemec, Bethany. "Oregon Trail Chronology." End of the Oregon Trail, April 3, 2019.
https://historicoregoncity.org/2019/04/03/oregon-trail-chronology/.

North Platte Telegraph. "Patricia Ann (Meyer) Evans," June 26, 2019. nptelegraph.
com/obituaries/patricia-ann-meyer-evans/article_5ed2d0b0-4a34-11e6-bb82
-e381bf369227.html.

Oregon-California Trails Association. "George Winslow." Accessed December 22, 2021.
https://octa-trails.org/people-places/george-winslow/.

Patee House Museum and Jesse James Home. "Home Page." Accessed December 22,
2021. http://ponyexpressjessejames.com.

Pedal Chile. "Why Is a Bicycle Seat Called a Saddle?" April 20, 2020. https://pedalchile
.com/blog/mtb-seat.

Pony Express National Museum. "Experience the Ride." Accessed December 22, 2021.
https://www.ponyexpress.org.

————. "Historical Timeline." Accessed December 11, 2021. https://www.ponyexpress .org/historical-timeline.

Taylor, Stephen J. "Go West Young Man: The Mystery Behind the Famous Phrase." Hoosier State Chronicles: Indiana's Digital Newspaper Program, July 9, 2015. https://blog.newspapers.library.in.gov/go-west-young-man-the-mystery-behind -the-famous-phrase/.

Theodore, Lauren. "Historian Has Reason for Saddle Soreness." *Tahoe Daily Tribune*, December 19, 2001. https://www.tahoedailytribune.com/news/historian-has-rea son-for-saddle-soreness/.

Thompson, Don. "Historian Finds Pony Express Ad." *San Diego Union Tribune*, May 20, 2005. https://web.archive.org/web/20120313183122/http://legacy.signonsandiego .com/uniontrib/20050320/news_1n20ponyexp.html.

Town of Julesburg. "Welcome to Our Town." Accessed November 19, 2021. https:// townofjulesburg.com/about-us/.

Trimble, Marshall. "Arbuckles Coffee." *True West*, August 30, 2017. https://truewestmag azine.com/article/arbuckles-coffee-2/.

Visit Nebraska. "Dalton Prairie Schooner Museum." Accessed January 25, 2022. https:// visitnebraska.com/dalton/dalton-prairie-schooner-museum.

————. "Nebraska Tourism Launches Spring/Summer Campaign: 'Nebraska. Honestly, It's Not for Everyone.'" Accessed December 12, 2021. https://visitnebraska.com /press-releases/nebraska-tourism-launches-springsummer-campaign-nebraska -honestly-its-not-everyone.

————. "Oregon Trail Marker." Accessed December 14, 2021. https://visitnebraska.com /odell/oregon-trail-marker.

Visit North Platte. "McDonald Ranch." Accessed January 5, 2022. https://visitnorth platte.com/directory-posts/mcdonald-ranch.

Visit Sidney, Nebraska. "Fort Lookout." Accessed January 25, 2022. https://www.visitsid neyne.com/attractions/listing/camp-lookout.

Weingroff, Richard F. "The Lincoln Highway." Federal Highway Administration. Accessed November 15, 2021. https://www.fhwa.dot.gov/infrastructure/lincoln .cfm.

Wikipedia. "Fakelore," November 11, 2021. https://en.wikipedia.org/wiki/Fakelore.

————. "Fort McPherson, Nebraska," November 13, 2021.

————. "O'Fallons Bluff," October 15, 2021. https://en.wikipedia.org/wiki/O%27Fal lons_Bluff.

Williams, Jasmin K. "The Pony Express." *New York Post*, November 1, 2007. https:// nypost.com/2007/11/01/the-pony-express/.

Willis, Josh. "The Story of Arbuckle Coffee." Arbuckles', September 17, 2018. https:// arbucklecoffee.com/blogs/news/the-arbuckle-blog-vol-1-issue-1.

About the Author

Scott Alumbaugh is an avid cyclist who has ridden multiple ultra-distance events. He also teaches sailing in San Francisco Bay and skippers vacation charter yachts around the world. His previous publications include a novella, *Will Kill for Food*, as well as short fiction published in *StoryQuarterly*, *Kestrel*, *Hunger Mountain Review*, *Black Fork Review*, and *Meat for Tea*. His stories have been read onstage by professional actors at Stories on Stage Davis and Stories on Stage Sacramento. He practiced business litigation in Los Angeles and San Francisco, California, for a number of years before leaving the profession to pursue other interests. He lives with his partner, Lisa Ikemoto, in Davis, California.